Technological Competition and Interdependence

Technological Competition and Interdependence

The Search for Policy in the United States, West Germany, and Japan

Edited by
Günter Heiduk *and* Kozo Yamamura

UNIVERSITY OF WASHINGTON PRESS
Seattle and London

UNIVERSITY OF TOKYO PRESS

This book is sponsored by The Committee on Japanese Economic Studies and the Forschungsinstitut für wirtschaftlich-technische Entwicklungen in Japan und im Pazifikraum e.V. of Universität Duisburg, with the financial assistance of the United States–Japan Foundation, the Peter Klöckner Foundation, the Japan Foundation, and the Nomura Foundation. The publication of this book is made possible by a subvention provided by the Verein zur Förderung der kulturellen und wissenschaftlichen Beziehungen zwischen Japan und der Bundesrepublic Deutschland.

Published in Japan and Asia by University of Tokyo Press.   ISBN 4-13-047047-7
Distributed in Germany by Nomos Verlagsgesellschaft MBH und Co. KG, P.O. Box 610, 7570 Baden-Baden, FRG.   ISBN 3-7890-2133-4

Library of Congress Cataloging-in-Publication Data

Technological competition and interdependence : the search for policy in the United
  States, West Germany, and Japan / edited by Günter Heiduk and Kōzō Yamamura.
  p. cm.
  Revised papers originally presented at a symposium held in Duisburg, West
  Germany in August 1987 which was sponsored by the Committee on Japanese
  Economic Studies of the United States and the Forschungsinstitut für wirtschaftlich-
  technische Entwicklungen in Japan und im Pazifikraum e.V. of Duisburg University.
  ISBN 0-295-96931-8
  1. Technology and state—United States.   2. Technology and state—Germany
  (West)   3. Technology and state—Japan.   4. Competition. International.   I. Heiduk,
  Günter.   II. Yamamura, Kōzō.   III. Committee on Japanese Economic Studies
  (U.S.)   IV. Forschungsinstitut für wirtschaftlich-technische Entwicklungen in Japan
  und im Pazifikraum e.V.
  T21.T39   1990   89-28169
  338.97306—dc20   CIP

The paper used in this publication meets the minimum requirements of American National Standard for Information Sciences—Permanence of Paper for Printed Library Materials, ANSI Z39.48–1984. ⊗

Contents

Preface

This volume is the result of a symposium held in Duisburg, West Germany, in August 1987 and attended by economists and political scientists of Japan, West Germany, and the United States. Because the symposium was both international and interdisciplinary with ambitious goals as described in the Introduction, preparing this volume for publication took much more time than the editors and participants had anticipated and hoped. To benefit from comments and criticisms made on their papers at the symposium, all authors felt it necessary to revise the papers they had originally presented. Although time-consuming, this was a process the editors welcomed because it attested to the liveliness and usefulness of the interdisciplinary and international exchange of views that occurred at the symposium. The very process of editing the final manuscripts also proved time-consuming because these works of economists and political scientists represented three different nationalities with styles of exposition that varied widely.

The editors and participants alike hope that what is presented in this volume justifies the nearly two years of collaborative efforts across the Pacific and Atlantic oceans and that despite the delay in publication, readers will find the issues raised and analyses offered in this volume useful and stimulating not only in better understanding and in conducting analytic studies of the issues examined but also in formulating public policy to promote technological progress at home and to increase cooperation and minimize conflicts among the technological leaders.

An international conference such as this requires the cooperation and assistance of many organizations and individuals and the funding provided by several sources in all three nations. The symposium was conceived, planned, and administered as a joint project of the Forschungsinstitut für wirtschaftlich-technische Entwicklungen in Japan und im Pazifikraum e.V. (FJP) of Duisburg University and the Committee on Japanese Economic Studies of the United States (Masahiko Aoki, Stanford University; Koichi Hamada, Yale University; Solomon Levine, University of Wisconsin; Hugh Patrick, Columbia University; Henry Rosovsky, Harvard University; Kazuo Sato, Rutgers University; Gary Saxonhouse, University of Michigan; and Kozo Yamamura, University of Washington). The primary goal of the former, the only such institute in West Germany, is to promote understanding of the economies and technological developments in Japan and other Asian nations. The latter is a committee of American specialists of the Japanese economy, organized to undertake and sponsor research and other education projects to increase understanding of the Japanese economy and its relations with the United States and other nations. Since its creation a decade ago, the committee has organized conferences that have resulted in several publications, all published by the University of Washington Press: Kozo Yamamura, ed., *Policy and Trade Issues of the Japanese Economy: American and Japanese Perspectives* (1982); Gary R. Saxonhouse and Kozo Yamamura, eds., *Law and Trade Issues of the Japanese Economy: American and Japanese Perspectives* (1986); and Hugh Patrick, ed., *Japan's High Technology Industries: Lessons and Limitations of Industrial Policy* (1986).

The coeditors of this volume are most grateful to all who contributed in various ways to make the publication of this volume possible. We first wish to express our sincere appreciation to Professors Kuniko Inoguchi, Erich Kaufer, Wolfgang Klenner, Klaus Müller, Dieter Cassel, Ingo Böbel, and Willy Kraus, who participated in the symposium and contributed actively to the discussion and debate, and to the FJP and the committee, which endorsed and supported this symposium. Heiduk wishes to thank Rektor Gernot Born of Duisburg University, who gave the symposium his unqualified support. Yamamura is most appreciative of the active support Gary Saxonhouse, chairman of the committee, provided from the earliest stage of organizing the symposium and also as an active participant.

Our deep appreciation is due to the foundations that supported the symposium. Generous funding provided by the United States–Japan Foundation enabled the committee to fund a large part of the cost of inviting American and Japanese scholars. The Peter Klöckner Foundation made a substantial grant to enable the cosponsors of the symposium to invite German scholars and to defray a significant part of the costs of the symposium proceedings. Our special thanks are due to the Verein zur Förderung der kulturellen und wissenschaftlichen Beziehungen zwischen Japan und der Bundesrepublik Deutschland for providing publication assistance for this volume. In addition, we are most appreciative of financial assistance received from the Japan Foundation and the Nomura Foundation, each of which provided crucial assistance in meeting various expenses of the symposium. Heiduk also wishes to acknowledge the crucial continuing support that is given by Gesellschaft der Freunde der Niederrheinischen Universität Duisburg to the FJP, making the activities of FJP, including this symposium, possible.

In the long process that extended from the initial conception of the symposium to the preparation of the manuscripts, we incurred many debts to many persons. Martha Lane assisted with her usual efficiency in taking principal responsibility for the administration of the symposium and in acting as a rapporteur who also had the responsibility of producing the final report of the rapporteurs. Karla Pearson provided indispensable assistance in manuscript preparation as well as in tending to the organizing activities of the symposium. We are also grateful to Christina Messer, who with skill and grace assisted in the administration of the symposium and served as a rapporteur. Sabine Seidler, who is bilingual, as is Christina Messer, was an extremely valuable aide-de-camp who performed multiple roles, including that of rapporteur. Dr. Paul Welfens also served as an able rapporteur.

Heiduk wishes to express his special thanks also to Brigitte Dunkel and Sabine Ellerich, who assisted in preparing and organizing the symposium. Yamamura acknowledges with appreciation the advice and encouragement provided by Hugh T. Patrick, a member of the committee, and the patient and professional assistance of Naomi Pascal of the University of Washington Press, who again agreed to take on a multinational conference volume with all of its problems.

Finally, we express our thanks to those who attended the symposium on the current issues and future prospects of technological change in East Asian follower countries—the People's Republic of China and South Korea—held concurrently with our symposium. Interaction in and out of conference sessions with those who attended the "follower" symposium helped to enliven and enrich our discussion. Those who attended the follower symposium included Professors Takashi Inoguchi, Chuk-kyo Kim, Nicholas Lardy, Jinjoo Lee, Dwight Perkins, Thomas Rawski, Gary Saxonhouse, and Lin Zhou.

Introduction

The economies of advanced industrial nations face, today and in the coming decades, many difficult political and economic problems due to the accelerating pace and evolving character of technological change that cannot but further increase the interdependence as well as competition among them. Adopting new policies to cope with or solve these problems will significantly shape the future of each of these nations as well as that of all nations.

There are several important reasons why making policy decisions to address these problems will be difficult. First, within each of these nations, no political consensus exists as to the extent or types of desirable government involvement in promoting innovative activities and in increasing national capabilities to make the most effective use of technology. Some argue that active political intervention is called for to enhance international competitive abilities by promoting a nation's own innovative capabilities and by assisting national industries. Others sharply disagree and advocate that the future course of technological progress and national abilities to make effective use of new knowledge should be left to the dictates of market forces. Eclectic views are held by many between the two camps, and policy debates are often inconclusive because making accurate, objective estimates of the benefits and costs of a specific policy is extremely difficult, if not virtually impossible.

A second reason making selection of a policy course difficult is that the interests of technologically advanced nations conflict, often sharply, because of competition for current or future international market share and disagreement regarding the real or perceived effects that one nation's policies, practices, and institutions will have on its trading partners. Of course, this difficulty is due to the fact that the policy decisions of each nation are made in response to political demands of citizens. That is to say, a nation as a political entity is frequently incapable of adopting policies as an interdependent economic entity, the interests of which are better served by promoting international cooperation.

Yet a third reason, which makes the preceding two even more salient, is the sharp divergence of views regarding international technology transfer. Some are convinced of the desirability of the free flow of technology across international boundaries or of the futility of efforts to prevent such a flow. However, others argue with no less conviction that it is possible to restrict international transfers of technology. They say the transfer should

be restricted to the extent possible in order to enable domestic innovators and industries to capture maximum gains by exploiting the advantage, if even for a limited period, of being the innovator or possessor
of more advanced technology.

To examine and discuss these and other difficulties in the hope of contributing to their mitigation or solution, the intent of the organizers and
participants of the Duisburg symposium was to gather an international
group of scholars who would present papers on salient and pressing policy issues and offer insights useful in formulating the policies that could
best promote fair and fruitful competition and enhance equitable and
effective cooperation among the advanced industrial nations. To focus the
attention of the participants on policy issues, especially those faced by
the technological leaders, the papers presented and discussions to take
place at the symposium were to be not only policy oriented but limited
to the three major leaders: the United States, West Germany, and Japan. That is, while making use of analytic insights and remaining mindful
of broad international issues of interest to all advanced industrial nations,
the participants were to examine and debate intensively the policy issues
faced by these three nations.

As the organizers proceeded to assemble a list of economists and political scientists who could participate and began to explore the potential
agenda and format of the symposium, they were quickly made aware that
many participants lacked knowledge of the specific policy issues and the
political, economic, and institutional reasons for these issues faced respectively by the three nations. The organizers realized that given the
number and scope of the policy issues involved, it would be much more
fruitful to select participants who had already studied specific facets of
policy issues rather than to attempt to predetermine the issues and identify a participant.

On this basis, a format was developed for the symposium in which
three overview papers, two analytical papers, and four papers on specific
policy issues would be presented, with a summary paper written following the conclusion of the symposium. The overview papers were to describe each of the three nations' current and near-future technological
capabilities, reasons for policies in effect, the effects of both political and
economic institutions on current and likely future policies, and, to
the extent necessary to better understand all the foregoing, a descriptive
and comparative analysis of the recent history of technological change in
each of the nations. The main goal of these overview papers was to provide all participants with common knowledge as a foundation for discussion and debate of issues of common interest and concern.

The two analytical papers were to be written, respectively, by a political scientist whose expertise in international policy issues was well
established and by an economist well known for theoretical and policy-
oriented works in international economics. Their assigned tasks were to

describe and analyze from the perspectives of their disciplines what each regarded as the most significant policy issues raised by technological change and the international competition and cooperation that are being increased by it. The four papers on policy issues were to be written by scholars who, because of their ongoing research, were familiar with a specific policy issue or a number of closely related policy issues. These scholars were asked to analyze more narrowly defined policy issues in order to provide a basis for conference discussion. Finally, the task of the scholar writing the summary paper was to highlight what he regarded as the principal insights gained and lessons learned from the conference.

We will now present brief summaries of each paper to highlight the observations and analyses offered and the issues raised and examined by each author. These summaries will be followed by the editors' own assessment of and reflections on the proceedings of the symposium.

In the overview paper on the United States, entitled "What Has Happened to U.S. Technological Leadership?" Richard R. Nelson describes the historical trend toward convergence in technological performance and predicts that this trend will continue. His central observation is that after World War II the United States became the undisputed leader in virtually all areas of technology, a unique situation in modern world history, but the American lead began to slip away in the late 1960s just when Europeans became seriously concerned with the long-run dangers to Europe of continuing American technological dominance. In Nelson's view, convergence was inevitable due to the internationalization of science and technology, free trade of sophisticated goods and technical expertise, and the growing capabilities of other industrialized nations. The efforts required by the followers to catch up were far less demanding than those necessary for the leader to create new products or to improve existing technologies.

In addition, Nelson argues that the large share of research and development (R&D) resources allocated for defense and space research in the United States reduced the R&D resources that could have otherwise been used in civilian research. Moreover, the spillover effects of defense-related research to civilian technology declined sharply over time. In general, this development by itself, he argues, would not have been cause for serious concern were it not for two "outlier phenomena." One is Japan's rapid technological progress. Japan has not only caught up with the United States but in some areas has taken the lead. The other is an extremely slow rate of growth in productivity in the United States, measured for all input or for labor alone, since 1970. He expects, however, that American companies and the U.S. government will not allow civilian R&D to fall significantly below Japanese and European levels.

In assessing the future course of American productivity advances, he also expresses serious concern with the short time horizon of American investors and management as well as with the declining quality of American education, which once played a crucial role in enabling the United States to achieve high rates of productivity growth. On the other hand, he sees American advantages over other nations in the high level of university research, in seemingly more productive university-industry relationships, and in the supply of venture capital to finance risky innovation investment. Thus, Nelson's tone is optimistic when he directs the reader's attention to the demonstrated ability of Americans to mix entrepreneurial firms, giant corporations, universities, and industry in a way unmatched by other nations.

An assessment of Japan's current technological capabilities and its capacity to innovate is presented by Sully Taylor and Kozo Yamamura in their overview paper "Japan's Technological Capabilities and Its Future." The authors survey the Japanese commitment to key technological sectors such as semiconductors, telecommunications, biotechnology, and carbon fibers. Their study reveals that Japan has already achieved a strong position in many areas and has of late become increasingly capable of making significant innovations of its own.

Taylor and Yamamura regard four variables as most influential for the process of innovation in postwar Japan: industrial policy, which they believe changed significantly over time and is less important today than before; firm organization, which both contributed to and detracted from Japanese firms' ability to innovate; institutions and management of labor, which also affect Japan's technological capabilities both positively and negatively; and the international trade system, which is crucial in determining Japan's technological future.

They also give special attention to the current weakness of basic research in Japan. They stress that the Japanese educational system, better suited to the process of catch-up than to fostering innovative skills, presents a problem of its own; that the flexibility of Japanese firm organization is a significant asset in the current technology competition; and that labor market conditions are creating problems as Japanese workers are on average getting older and the number of women seeking employment is steadily increasing. The authors emphasize that the future international trade system will play a vital role in Japanese innovative capabilities because protectionism and restricted technology transfer can still significantly threaten Japan's technological development in the coming decades. They argue, therefore, that Japan must pursue a policy of internationalization and allow broad access to domestic markets in an attempt to settle current trade disputes.

The position of West Germany is very similar to that of several other European countries. All indicators of economic and technological development for Europe show that the process of catch-up with the United States has ended in certain respects. This view is expressed in the third overview paper, which is by Ernst-Jürgen Horn and is entitled "West

German Technology in the 1980s: Perceptions, Evidence, and Policy Issues." In noting the end of catch-up in Europe, the slow decline in U.S. leadership, and the dynamic technological and economic performance of Japan, his view is consistent with that expressed by Nelson.

Horn is not sanguine about the capability of West Germany to retain the leadership role it now enjoys. Institutional weaknesses such as the lack of venture capital, the regulation of markets with high growth potential (e.g., telecommunications), and continuing subsidies to declining industries such as shipbuilding, steel, and coal mining are likely to retard German innovative capacities. He is also doubtful of the efficiency of industrial policy, because West Germany's comparative advantages do not lie in the creation of new products but rather in their quick imitation and incorporation into production processes (a point seconded by Legler in his paper). Thus, a better strategy, according to Horn, is the improvement of overall economic conditions.

In the first theoretical paper, "The Impact of Industrial Structure and Industrial Policy on International Trade," Motoshige Itoh presents a non-mathematical survey of a recent theory often referred to as the new international trade theory and applies it to Japan. As more theorists are attempting today, he challenges the traditional Heckscher-Ohlin theory, in which exogenous factors such as factor endowments and natural resources determine the patterns of international trade. He argues that the industrial structure of a nation plays a determining role in explaining its pattern of international trade and that the industrial structure of a nation is in turn determined, to a large degree, by technological developments that can be fostered by economic policy.

In his model of two countries and three goods (seen as a continuum of goods ranging from the low to the middle to the high end of a technology-intensity scale), trade partners can influence their relative income positions by increasing output and exports of a certain product category. The model assumes the existence of a bilateral relationship in which one party chooses to adopt a certain structure and the other accepts (without taking countermeasures) the decision of the former in order to avoid trade conflicts. The key to his analysis is that if country A succeeds in diminishing its propensity to import, it gains a relative income advantage. Moreover, dynamic economies of scale due to the various effects of technological progress and learning-curve effects create a situation dramatically different from that of perfect competition. According to Itoh, oligopolistic market structure allows scope for policy intervention to keep oligopolistic rents within the country. Nevertheless, as in the optimal tariff case, potential foreign repercussions must be considered. That is, it is possible to conclude an international agreement to provide subsidies to improve economic welfare on a global scale.

However, as Itoh himself admits, policy to promote an industry in this manner is not likely to proceed smoothly in the real world due to the reactions of trade partners and because oligopolistic firms will involve themselves in the policy in order to obtain subsidies. He also notes that there exists the problem of information: how can governments predict future developments better than firms themselves? As in the case of the debate relating to various forms of industrial policy and the so-called strategic international trade policy, there are still many unanswered questions with regard to the analytic issues raised by imperfect market conditions and their effects on international trade.

The relative decline of U.S. leadership and changes in the international industrial structure have shifted the relative economic power of the largest industrial nations and therefore of interests in favor of a certain international economic order. Peter F. Cowhey, a political scientist presenting the other analytic paper, constructs a theory of the rise of specific international economic orders in "The Agenda of the Leading Nations for the World Economy: A Theory of International Economic Regimes." Three principles are seen to dominate in building the international trade system desired by the leaders of industrial economies. First, there must be a leading or a few leading economic powers to guarantee an open and smoothly functioning system. Second, power alone is not enough to persuade other countries to join the system. The leading country has to provide "credible commitments" for the less strong. This means it must recognize the interests of the latter. Third, the degree and kind of openness of the system reflect, in essence, those found in the domestic system of the leader.

Cowhey applies this scheme to the international economy of the nineteenth century, in which Great Britain favored the gold standard and constructed a liberal trade system modeled on its domestic order. The concepts of Keynesian macroeconomic demand management and microeconomic nonintervention that characterized the postwar U.S. domestic economic order were found again in the General Agreement on Tariffs and Trade and the Bretton Woods agreement, which provided the foundation for the postwar international economic system.

Two developments have eroded the U.S.-dominated regime. First, the Japanese and West German economies grew rapidly. Cowhey asserts that neither country distinguishes between macroeconomic and microeconomic management; instead, they pursue an industrial policy to promote oligopolistic industries through various means. Second, the power of multinational enterprises (MNE), which sometimes behave like independent agents in international trade, is growing. Cowhey addresses this phenomenon in the principal-agent context. The parties—Japan, West Germany, and the MNEs—are all export oriented and want to remain so. MNEs themselves are products of the internationalization of world markets, but, Cowhey adds, they all favor different rules for the international trade regime, especially with respect to industrial policy.

In the papers on specific policy issues, Iwao Nakatani sees, as does

Itoh, technology as an endogenous factor dependent on industrial structure. Taking Japan as an example, he first undertakes an empirical survey of the extent and kinds of groupings of firms in Japan in his paper
"Effectiveness in Technological Innovation: *Keiretsu* versus Conglomerates." The main thrust of his paper is to argue that the success of the
keiretsu (horizontally organized groups) lies in their ability to better dis-
tribute risk and to gain preferential access to capital markets. This is
shown by a smaller variance in profits, sales, and interest payments seen
for the firms in keiretsu vis-à-vis those that do not belong to keiretsu.
He thus argues that the firms in keiretsu can make larger R&D expenditures and can undertake riskier and longer-term projects in their efforts
to increase their technological capabilities.

Nakatani argues that vertical integration yields benefits to firms in a
different way. The close relationship between a parent firm and a number of subcontractors allows management to plan and carry out mutually
beneficial innovations without creating excess organizational slack and in-
curring large external transaction costs. Nakatani believes that these relationships favor above all "continuous refinements and improvements of
existing products" or "new products related to existing ones." In short,
Nakatani directs our attention to the importance of the type of firm group,
as well as the existence of the groups themselves, in analyzing firms'
ability to make technological progress.

"The German Competitive Position in Trade of Technology-Intensive
Products," by Harald Legler, reveals those areas in which West Germany enjoys a competitive edge. This empirical analysis allows the reader
to examine whether and to what extent market competition contributed
to technological competitive capability in West Germany.

Legler shows that the West German competitive position in semiconductors and computers (compared with electronics and informatics) is rather
weak, and he cites several discrepancies between expressed targets and
actual West German performance. Most useful in his study are his efforts
to separate high technology goods, defined as those with an R&D share
of total costs of more than 8 percent, from "high commodities" (*gehobene
Gebrauchstechnologie*), having an R&D share of 3 to 8 percent. Using
the concepts of relative world trade share and revealed comparative advantage, he determines the positions of the United States, Japan, and
West Germany in several industrial sectors. His findings indicate that
the United States maintains a dominant position in high technology goods,
whereas Japan is slowly moving away from high commodities into high
technology goods. West Germany holds a strong position in high commodities and a rather weak position in high technology. In addition, Legler finds that West Germany has a disadvantage in many of its targeted
sectors in both categories.

An assessment of U.S. technological capabilities combined with an
analysis of the social benefits (welfare gains) of being a leader is found

in "The Challenge to U.S. Leadership in High Technology Industries" by Rachel McCulloch. She, like Itoh, justifies public intervention in high technology markets in order to promote national welfare. She does caution, however, that technological capabilities are firm specific and can be transferred abroad via direct investment and licenses. This is the main reason, as Nelson also stresses, the United States has lost some of its dominance in the world markets. However, in this context it is important to note, she argues, that the share of world production by U.S. firms has remained constant if the output of American MNEs is included. This is especially the case in the high technology sector, in which the share of U.S. firms has even been increasing.

In general, McCulloch does not regard the overall performance of the United States in the high technology sector as dismal. She emphasizes that technological leadership by itself does not improve economic welfare but rather that the technological standard of a nation's industries does. If trade partners also have a similar standard, it allows for profitable two-way trade. Why then is technological leadership considered an important goal? McCulloch outlines several reasons, including national prestige and military considerations. Another incentive to strive for technological dominance and domestic technological development is the desire for technological independence. However, this desire is seen as reasonable by McCulloch only in regard to a few special goods produced by just a few firms that dominate the entire world market.

In his paper "Geography Is Not Destiny: The Changing Character of Competitive Advantage in Automobiles," George C. Eads emphasizes, as does McCulloch, the role of individual firms in using and developing specific technology. That is, he regards analyses of technological transfer at country level as outdated and unrewarding. He also argues that overall factor endowment and returns to factors of production are poor guides in determining and forecasting future trade and investment patterns. Using the case of the motor vehicle industry, Eads demonstrates the importance of scrutinizing the specific capabilities of individual firms of all nations to remain competitive instead of explaining, as is often done, the international shift in production capacity as due to wage differentials. Thus, he argues the need to recognize the advantage that some Japanese firms have in their highly efficient internal organization, which allows flexibility and continuing product improvement, as well as the need to realize that there are large differences in efficiency among Japanese firms. Traditional suppliers in the United States and Europe have to cope with high factor costs (as the Japanese do now as well), and they react quite differently to this challenge—some by relying heavily on automation. Third World firms have labor cost advantages but sometimes inadequate technology and worker skills to produce the quality demanded. Eads asserts that none of these advantages alone will be sufficient to remain competitive. Even Japanese firms—which have so far proved to be the most dynamic—must strengthen their automation efforts for continuing competitiveness. On the other hand, U.S. firms must improve organization. Eads expects some kind of convergence between the two since Japanese automobile firms have shifted production to sites in the United States and have thus allowed a transfer of organizational expertise.

The final contribution is a summary essay by Merton J. Peck entitled "The Benefits and Burdens of the Technological Leaders." Peck reviews the discussions among participants on the uncertainty of the rewards of being a technological leader; on the reasons for, and the significance of, the decline of the United States as the dominant technological power; the rise of Japan as a challenger to the United States; and the current performance of West Germany. According to Peck, West Germany needs to be considered an in-between case, since it is neither a leader nor a challenger but still plays an important role in technological competition. Thus, in reviewing the development of technological competition among these nations, Peck makes an observation having significant implications for policymakers of technological leaders: unlike in the past, today no single nation can be the dominant technological power, as the United States was in the postwar decades. This is because given the diversity of technological change, we have entered an era in which many nations have technological power in one or more sectors, but no longer will all sectors be dominated by one power.

As is evident from the preceding descriptions, the Duisburg symposium had two ingredients that could not but make the conference a lively one. One was the large, multifaceted topic addressed that raised many important analytic questions and difficult policy issues; the other was participants from three nations whose research interests and expertise differed widely. The result was an even livelier—and more fruitful—symposium than the organizers and participants had hoped.

One of the most frequently debated questions was, What role should governments play to enhance the technological capabilities and competitiveness of their industries? The question became a central topic of debate and was dealt with in several of the papers presented from various perspectives, each focusing on a different set of policies. The discussion and debate became "energetic" at times because of differences in the views among the participants on (1) causal links between the policy adopted (and resources allocated) and the policy goal achieved; (2) the extent to which resources allocated by one nation to promote innovative activities were producing a "public good" for the world; and (3) desirable political solutions to the conflict between the recent political trend of several large industrial nations (including Japan, West Germany, and the United States) to place increased reliance on the market (to the point of deregulating formerly regulated industries) and the economic reality of some important high technologies (especially those determining the character of telecommunications and data processing) that appear to require further gov-

ernmental involvement in the difficult tasks of dealing with, and even
regulating, increasingly intensive domestic and international competition.

Summarized briefly, although the participants reached a broad consensus on the desirability, in most cases, of adopting policies intended
to make use of the competitive forces of the market, many believed that
governments have distinct roles to perform in promoting technological
progress. Stated alternatively, many shared the view that although it is
not justified to think that any country can maintain technological leadership for a long period, countries should adopt policies intended to keep
up with others at the frontier of technological change. Such policies should
maintain a climate favorable to investment and R&D, effective and cost-
efficient support for R&D, and a good educational system in order to
increase investment in human capital.

Beyond this broad consensus, however, there remained differences of
opinion as to the specific meaning of such adjectives as *favorable*, *effective*, and *good* used in the preceding paragraph. This was due to differing assessments of the degree and rapidity of the internationalization
of scientific knowledge and technology, that is, the extent to which the
resources allocated to carry out a policy may yield outcomes favorable
(and for a sufficiently long time) to the nation adopting the policy so that
it can realize adequate returns, especially increasing international competitiveness, to those resources.

Some participants were more inclined than others to believe in the
"borderlessness" of scientific knowledge and technology. For some, it is
no longer meaningful even to identify specific technology with nationality
in the age of increasingly larger and more global multinationals, joint
ventures, and other means that are making many large firms truly international rather than American, German, or Japanese. Other participants, however, were more inclined to think that the gains resulting from
resources allocated by a nation to R&D and education can still be significant in terms of gaining the advantage of "lead time" and in more
effectively sustaining the pace of technological progress; that is, technological progress is the result of many capabilities of a society, not all
of which are easily transferable across national boundaries.

Discussion of this issue was carried on as a debate on the desirability
and effects of industrial policy, which participants generally understood
to mean subsidies of various types (including R&D assistance and tax
preferences) and various forms of protection for targeted industries. Some
participants argued that such a policy may be useful in assisting a nation's industries to gain and maintain competitiveness so long as it did
not have the effect of limiting market competition in the domestic market. Japanese and other participants cited the case of Japan to argue the
possibility of a government's providing modest but critical assistance
without restricting market competition. Others took issue with this view,
arguing that such a policy could not but foster the oligopolistic market

power of firms favored by the policy and that such a policy would induce retaliatory action by trading partners and might have adverse effects on income distribution within the economy in which this policy was adopted. Even those in support of some type of industrial policy acknowledged that Japanese-style industrial policy was effective in the rapid-growth decades of the 1950s and 1960s primarily because Japan was catching up with the West (borrowing technology) and that in Japan today industrial policy has lost many of its tools and has become significantly less effective.

Discussion of the roles of government and especially of industrial policy became wide ranging and prolonged due substantially to the facts that the established theory of trade is of decreasing relevance today, when technological changes are rapidly continuing and several basic assumptions of the theory no longer hold, and that recent attempts to replace the theory have not yet succeeded in advancing a theory free of serious analytical weaknesses. The recent theoretical attempt—the so-called theory of strategic trade policy—is based on three features: (1) oligopolistic market structure (in contrast to competitive market structure, assumed in the traditional theory); (2) government policy adopted to subsidize or protect targeted industries or both; and (3) because of feature 2, oligopolistic firms having sufficient market power and size (needed to adopt new technology) to adopt new technology and realize the gains of learning by doing in order to become internationally competitive. That is, dynamic comparative advantage can be *created* by policy.

This description, attractive to some policymakers and theorists wishing to stress the importance of these features lacking in the traditional theory, is based, however, on making what many regard as unacceptably strong assumptions. These include the assumptions that oligopolistic firms in other nations either will fail to react or will have only certain predictable reactions to the output and price decisions of the oligopolistic firm of the nation adopting the policy; that trading partners will not adopt counterpolicy; and that the economy as a whole will gain by promoting the comparative advantages of the targeted firms, which become beneficiaries of what the policy provides.

The participants did not engage in protracted discussion of theoretical issues since the symposium was not intended to deal with purely theoretical issues. However, as noted above, much of the debate relating to the role of governments made it clear to all participants that theoretical development is today attempting to catch up with reality, which is undergoing rapid changes because of the accelerating pace of technological change, the ever-increasing size and importance of multinationals, and the internationalization of science and technology, which seems to be proceeding at an increasing rate.

Closely connected to internationalization and the debate concerning the role of governments was a discussion of the present and future of the international trade regime. The central question was, What policies must the technological leaders adopt in order both to maintain stable trading relations and to nurture the systems of competition and cooperation that are most desirable for all concerned? The significance of the decline in the dominance of the American economy and technology was discussed at length, and many participants agreed that it was no longer possible or desirable for both West Germany and Japan to accept American models in creating a stable and harmonious trade regime. What is needed are conscious efforts, despite unavoidable conflicts, to evolve systems that are acceptable to both Americans and their primary challengers, especially the Germans and Japanese. Specific cases of telecommunications, high-speed computers, and other high technology products were discussed extensively by the participants.

Despite the fact that the participants were discussing issues involving the technological leaders, a considerable amount of discussion took place on the effects that the technological competition and cooperation among the leaders and the policies these leaders adopt will have on the technological followers of today. (Of course, this was in part due to the fact, as noted in the Preface, that several Western scholars specializing in Korea and China and scholars from these countries participated in the proceedings.) The main questions discussed included such conflicting concerns as, Will the "rent-seeking" behavior and policies of technologically advanced multinational firms and nations retard the technological progress of the followers? And, how and how well will the followers benefit from the internationalization of technology and science? These and other questions discussed reminded the participants of the clear need to consider the effects of policy and behavior of the technological leaders in global terms. Today it is much less likely for the followers to benefit, as Japan did after 1945, from what proved to be attractive terms (costs and conditions) for technological transfer, from virtually unrestricted access to sources of technology (research institutions, university research activities, and even corporate research activities), and from open markets of the technological leaders (the leaders' markets have become increasingly protected by various measures).

The participants also discussed such topics as the measurement problems involved in defining a product as either a high, medium, or low technology product for the purposes of theoretical and policy analyses; the increasing difficulties and their consequences involved in distinguishing "pure" scientific research from applied research useful in product development; and the effects that nation-specific forms of interfirm organization (such as enterprise groups in Japan vis-à-vis conglomerates in the United States) have on a nation's ability to make technological progress.

Here we must acknowledge, to our regret, that discussions at the symposium failed to delve into an important set of questions regarding how domestic and international policies are formulated and how the specific character of the policies is determined. This is to say, beyond broad discussions concerning the process of making international policy that were stimulated by Peter Cowhey's paper, the participants engaged in little substantive discussion of such questions as, How do interest groups bring pressure to bear on policy outcomes? How do the differences in political institutions among the three nations affect policy outcomes? What factors—such as the character of the technology in the industry at issue, the relative importance of the industry within the domestic economy and in international trade, the current and expected competition and cooperation between the same industries of different technological leaders— determine the strength of their pressure and the nature of the policy adopted? To be sure, this missed opportunity was due mainly to the lack of perspicacity on the part of the organizers, whose choice of participants did not include more political scientists.

Finally, we conclude this Introduction by noting that what became apparent to us through the papers presented and the active discussion at the symposium was that all three nations are today in search of policy, both domestic and international, that can sustain technological progress at home and keep them internationally competitive. And, if we have correctly interpreted the expressed concerns of the scholars of each of the three nations, the search is being motivated by the uneasiness each nation feels in its ability to remain a technological leader.

The United States, in facing the historical fact that the postwar process of technological convergence has deprived it of the dominance it once enjoyed, is experiencing a loss of confidence. It is being forced to reevaluate its educational system, the costs of resources allocated for defense-related R&D efforts, the legal system protecting proprietary rights of scientific knowledge and technological discoveries, and many other practices and policies. The loss of confidence also appears in the form of selective protectionism.

Some participants argued that the technological prowess of the United States is still substantial, as evidenced by its ability to undertake basic research, to provide risk capital for fledgling ventures, and to educate the next generation of Nobel Prize winners. Others note that the share in the world market of high technology and other manufacturing products produced by American MNEs has not declined in the past few decades, attesting to the resiliency of American technological capabilities. But these observations are efforts to enumerate remaining American strengths and do not reflect a confidence shaken by deteriorating trade statistics and by the growing market shares of foreign firms in the domestic market.

West Germany too is far from confident of its technological future, as was repeatedly noted by the German participants. Despite their demonstrated performance in the international market and in the increasing number of international patents won, the nation clearly is also uneasy and not confident of meeting the technological challenges of the United States and Japan. The debate within West Germany is intense on the issues surrounding the extent government is to intrude in the market, the deregulation of industries, its relations with its European Community (EC) partners and resource commitments to joint EC projects to promote its own technological capabilities as well as those of other EC members, and its educational systems, which are primarily administered by its eleven states.

Trade surpluses notwithstanding, German concerns for the increasing international competition are real. They do feel they are slowly losing ground, especially to Japan, in the competition for high technology products. Thus, for them, the critical questions arising are, How much longer will West Germany be able to maintain its policy of opening its doors wider than its fellow Western European nations to Japanese firms, products, and capital? How will its declining but still high unemployment rate affect the policy? What should West Germany do to regain the undisputed scientific and technological leadership it once enjoyed in many areas?

One would expect that the Japanese would be confident of their technological future and ability to enlarge their share in the world market of high technology products. The abundant evidence, ranging from rapidly increasing international patents and a large number of trained engineers and other technical personnel to trade and investment data, suggests the reasonableness of such an expectation. And, indeed, some Japanese are confident. However, it is decidedly inaccurate to characterize the feeling of a large majority of Japanese as confident of their technological future or their ability to maintain the current pace of performance in international markets for high technology products.

The reasons for their uneasiness are many. They are fully aware that although their capabilities are improving, they still lag behind other countries, especially the United States, in basic research. Their educational system has well-known weaknesses (overemphasis on examinations requiring a significant amount of rote memorization, rigidities permitting little individual initiative and experimentation, and so on). There is extreme difficulty in obtaining venture capital, and although their oft-discussed labor management practices have several useful characteristics for promoting technological progress, they nevertheless are not supportive of innovation. Of course, the Japanese ability to remain a technological leader would be threatened seriously were its trading partners and others to limit access to their markets, natural resources, scientific knowledge, and technology. Furthermore, one should recall the fact that many of Japan's past policies that aided technological progress are today either unavailable or ineffective.

These are very broad descriptions of the uneasiness—the lack of confidence—each of the three nations manifests today. When read with the observations and analyses contained in the chapters to follow, these descriptions are sufficient to make the point that these nations, the technological leaders of today, are in search of the policy that can best boost their confidence. But as we have indicated earlier, such policies are hard to come by.

To recapitulate, the uneasiness and difficulties in finding effective policies are to be expected. This is because ours is a world in which technological change is rapid and the direction, speed, and consequences of the changes are difficult to anticipate; knowledge and information of all types are exchanged across international boundaries with the speed of a jet or even of electronic communication; economic interdependence among nations, especially among the technological leaders, has become much more intense and extensive than ever before; and several crucial modi vivendi of the international trade regime, necessary in maintaining its functions and harmony, are yet to evolve.

The symposium was but a minute collective step taken by the participants to learn from each other what policy questions and analytic issues each believed to be most salient and how each must proceed in attempting to answer these questions or resolve these issues. In the earnestness and frankness shown in the discussion and debate, it was evident that the participants learned a great deal from one another and came to have a far better sense of the most important questions and issues affecting the future of their nations as well as that of other nations. In Duisburg, there were often either too many answers or no answers at all. But all participants became more convinced that in our attempts to find the correct answers, an international forum such as that held in Duisburg was one of the most meaningful and rewarding ways.

GÜNTER HEIDUK

KOZO YAMAMURA

Part One

OVERVIEW

1

What Has Happened
to U.S. Technological Leadership?

RICHARD R. NELSON

A scholar charged with writing a paper on the "technological capabilities and problems of the United States" cannot help but attempt to address the question, What has happened to U.S. technological leadership? A dry account, even a diagnosis, focused strictly on the current situation simply will not suffice.

During the first quarter-century after World War II, the rest of the world came to regard the United States as the undisputed technological leader in most, if not all, fields of industry. Labor productivity in the United States was considerably higher than in any other industrial nation, as was total factor productivity. U.S. firms pioneered in the leading-edge industries, and the resultant manufacturing exports dominated world markets. The research and development (R&D) and educational systems of the United States became objects of envy and emulation by other nations. The sophistication and aggressiveness of American management and the literacy and flexibility of American labor were also highly touted.

This is no longer the case. What has happened over the past fifteen years, and what does it forebode? These are important questions, but they require analysis in terms of a dynamic picture that takes us up to the present rather than a static snapshot of the current situation.

Accordingly, I begin this paper with some analytic history. When and how did the sources of American technological leadership of the 1950s and 1960s come into being? What are the factors behind its obvious erosion in the 1970s and 1980s? Only after struggling with these questions do I turn to the current picture and present statistics that describe the present U.S. standing. Finally, I will assess the current strengths and weaknesses of technology in the United States and present alternative scenarios for the future.

THE AMERICAN HALF-CENTURY, OR WAS IT A CENTURY?

A number of foreigners, principally Europeans, reflecting on the post–World War II American economic and technological dominance, wrote as if the phenomenon were new. Others wrote as if the conditions were long-standing. Both positions are partly correct.

While Great Britain is correctly regarded as the pioneer and dominant technological power of the first industrial revolution, the Americans caught on quickly, in a number of ways and in a number of fields. As early as 1835, de Tocqueville noted that the Americans were superior to the British in shipbuilding and shipping.[1] Habakkuk observes that "there is a substantial body of comment, by English visitors to America in the first half of the 19th century, which suggests that in a number of industries American equipment was in some sense superior to the English even at this period."[2]

The evidence is clear that by the middle of the nineteenth century, the United States was a major source of mechanical invention. American leadership appears to have been concentrated in technologies used significantly more on the American scene than the European, like steamboats and machines to process American agricultural products and, more generally, machinery and technology suited to the American context of scarce and expensive skilled labor and abundant land and raw materials.

During the last quarter of the nineteenth century, a combination of a mass market of relatively well-to-do households and a rail and communications network that broke down distance barriers led to the rise of a large-scale mass production and marketing industry in a variety of fields. Chandler has chronicled and analyzed their development. In most cases the new technology involved special-purpose machinery associated with the fine division of labor and a tightly organized work flow. In many of these industries, American firms developed a clear lead in process technology or product design or both over British and Continental firms. For example, U.S. firms dominated world production and trade in sewing machines, matches, and refrigerated meat.[3]

Also, although many observers looked upon the post–World War II wave of direct investment by U.S. manufacturing companies in Europe as a new phenomenon, it was not. During the late nineteenth and early twentieth centuries, the dominant American firms in the above industries often located plants in Europe and controlled the European market in that way rather than through exports.[4]

The leading-edge technologies of the first industrial revolution were largely mechanical, and no particular formal science training was essential to their invention. Private inventors working alone, or with a few collaborators, were the principal locus of nineteenth-century mechanical invention. The late nineteenth century, however, saw a significant change in the nature and locus of leading-edge technological change.

By 1860 the science of chemistry had developed to a point where only trained chemists could understand aspects of various manufacturing processes. Chemists began to play a central role in technological innovation in iron and steelmaking, in the making of traditional inorganic chemicals such as soda and new organic chemical substances such as dyes and, later, plastics, and in a variety of other fields.[5] Shortly after, understanding of electricity and magnetism also reached a similar stage, and scientifically trained people came to dominate innovation and problem solving in these fields as well. In both the new chemical and the new electrical industries, technological advance became dependent upon the availability of trained specialists and, thus, on the university systems providing scientific training. Technological advance in these fields began to take place increasingly in industrial R&D laboratories staffed by university-trained scientists.

Germany, rather than the United States or Great Britain, initially took the forefront in the new chemical technologies. Germany's university system was the first to incorporate instruction and research in chemistry, and German universities became the locus of training not only for German chemists but also for British and American. The Americans who went home, however, had much better luck than did their British counterparts in establishing academic chemistry in their home country. And relatively quickly the new American chemical companies had an available supply of trained chemists that was nearly on a par with that available to the German companies.[6]

In the field of electricity, American universities were nearly as quick as German universities to establish training programs. From the beginning, American companies exploiting electrical technologies had available to them American-trained personnel, while the British and French lagged behind.[7]

It is difficult to document at exactly what point American productivity and income surged above those in England. Some place the time well before the turn of the century, while others write as if the United States established its economic lead during the interwar period. However, the latter period is surely too late.

There is strong evidence that by 1914 worker productivity and per capita income in the United States were significantly higher than in England, and higher still than in the rest of Europe.[8] This was partly the result of the high productivity of American agriculture, but it is apparent that productivity in American manufacturing was also higher than in most European industries. Productivity was higher for at least two reasons. By that time, American industry was operating with a significantly higher capital-labor ratio than European industry. This was both the result and the cause of the significantly higher wage rate in U.S. industry. But total factor productivity was undoubtedly higher too. If it were simply greater capital intensity with comparable total factor productivity, the rate of return on capital would have been significantly lower in the United States than in Europe. The limited evidence suggests, rather, that it was higher.

The interwar period, then, is better regarded as the period during which the United States consolidated and increased its lead in manufacturing technology. However, there were two new developments and features of this period that became of increased importance.

One was the growing importance of the American mass market in an era when much of technological advance in manufacture amounted to the progressive exploitation of latent scale economies through the further development of mass production methods. As noted earlier, even during the nineteenth century this feature of the American situation played an important role. But because the interwar period was marked by restraints on international trade that hindered the ability of the other manufacturing powers to exploit latent scale economies, the American mass market undoubtedly provided an enormous advantage for American firms.

The second development was in American education. The interwar period saw a dramatic increase in the percentage of American youth who went on beyond primary school to secondary school, with many going on to college. Nothing like this occurred in Europe in this period.

So, European observers of post–World War II American technological primacy who presumed this leadership to be a long-standing phenomenon certainly were correct, at least in terms of certain dimensions. But so, too, were the European commentators who saw American technological primacy as something fundamentally new.

Although during the interwar period America was the undisputed leader in productivity and technology in many mass production industries, this was not the case in organic chemical products, chemical process equipment, and electronics. The technologies of the electronics industry were arguably the most sophisticated technologies of the era. The Americans lagged behind Germany in developing new chemical industries, as noted earlier. By the late 1930s there was no longer any evidence of a major technological gap, but German companies were still obtaining more patents than American firms.[9] And certain British companies were clearly at the forefront. Similarly, although the major American electrical equipment companies were clearly in the vanguard, there were companies of at least equal technological competence in Germany and Britain. American university training and research in the leading-edge sciences and technologies of that time were clearly world class. In many fields, however, German training and research (and, in some fields, British) were widely regarded as equal or even superior.

THE POSTWAR ERA:
THE AMERICAN BREAKAWAY AT THE TECHNOLOGICAL FRONTIERS

Just as after World War I, the United States came out of World War II buoyant, its technological capabilities stretched by the wartime production experience, while Europe emerged prostrate. Japan, too, was a demolished economy and nation, unlike its experience following World War I.

However, it is wrong to ascribe the U.S. technological dominance in the new high technology industries of the postwar era solely to U.S. capabilities acquired prior to and during the war and the virtual destruction of the capabilities of other industrial powers. In particular, there were three interdependent but distinguishable developments worth noting.

One was the dramatic increase in the percentage of American high school graduates who went on to college. Earlier I noted the American lead in the 1920s and 1930s over the rest of the world in the percentage of youth attending secondary school. After World War II, as other industrial countries began to catch up with the United States in secondary education, the United States pulled ahead of the pack in college education. In part, this was simply the result of the relative affluence of Americans. However, government policies further encouraged higher education. The GI bill of rights, which guaranteed educational funding to all qualified veterans, was both emblematic and an important factor in its own right. College fellowships were also made available through a number of public programs. In addition, the state-supported "public" side of the American higher education system enormously subsidized higher education.

Second, during the half-decade following World War II, the United States for the first time put government machinery into place to provide massive funding for university research. As noted earlier, by the beginning of World War II, the American system of university scientific research was world class, but had by no means outdistanced those in Europe. The new university research support programs of the National Science Foundation and the National Institutes of Health provided public funding for university basic research across a wide spectrum of fields. The Atomic Energy Commission and the Department of Defense provided large-scale funding for university research in fields of particular interest to those agencies. And, the support was not just for basic research. The mission-oriented agencies and, particularly, the Department of Defense provided funding that involved university applied science and engineering departments in work at the forefront of materials and electronics technologies.

It took some time for the European countries to mount similar programs of government university research support. During the interim, the American research universities clearly pulled ahead of those of the rest of the world in most fields. Just as young American scholars flocked to German universities to learn science during the late nineteenth century, young Europeans and Japanese students came to the United States for scientific training during the 1950s and 1960s and even still today.

The third major development was the establishment of massive Department of Defense, and later National Aeronautics and Space Administration (NASA), support of industrial research on systems and related technologies of interest to them. As noted, the Department of Defense during the early postwar period became a major supporter of university research in certain fields; however, the bulk of its R&D funding went to industry. During the 1950s and through the 1960s, the Department of Defense and NASA accounted for roughly a half of total industrial R&D expenditures.

Whereas some foreign observers of the postwar American scene have focused on Department of Defense R&D support as the fundamental source of American technological dominance, Americans have tended to play this down. Although Department of Defense R&D support played a central role in certain technologies, increased college attendance and massive government funding of university research were more important factors.

It was American dominance in computer and semiconductor technologies that most interested and concerned European analysts during the 1950s and 1960s. These were considered to be the leading-edge technologies of the postwar era. It was here that for the first time the United States established clear technological primacy at the frontier. Military and, to a lesser extent, space R&D support certainly was an important contributor.[10]

During the 1930s, those concerned with the capabilities of the armed forces, both in Europe and in the United States, were strikingly aware of the advantages that could be gained by enhanced ability to solve complex equation systems rapidly. Ballistics calculations were perhaps the dominant concern, but there were others as well. Prior to and during World War II, the German and British, as well as the U.S. government, funded research aimed at developing a rapid computer. However, it is clear that during and shortly after World War II, by which time the feasibility of electronic computers had been established, the United States had vastly outspent other governments in bringing this embryonic technology into operational form in terms of military applications. It is interesting that early assessments predicted that the civilian demand for computers would be very small. By 1960, however, it was apparent that the nonmilitary demand would be very large, and it turned out that the design experience that the major U.S. companies had had in working on military systems was directly relevant to civilian systems.

The case of semiconductors is somewhat different. While military funds had gone into research on semiconductor devices, it was the Bell Telephone Laboratories that made the critical discoveries and inventions, using their own funds and motivated by the telephone system, not military demand. Once the potential of semiconductor technology had been demonstrated, the armed services and, later, NASA quickly recognized the relevance of this technology to their needs. Significant government R&D funds went into supporting technical advance in semiconductors, and perhaps more important as it turns out, the Department of Defense and

NASA indicated they would be large potential purchasers of transistors. The evidence is clear that huge amounts of private R&D funds went into trying to advance semiconductor technology in anticipation of a large government market if the efforts were successful. And in the field of semiconductor technology as well as computer technology, it turned out that in the early stages at least, the transistors and later the integrated circuits that were of high value to the military also became the workhorses for civilian products.

All of these forces were reflected in a dramatic increase in the United States in scientists and engineers as a percentage of the work force and R&D as a fraction of gross national product (GNP). By 1960 these two measures of technological input stood far above those of other nations.

The American postwar technological lead is unquestioned, especially in the high technology industries but generally in manufacturing technology. Foreign concern over American technological dominance built up slowly in the postwar era, perhaps reflecting the belief of many Europeans that the dominance would dissolve as their economies recovered from the devastation of the war. This did not occur, at least not right away, and by the late 1960s, European concerns reached a peak regarding the long-run dangers to Europe of continuing American technological dominance. Ironically, by that time the evidence is clear that the U.S. dominance was shrinking rapidly.

THE CLOSING GAP

The period since the mid-1960s had seen a dramatic closing of the economic and technological gaps among the major industrial powers. The closing of the productivity and income gap is at once the broadest and the most fundamental manifestation of convergence. In the 1950s gross domestic product (GDP) per person employed in the United States was roughly double those of the major European countries and nearly five times that of Japan (table 1.1). While U.S. productivity grew at a respectable rate during the 1950s and 1960s, European productivity grew at a historically unprecedented rate, and the rate of productivity growth in Japan was even higher. The early 1970s marked a slowdown in productivity growth worldwide, but the discrepancies between the rates of growth persisted. By the early 1980s, GDPs per person employed in West Germany and France were very close to U.S. levels, and Japan was nearly there. The exact rankings since that time have been very sensitive to the price deflators used, suggesting that for all practical purposes the countries are now very close in overall productivity and income levels.

Tables 1.2 and 1.3 show the convergence in a different set of dimensions—exports and imports of high technology products—and the cross-country picture is somewhat different. The U.S. share of exports of high

TABLE 1.1
Real Gross Domestic Product per Employed Person
(in Constant 1972 U.S. Dollars)

Year	United States	Japan	West Germany	France	United Kingdom
1950	8,794	1,536	3,485	3,858	4,716
1955	10,028	2,113	4,784	4,713	5,234
1960	10,733	2,883	6,463	5,974	5,802
1965	12,503	4,365	8,002	7,755	6,526
1970	13,184	6,852	9,884	9,687	7,510
1971	13,563	7,120	10,129	10,165	7,839
1972	13,911	7,731	10,581	10,709	7,932
1973	14,203	8,198	10,988	11,144	8,422
1974	13,927	8,144	11,193	11,416	8,256
1975	13,856	8,364	11,329	11,549	8,207
1976	14,133	8,725	12,049	12,065	8,475
1977	14,391	9,063	12,438	12,335	8,640
1978	14,475	9,403	12,741	12,762	8,912
1979	14,423	9,764	13,104	13,188	9,018
1980	14,315	10,142	13,208	13,342	8,894
1981	14,537	10,483	13,262	13,482	9,065
1982 (prel.)	14,400	10,691	13,345	13,742	9,409
1983 (est.)	14,712	10,836	13,805	13,875	9,715

SOURCE: National Science Board, *Science Indicators: The 1985 Report* (Washington, D.C.: U.S. Government Printing Office, 1985).
NOTE: GNP implicit price deflators were used to convert current dollars to constant 1972 dollars. International price weights were used in currency conversions to enable cross-country comparisons.

technology products fell significantly during the 1960s, when foreign concern over American dominance was at a peak. However, U.S. export shares held up reasonably well over the 1970s and into the 1980s. During this period the most dramatic change is in the position of Japan relative to Europe. Japan's share rose significantly, while those of the European countries tended to decline. On the import side, the striking story is the sharp rise in U.S. imports and the slow growth of Japanese imports. It is the growth of U.S. imports, particularly since 1982, not a decline of export performance, that is the principal source of the erosion of the U.S. high technology trade balance.

The data on patent applications and grants presented in tables 1.4 and 1.5 display a similar pattern to that seen in export shares of high technology products. From the mid-1960s to the mid-1980s, the share of American patent grants has been relatively constant. Japan's share has risen dramatically, primarily at the expense of Europe. Many analysts have noted that U.S. patenting has shown an absolute decline since the late

TABLE 1.2
Trade in Technology-Intensive Products

Year	United States	Japan	West Germany	France	United Kingdom
		High Technology Imports[a]			
1970	5,861	2,017	4,140	3,304	3,043
1971	6,371	2,026	4,538	3,441	3,288
1972	7,917	2,193	5,105	4,222	3,948
1973	9,570	2,861	6,665	5,567	5,374
1974	10,298	3,618	7,475	6,510	6,127
1975	9,219	2,889	7,791	6,198	5,671
1976	12,199	3,185	9,127	7,171	5,879
1977	13,299	3,297	10,359	7,532	6,755
1978	16,744	3,927	12,427	8,770	8,908
1979	17,271	4,801	14,860	10,504	10,883
1980	18,728	5,378	15,843	11,878	12,077
1981	20,169	5,284	13,962	9,947	10,209
1982	19,787	4,888	13,267	9,220	10,049
		High Technology Exports[a]			
1970	12,527	5,088	7,774	3,276	4,499
1971	13,012	5,793	8,200	3,511	5,086
1972	13,299	7,180	9,537	4,134	5,586
1973	16,803	8,876	13,030	5,425	6,484
1974	21,246	10,525	15,748	6,534	7,631
1975	20,810	9,870	14,294	7,124	8,141
1976	21,808	12,733	16,021	7,830	7,990
1977	21,990	14,520	17,652	8,386	9,069
1978	25,475	17,359	20,297	9,693	11,025
1979	29,161	17,420	22,428	11,902	12,581
1980	33,468	20,156	22,847	11,926	15,056
1981	33,364	22,684	19,207	10,239	11,694
1982	30,663	19,642	18,736	10,080	11,315

SOURCE: National Science Board, *Science Indicators: The 1985 Report* (Washington, D.C.: U.S. Government Printing Office, 1985).

NOTE: Technology-intensive products are defined as those for which R&D expenditures exceed 2.36 percent of value-added.

[a]In millions of constant 1972 U.S. dollars. Currency conversion was based on purchasing-power parities. GNP implicit price deflators were used to convert current dollars to constant 1972 dollars.

TABLE 1.3
Export Market Shares in Technology-Intensive Products (OECD = 100)

	1970	1980	1984
United States	28.3	24.1	25.6
Japan	12.0	16.8	24.5
West Germany	16.0	15.6	12.9
France	7.0	7.7	6.9
United Kingdom	9.5	10.8	8.3

SOURCE: Organisation for Economic Cooperation and Development, *OECD Science and Technology Indicators* (Paris: OECD, 1986).

1960s. That is so, but the level of patenting of the major European nations has also declined. Of the major industrial nations, only Japan has experienced an increase in patenting. A similar trend is seen in external patent applications (those filed abroad), which indicate the extent of technology dissemination abroad.

In view of the convergence of general levels of productivity across the major industrial nations and the attainment of U.S. levels of R&D intensity by some of the European nations, as well as Japan, it is somehow surprising that the U.S. export share of high technology products has

TABLE 1.4
External Patent Applications by Inventors

Year	United States	Japan	West Germany	France	United Kingdom
1969	131,287	23,815	72,028	26,807	37,275
1970	123,724	26,568	70,137	24,422	33,463
1971	116,052	28,142	70,798	25,586	31,700
1972	119,984	25,760	70,636	27,887	33,324
1973	116,581	31,945	74,073	27,793	33,075
1974	102,711	33,463	67,335	22,821	28,968
1975	93,042	27,666	60,810	23,433	24,402
1976	93,356	29,340	58,310	23,356	24,185
1977	95,749	29,047	59,517	22,967	23,202
1978	85,352	30,182	53,657	22,073	21,286
1979	80,744	33,766	49,539	19,276	18,701
1980	79,078	35,945	48,650	18,839	17,400
1981	73,895	34,903	42,323	15,533	16,890
1982	65,335	36,901	38,985	15,498	16,144

SOURCE: National Science Board, *Science Indicators: The 1985 Report* (Washington, D.C.: U.S. Government Printing Office, 1985).

TABLE 1.5
Patent Grants: Country Shares (OECD = 100)

	1965	1970	1975	1980	1982
United States	20.2	19.8	24.2	22.9	21.8
Japan	8.7	9.5	15.8	17.1	19.0
West Germany	5.4	4.0	6.2	7.5	6.1
France	13.5	8.1	4.8	10.4	9.0
United Kingdom	10.9	12.6	13.8	8.8	11.1

SOURCE: Organisation for Economic Cooperation and Development, *OECD Science and Technology Indicators* (Paris: OECD, 1986).

not fallen further. I believe that this statistical "fact" is highly sensitive to the rather narrow definition employed for "high technology industries." A number of industries whose process and product technologies involve high levels of sophistication, such as automobiles, machine tools, and other kinds of mechanical machinery, are not considred high technology industries. When these industries are considered along with the so-called high technology ones, the U.S. export share suffers significant erosion, and Europe does not do nearly as badly as indicated by the statistics on the industries conventionally labeled "high technology."

Within the so-called high technology group of industries, more detailed analysis displays a somewhat variegated picture regarding U.S. performance.[11] Between the mid-1960s and the mid-1980s, the U.S. export share held up well in aircraft, aircraft engines and turbines, computing and other office machinery, and several classes of chemical products, but the export share declined significantly in professional and scientific instruments and in telecommunications. U.S. firms were routed in consumer electronics. The data on trends in national patenting in the different high technology areas, published by the National Science Foundation (NSF) and the Organisation for Economic Cooperation and Development (OECD), show a pattern very similar to that of export shares in the different industries. By and large, U.S. export shares have held up in industries where U.S. patenting has held up and declined where patents by citizens of other countries have risen sharply relative to American patents.

This more variegated picture of competition at the frontier is not surprising, given that by the 1980s the major industrial powers were roughly on a par regarding overall economic levels and R&D expenditures as a percentage of GNP. Due to differences in the nature of national markets, differences in choices made by key corporations, and matters of chance, one would have been surprised had one not found some differences across nations in areas of special strength.

The interesting question, of course, is how did this essential economic and technological equality come about? What were the factors behind the convergence?

Many analysts have stressed that convergence should be no surprise. After all, Europe and Japan had been heavily damaged by the war; the early post–World War II advantages of the United States had to erode with their recovery. This observation has a lot of merit, but it does not answer the question. As I have tried to document, U.S. economic leadership was not solely a result of the immediate post–World War II situation. The United States had had significantly higher productivity levels than Europe and Japan for at least half a century. As I argued in the previous section, the domination of high technology industry by the United States in the quarter-century after World War II was largely a result of investment and policy decisions in the United States rather than European and Japanese backwardness. The "recovery was inevitable" proposition explains why one should have expected some closure, but it does not explain the virtually total elimination of the long-standing and structurally rooted American lead.

What are the key factors behind the virtual close, rather than partial closing, of the gaps? I would stress four primary factors. First, the free flow of world trade has eroded the advantages U.S. firms used to have in serving the world's largest market. Second, the internationalization of business associated with greater openness of the world economies was part and parcel of a set of developments that led to the internationalization of technology. Third, other major industrial powers have significantly increased the percentage of their work force trained in science and engineering and the percentage of GNP allocated to R&D, thus establishing strong endogenous competence to exploit the now more accessible technology, as well as to create new technology. Indeed, if one considers nonmilitary R&D as a percentage of GNP, by 1980 a number of nations were spending more than the United States. This is important, because the fourth major factor behind the convergence was a sharp decline in the importance of the spillover from military R&D into civilian technology.

The percentage of manufactured products traded has grown rapidly since 1955 in all major industrial countries. In the post–World War II era, efficient companies producing attractive products have increasingly faced a world, rather than a national, market. Earlier, I suggested that American business had a significant advantage during the late nineteenth century and the first half of the twentieth by residing in the world's largest common market. By 1970 the world became, largely, a common market.

At the same time, business has become increasingly international. I observed that technologically progressive American companies established branches in Europe even during the late nineteenth century. During the 1950s and 1960s, American overseas direct investment surged dramatically. In *The American Challenge*, J. J. Servan-Schreiber expressed concern that American companies were taking over the European economy at least as much by investing there as by exporting.[12] By the late 1960s, Europe was beginning to return the favor by establishing branches or buying plants in the United States. Recently, Japanese companies, too, have become increasingly international.

The internationalization of business has greatly complicated the interpretation of international trade statistics. For example, a not-insignificant percentage of the rising U.S. imports of high technology goods are imports from foreign subsidiaries of U.S.-owned companies. It is interesting that while the U.S. share of world manufacturing exports (low and middle technology as well as high technology) fell somewhat from the mid-1960s to the mid-1980s, the export share of U.S. *firms* held up, with gains in exports from foreign branches matching declines in exports from U.S.-owned plants based in the United States.[13]

The internationalization of trade and business has been part of the second postwar development that I want to highlight: the erosion of national borders and national status as factors obstructing or channeling access to technology.

Modern science has always been an international activity; British and French scientists continued to communicate even during the Napoleonic Wars. This is because the ethos of science has always stressed the public and international nature of scientific knowledge. Attempts by national governments to define and keep separate a particular national science have been condemned by the scientific community as antisocial and counterproductive, except in wartime. Even in wartime, as the example above indicates, science has been able to resist nationalization.

In contrast, the notion that individuals and firms have property rights to the inventions they develop has been accepted as appropriate for many centuries, and so, too, the idea that it is appropriate for a nation to try to gain an advantage from the inventive work of its nationals. Nations have also tried zealously to keep national technology within their borders and to prevent it from leaking over into foreign nations. While in many cases these efforts have proved futile, they have always been accepted as legitimate. While technologists from different countries have traditionally communicated with each other and formed something of a worldwide community, until recently the notion that best-practice technology was available to any nation with requisite resources was most likely incorrect. While some analysts stress patent protection of technology, I believe expertise and experience, which are innately privy, are much more important. The networks of technologists exchanging information have been largely national.

The post–World War II era has seen increasing communication among technologists in different countries. One important reason for this is that technologies have become much more like sciences than they were previously. A considerable portion of the generic knowledge relevant to a technology is now written down, published in journals, discussed at national and international meetings, taught in schools of engineering and applied science, and the like. International communication in the postwar era is so much easier, quicker, and cheaper than ever before. Letters and journals circulate quickly and easily. International air travel permits technologists to attend conferences around the world. New technological developments by a single company are published much more quickly and more widely than they used to be, and while I have no direct data to support this, the growing sense among technologists that they are part of a worldwide community encourages more open questioning and answering about what is new.

And, of course, the internationalization of business has been an important contributing factor. Europeans can observe American technology in operation in their home countries and even purchase operating American firms. Companies like IBM have industrial research laboratories in a number of different countries, each employing a mix of nationals. In turn, scientists from IBM and scientists from Philips and Fujitsu meet at conferences to exchange papers and ideas.

I stress the presence of these international networks of highly trained scientists and engineers employed in universities and industry undertaking significant R&D efforts to correct a widely held misconception that aside from matters shielded by patents or secrecy, technology is basically a public good. The generic technological knowledge taught in graduate school, published in books and articles, and exchanged among high-level professionals does indeed have strong attributes of a public good. But even here access is limited to those with the requisite training, and in many cases, only a researcher in a particular field can understand the publications bearing on that field. In order to take industrial advantage of generic knowledge or technology licensed from another company, or merely to understand what another company has done and how, generally requires significant inputs of trained scientists and engineers and often involves R&D aimed to tailor what has been learned to specific uses.

Thus, the growing convergence among the advanced industrial nations in the percentage of young people going on to college, in scientists and engineers as a percentage of the work force, and in R&D expenditures as a percentage of GNP is an essential part of, and a complement to, the internationalization of technology (tables 1.6–1.8). It is important to recognize that while there has been a convergence among those nations with modern educational systems, strong internal scientific and engineering communities, and sophisticated industrial enterprises, nations without these attributes have tended to fall farther and farther behind the frontiers. While there are now few important technological secrets, a major investment is required to command a technology.

Military technology, however, is something of an exception to what I

TABLE 1.6
Higher Education

A. Diplomas Giving Access to Higher Education as Proportion of Age-Group	
Japan (1981)	87
Sweden (1982)	82
United States (1980)	72
West Germany (1982)	26
Denmark (1980)	25
France (1983)	28
Italy (1981)	39
United Kingdom (1981)	26
Finland (1980)	38
Austria (1978)	13
Netherlands (1981)	44

B. Proportion of Age-Group Entering Higher Education	
Japan	62
United States	62
Sweden	25
West Germany	20
Denmark	33
France	34
Italy	25
Finland	10
Netherlands	26
United Kingdom	29

SOURCE: Henry Ergas, "Does Technology Policy Matter?" in Bruce R. Guile and Harvey Brooks, eds., *Technology and Global Industry: Companies and Nations in the World Economy* (Washington, D.C.: National Academy of Engineering, 1987).

have been describing. The major military powers, especially the United States, continue to make strong efforts to prevent military technology from leaking away to other, potentially hostile nations or to nations who might serve as conduits of military technology to hostile nations. The success of the United States in restricting foreign access to American military technology has been mixed. I suspect that the major reason the Soviet Union is unable to match American military technology in many areas is not so much that Americans keep military technology secret but rather that Russian technological competences are not strong enough to take advantage of the copious knowledge that does become public and to learn how to command those technologies. Military technology, however, certainly continues to be confined much more to a national level than civilian technology.

TABLE 1.7

Scientists and Engineers Engaged in R&D per 10,000 Labor Force Population

Year	United States	Japan	West Germany	France	United Kingdom
1965	64.7	24.6	22.7	21.0	19.6
1966	66.9	26.4	22.4	23.3	NA
1967	67.2	27.8	24.9	25.3	NA
1968	68.0	31.2	26.2	26.4	20.8
1969	66.9	30.8	28.4	27.1	NA
1970	64.4	33.4	30.8	27.3	NA
1971	61.0	37.5	33.4	27.9	NA
1972	58.3	38.1	35.6	28.2	30.4
1973	56.8	42.5	37.1	28.5	NA
1974	56.1	44.9	37.8	28.9	NA
1975	55.8	47.9	38.6	29.4	31.2
1976	55.8	48.4	39.2	29.9	NA
1977	56.4	49.9	41.8	30.0	NA
1978	57.2	49.4	NA	31.0	33.2
1979	58.4	50.4	45.3	31.6	NA
1980	60.7	53.6	NA	32.4	NA
1981	62.7	55.6	46.8	36.3	35.8
1982	64.6	57.1	47.8	37.9	NA
1983	66.2	58.1	NA	39.1	NA

SOURCE: National Science Board, *Science Indicators: The 1985 Report* (Washington, D.C.: U.S. Government Printing Office, 1985).

NOTE: Includes all scientists and engineers engaged in R&D on a full-time-equivalent basis (except for Japan, where the data include persons primarily employed in R&D [excluding social scientists], and the United Kingdom, where the data include only the government and industry sectors).

NA = not available.

Although American dominance of the frontiers of military technology gave the United States significant civilian technological advantages during the 1950s and 1960s, today that dominance buys very little outside the military sphere. Thus, in terms of access to technology that affects productivity in the broadly defined manufacturing industry and competitiveness of products sold on international markets, it matters little that American companies are engaged in military R&D to a much greater extent than those in Europe or Japan and that access to that technology is difficult, if not closed. For the most part since the late 1960s, advances in military technology have had very few spillover effects into civilian technology. Indeed, it can be argued the other way. Since the late 1960s, the cutting edge of semiconductor and computer technology has been concentrated primarily on civilian applications, and funding has been provided primarily by companies or civil government agencies, with the

TABLE 1.8
R&D Expenditures as a Percentage of Gross National Product

Year	United States	Japan	West Germany	France[a]	United Kingdom
Total R&D Expenditures					
1971	2.48	1.85	2.18	1.90	NA
1972	2.40	1.86	2.20	1.90	2.11
1973	2.31	1.90	2.09	1.77	NA
1974	2.29	1.97	2.13	1.79	NA
1975	2.27	1.96	2.22	1.80	2.19
1976	2.27	1.95	2.15	1.78	NA
1977	2.23	1.93	2.14	1.76	NA
1978	2.22	2.00	2.24	1.76	2.24
1979	2.27	2.09	2.40	1.81	NA
1980	2.38	2.22	2.42	1.84	NA
1981	2.43	2.38	2.49	2.01	2.41
1982	2.58	2.47	2.58	2.10	NA
1983	2.62	2.61	2.57	2.15	2.24
1984	2.62	2.60	2.60	2.22	NA
1985	2.70	2.70	2.60	2.27	NA
Nondefense R&D Expenditures					
1971	1.68	1.84	2.03	1.46	NA
1972	1.63	1.84	2.08	1.50	1.50
1973	1.62	1.89	1.94	1.38	NA
1974	1.69	1.96	1.98	1.43	NA
1975	1.68	1.95	2.08	1.46	1.41
1976	1.68	1.94	2.01	1.44	NA
1977	1.67	1.92	2.01	1.44	NA
1978	1.69	1.98	2.10	1.41	1.51
1979	1.75	2.08	2.27	1.42	NA
1980	1.86	2.21	2.30	1.43	NA
1981	1.87	2.37	2.38	1.51	1.72
1982	1.94	2.46	2.48	1.63	NA
1983	1.91	2.60	2.47	1.69	1.61
1984	1.86	2.60	2.50	1.76	NA
1985	1.89	2.70	2.50	1.80	NA

SOURCE: National Science Board, *Science Indicators: The 1985 Report* (Washington, D.C.: U.S. Government Printing Office, 1985).
NOTE: NA = not available.
[a]Gross domestic product.

spillover occurring largely from civilian to military applications. Thus, while military technology does not share the international characteristics of civilian technology, this does not matter much in terms of economic growth and competitiveness. Therefore, military technology has not been a major obstacle in the path of convergence.

Although the general pattern of economic and technological development among the major industrial powers since the mid-1960s can be characterized as convergent, the growth records of Japan and the United States require special attention because they represent unusual cases. Japan's economic and technological performance has been significantly stronger than might have been predicted given the general forces just described, while the economic performance of the United States has been weak, both absolutely and relatively. These two different performances have strongly influenced world perceptions of the events of the last twenty years.

Table 1.1 outlines the dramatic developmental performance of Japan since 1950. Japan's rate of productivity growth has been not only higher than that of the United States but also significantly higher than those of the major European powers. Japan has experienced much slower growth since the early 1970s, along with other nations, but the productivity growth rate of Japan continues to be at the top of the league. At least as dramatic, perhaps even more so, has been Japan's coming of age as a world technological leader. Tables 1.2 and 1.3 illustrate Japan's rise as an exporter of high technology products. Tables 1.4 and 1.5 show the patent data.

The rapid development of Japan and in particular the surpassing of the major European powers in terms of various measures of technological performance during this period have strongly colored European perceptions of events. Above I stressed convergence, and there is no doubt that the major European nations have come much closer to the United States in terms of levels of productivity and various measures of technological performance. Europeans, however, tend not to think in those terms but rather to concentrate on the fact that by the late 1970s, they were not only behind the United States but behind Japan as well. This has taken attention away from the strong technological performance of a number of European countries during the 1970s. A lot has changed in Europe since the days of concern over an across-the-board technology gap with the United States, but the subsequent rise of Japan has shifted attention away from these accomplishments.

The rise of Japan has also had a significant effect on the U.S. perceptions of events. Because of the strong Japanese performance, Americans have not seen convergence so much as the taking over of technological leadership by another nation.

As I suggested above, the U.S. performance over this period was unusual. Not only were other nations catching up to the United States, but

American growth performance significantly deteriorated during the 1970s compared with the 1960s and still has not recovered. While productivity growth has also declined in other countries, in the United States the growth rate of total factor productivity has been close to zero. The collapse of growth of total factor productivity in the United States is a real puzzle, and economists are divided on the appropriate interpretation.

The question of how to interpret these outliers—the superb performance of Japan and the poor performance of the United States—is a fundamental one. One could posit that these are temporary phenomena, features of no durable importance. On the other hand, one could posit that the performance of these two outliers is fundamental, that Japan is indeed coming into a position of economic and technological ascendancy and that the United States will follow the same path of relative decline that England did a century ago. In the final section of this paper I turn to these possibilities.

WHAT LIES AHEAD?

There are now a number of studies aiming to assess U.S. technological performance relative to that of other countries, to identify where it is weak and where strong, and to hazard a look into the future. Perhaps the most thoughtful such study is by Patel and Pavitt.[14] The authors identify U.S. strengths as lying in aerospace, electronics broadly defined, and the agricultural processing industries. They also point to possible U.S. weaknesses in the chemical industry complex and pharmaceuticals. However, their own data point in a variety of different directions.

I believe that it is hazardous to make industry-by-industry forecasts and further propose that what happens in any particular industry does not matter very much. After all, a nation cannot have a comparative advantage in everything, and within limits, it does not matter much to national well-being whether X is imported and Y is exported or vice versa. Semiconductor and computer technology may or may not be an exception. These clearly are strategic industries, but they are also populated by international companies who sell in a world rather than a national market and whose production and, in many cases, even design capabilities are often located near their markets. With respect to defense needs, it is almost certain that the Department of Defense will not permit the capabilities of U.S.-owned firms to collapse.

Without an in-depth analysis of particular industries, then, what lies ahead for the United States regarding competence in high technology industries in general? If I limit discussion to the major industrial powers, it is now a world of near-equals in which the forces for continuing convergence are strong.

I see no reason to modify my earlier arguments concerning the internationalization of technology. The forces of international technical professionalism and of international business look strong and durable. The market for most manufacturing goods will continue to be more global than national, despite pockets of protectionism. Similarly, I expect that national R&D systems and investment will continue to be, aside from the scale factor, remarkably similar. Governments are watching other countries to an unprecedented degree. Institutional features seen as characterizing leading nations will be quickly adopted, whether or not they prove effective.

As during the 1970s, the defense establishment of the United States is likely to be an exception, and spending will exceed that of any other nation. This, however, will have little influence on civilian technology. On the one hand, I suspect that spillover will be minor. On the other hand, I expect that American companies and the U.S. government will not allow civilian R&D to fall significantly below the levels in Japan and Europe.

I confess, however, to a great deal of subjective variance around my best-bet forecast. I do see a significant downside risk for the United States that is linked to the high cost of capital in the United States, the dependence of large companies on the stock market for funding beyond retained earnings, and their resultant vulnerability to takeover bids and hence sensitivity to such potentialities.

Due to the particularities of the American capital market, American firms may well operate with short-run horizons relative to firms in Japan and Europe. This environment may hinder the ability of firms to pursue long-run strategies involving significant up-front investment. In particular, companies engaging in research that promises payoff only in the more distant future will feel threatened and may cut back on such endeavors. As a result, American companies may not be laying the foundations necessary to compete in the future and may find themselves at a disadvantage relative to companies in Japan (and in Europe?), who feel secure about making such long-run investments.

Henry Ergas has suggested that the ability of American capital and labor markets to shift resources between firms, while lending the United States a strong advantage in initiating technical change, may cost us in terms of staying power once a field has caught on.[15] Labor turnover diminishes the ability to retain the advantages of early experience. Capital mobility spurs withdrawal when competition becomes serious. Ergas also proposes that this can cost the United States heavily in competition with countries, like Japan, where there is more staying power to complement the newly enhanced innovating power. Although the notion that the United States is currently at a comparative disadvantage in industries where staying power is important is far from proved, it deserves serious consideration.

The American system of primary and secondary education may also present a negative factor. That system, which in earlier years was a source of strength for the United States, now looks weak in comparison with those of some of our major competitors in terms of turning out literate, arithmetically competent, and trainable young entrants into the work force. The United States still stands high on the list of countries in terms of the percentage of youth who finish secondary school (see table 1.6), but it is quality that presents the problem. I do not worry so much about our ability to turn out well-trained scientists and engineers as about our ability to train technicians and general blue-collar skills. The problem does not lie in higher education, where the United States arguably remains the strongest nation, but rather at the lower levels. This may prove serious in terms of enduring economic consequences.

There is also a more positive view regarding the future performance of the United States. Compared with any of the other major industrial powers, the United States has an unusual and promising combination of institutional ingredients. Although the United States may no longer lead the world in the ability to provide capital for enormous, multinational corporations, U.S. capital markets seem to do a much better job than those in other countries of funding new entrepreneurial firms and of enabling these and large established firms to form relationships.

The American university research system is still the world's strongest, and the lead in this area is not likely to close quickly. Moreover, this lead is not simply with respect to research and teaching (which other countries can tap through a variety of channels). The American university system is closely linked with American industry. University professors are consultants and entrepreneurs. Companies fund research and aid in innovation. The capability may not be of particular importance for many technologies, but it was important in the early days of microelectronics and is currently important for software and microbiology. This capability may give the United States a real advantage in these areas.

Many commentators have remarked on how uncoordinated the American government is regarding R&D support, but this may not be all bad. Although the Department of Defense is the elephant among government research funders, there is a remarkable pluralism of research support agencies in the United States, and various new policies can bubble up in a variety of different places. Who would have thought that the National Science Foundation, originally dedicated to basic academic research, could have come to the forefront of agencies supporting a significant increase in close university-industry relationships? That is, however, the case.

What a change this appraisal of U.S. strengths is from the appraisal given by such observers as J. J. Servan-Schreiber during the heyday of American dominance. Servan-Schreiber stressed size, mass resources, Department of Defense programs, large organizations, and good management. I highlight variety and the creativity and flexibility based on variety. In short, I propose that the United States possesses an apparent ability to mix entrepreneurial firms and giant corporations and university and business in a way unmatched by other nations. In some areas at least, this may be a significant advantage.

NOTES

1. Alexis de Tocqueville, *Democracy in America* (New York: G. Dearborn & Co., 1838; New York: Random House, Vintage Books, 1954), 2:165–66.

2. H. J. Habakkuk, *American and British Technology in the Nineteenth Century* (Cambridge: Cambridge University Press,. 1962), pp. 4–5.

3. Alfred Dupont Chandler, *The Visible Hand: The Managerial Revolution in American Business* (Cambridge: Harvard University Press, 1977).

4. Ibid.

5. See, for example, Nathan Rosenberg, "The Commercial Exploitation of Science by American Industry," in Kim B. Clark, Robert H. Hayes, and Christopher Lorenz, *The Uneasy Alliance: Managing the Productivity-Technology Dilemma* (Boston: Harvard Business School Press, 1985).

6. For a more thorough discussion of the German case, see David S. Landes, *The Unbound Prometheus* (Cambridge: Cambridge University Press, 1970). For a thorough discussion of the development of chemistry in the United States, see Arnold Thackray, *University-Industry Connections and Chemical Research: A Historical Perspective in University-Industry Research Relationships* (Washington, D.C.: National Science Board, 1982).

7. For a good discussion on both the rise of the electrical industry and the development of the chemical industry, see Christopher Freeman, *The Economics of Industrial Innovation* (London: Penguin Books, 1982).

8. See, for example, Angus Maddison, *Phases of Capitalist Development* (Oxford: Oxford University Press, 1982).

9. See Freeman, *The Economics of Industrial Innovation*.

10. For an analytic history, see Richard R. Nelson, ed., *Government and Technical Progress: A Cross-Industry Analysis* (New York: Pergamon Press, 1982); idem, *High Technology Policies: A Five Nation Comparison* (Washington, D.C.: American Enterprise Institute, 1984).

11. Data from the National Science Foundation.

12. Jean Jacques Servan-Schreiber, *The American Challenge* (New York: Atheneum, 1968).

13. Robert E. Lipsey and Irving B. Kravis, "The Competitive Position of U.S. Manufacturing Firms," *Banca Nazionale del Larono Quarterly Review*, June 1985.

14. Pari Patel and Keith Pavitt, *Measuring Europe's Technological Performance: Results and Prospects* (Brighton, East Sussex, U.K.: Science Policy Research Unit, University of Sussex, 1985).

15. Henry Ergas, "Does Technology Policy Matter?" in Bruce R. Guile and Harvey Brooks, eds., *Technology and Global Industry: Companies and Nations in the World Economy* (Washington, D.C.: National Academy of Engineering, 1987).

2

Japan's Technological Capabilities
and Its Future: Overview and Assessments

SULLY TAYLOR and KOZO YAMAMURA

It is widely acknowledged today that Japan is one of the leaders in the high technology industries that are rapidly transforming all the industrial economies in significant and profound ways. Despite the recent profusion of descriptions and analyses of Japan's technological capabilities, however, it is difficult to find a single source that offers a broad overview and assessment of Japan's present technological capabilities and of the many factors, such as changing business strategies, public policy, and the international political economic environment, that will crucially affect or can even determine its technological future. Thus, the central intent of this paper is to present an overview of Japan's current technological capabilities and discuss the problems and issues Japan faces and is likely to continue to face in the coming decades in its efforts to maintain and strengthen its technological capabilities.

Our endeavor, however, is necessarily circumscribed by the as yet ill-defined characters of two crucial realities confronting the industrial economies. One is that industrial economics and international competition have undergone fundamental changes of late as a result of what Drucker has called an "uncoupling" between the primary products economy and the industrial economy and between production and employment and because capital movements rather than trade itself have become the driving force behind global financial movements.[1] Such developments and others yet unanticipated will undoubtedly further change the nature of the "games" that all firms and nations must play, both at home and in the international arena, if they are to succeed in continuing to make technological progress into the twenty-first century. Thus, what we can describe and discuss concerning the technological future of Japan must be read with the awareness that our evaluation is also subject to reassessment as the forces of these developments continue to affect Japan's technological future.

The other reality, closely related to the first, is that the task of anticipating the effects of ongoing technological changes for the future has become even more difficult today than it was several decades ago. We have just entered into a new era, whose fundamental technological characteristics differ qualitatively from the technology of mass production that played a determining role in the economic growth of the past several decades. Briefly stated, the new high technology is distinct in that it makes use of and crucially depends on degrees of precision measured in millionths of seconds or millimeters, on a digital analytic construct that has no visually comprehensible analog, and on other complexities that are perceived, except by a very small number of highly trained specialists, as incomprehensible and even enigmatic.

Unlike the technology it is now replacing, high technology no longer requires a large quantity of energy or raw materials but rather requires many novel skills and behavior patterns, new kinds of specialists (including scientists, technicians, operators, and production workers), and a hitherto unfamiliar set of varied infrastructures such as multipurpose cables, huge data bases, and a new educational system. And, if we were to be ambitious in listing all the changes to occur in the future, we would have to also include changes in the character and distribution of the labor force, market structure, concepts of private property, and many more. In fact, some of these changes have already begun to occur. In attempting to discuss the technological future of Japan or any other nation, we must remember that we now have only a glimpse of the newly emerging century of high technology.

In the first section we present an overview of the present capabilities of the Japanese high technology industries. In the second section we discuss the parameters of continuing progress—the factors that affect and the problems that must be faced in Japan's efforts to remain a technological leader in the twenty-first century. The last section is devoted to our conclusions regarding the course Japan must follow if it is to remain a technological leader in the twenty-first century.

PRESENT CAPABILITIES

In our efforts to assess Japan's present technological capabilities and those that we can anticipate Japan to have in the very near future, we shall focus on what are commonly seen as the key future industries, that is, the broadly defined communications industry and the biotechnology and new materials industries. After briefly summarizing Japan's present commercial and technological strengths in these fields, we will examine cross-industry indicators of Japan's scientific prowess.

Current Japanese commercial and technological strength in the key industries of the future can be summarized in a few bold statements (the Appendix presents a more complete analysis supporting these general statements).

First, the Japanese have been making the most progress in fields in which incremental improvements on imported technology are possible, such as semiconductors. However, most expert opinion concerning the

Japanese capability to produce increasingly radical innovations has concluded that Japan has an increasing capability to do so, with the possible exception of computer software. Second, the Japanese have attained market strength in those high technology areas where wide commercial applications are possible, such as carbon fibers or DRAMs (dynamic random access memory). This is an important strategy, as it allows industry participants to finance out of present profits expensive basic research and development (R&D) into new areas.

And finally, the high technology industries chosen by the Japanese government as key to Japan's future show two key characteristics: (1) extremely high market growth potential and (2) the ability to link synergistically with technological advances in other industries. For example, the application of fine ceramics to industrial machinery combines with advances in the communications industry such as computer-aided design/computer-aided manufacturing (CAD/CAM) to produce a highly sophisticated and efficient manufacturing plant. The existence of any one high technology industry is reinforced by these synergistic linkages, and these in turn encourage Japanese technological innovations and commercialization of breakthroughs. Consequently, a nation like Japan with strength in a broad spectrum of high technology fields is most likely to make the intraindustry linkages that result in high production efficiency.

Evaluating present Japanese strength in high technology can be approached with a different set of measurement tools. That is, a variety of R&D input and output criteria can be used such as number of patents, number of Nobel Prize winners, technology exports versus imports, number of personnel presently engaged in R&D, and the extent of international research collaborations. Some of these measures can provide a cross-industry picture of Japan's scientific and technological strength.

The three most problematical measures are number of Japanese patent applications, number of Nobel Prizes, and the balance of technology flows. Because of problems with each of these measurements, an evaluation based entirely on them would result in a rather skewed and misleading picture of the present Japanese position. With regard to patents, for example, it is estimated that one U.S. patent is worth seven Japanese patents.[2] Japanese researchers tend to apply for patents for everything as proof of research activity, and as a consequence, over one-half of all patent applications in Japan by Japanese are rejected. Some firms offer relatively modest rewards for patent applications, which nevertheless are important signals of the firm's favor.[3] Thus patent activity is decidedly different between Japan and other countries participating in the high technology race, making comparisons difficult, at least with regard to number. In terms of number of Nobel Prizes, while Japan won only four between 1901 and 1981, it must be remembered that for much of that period the preferred strategy was to borrow technology from the West.

Technology flows can also be misleading. While Japan has become a net exporter of technology in recent years, over 40 percent goes to less-developed countries. When technology by type is examined, it becomes clear that Japan is selling off its technology in declining industries such as steel while continuing to be a net importer of technology in such areas as communication equipment, pharmaceuticals, and computer manufacturing.[4] This is consistent with the observation made earlier that most of Japan's present strength derives from incremental improvements on imported technology.

Other cross-industry measures are more useful. One is the number of personnel engaged in R&D. With regard to the total number of corporate, government, and university researchers per 10,000 people, the USSR leads with 53 per 10,000, followed by the United States with 31 and Japan with 29.[5] In addition, an overwhelming number of Japanese R&D personnel hold engineering rather than basic science degrees. In the United States, the physical and life sciences account for 56 percent of U.S. natural sciences and engineering first degrees, whereas in Japan they account for only 12 percent.[6] Moreover, until recently holders of advanced degrees in the natural sciences and engineering were found only in Japanese universities. In short, Japan has the human resource capability in R&D, but it is skewed toward applied research and lacks in-depth knowledge of specialized fields beyond that required for the individual's particular work setting. A final measure of research activity is publication of articles with researchers in other countries. Japanese participation in such cooperative scientific publications with the United States has been increasing, although it still lags far behind other U.S. international cooperative research, perhaps because of linguistic barriers.[7]

In sum, using industry-specific and cross-industry measures of technology, we can conclude that Japan is a strong player but not yet a dominant player in the new economic game. And even to remain a strong player possessing the skills needed for future competitiveness, there are a variety of problems with which Japan must deal. We turn our attention to these problems in the following section.

PARAMETERS OF CONTINUING PROGRESS

The problems and issues affecting future Japanese competitiveness in high technology can be divided into two categories. The first concerns those affecting Japan's ability to produce technological innovations, and the second deals with the effect of the international environment on Japan's ability to implement its technological strategy.

Factors Affecting Innovation

Can Japan make technological innovations of its own? This is a most crucial question, the answer to which will significantly determine whether or not Japan can remain a leading technological power and possibly strengthen its position among other technological leaders.

Modern trade theory suggests several reasons why innovation may be the most crucial skill of all. Many of the new high technology industries operate in imperfectly competitive markets in which there are only a few rivals, individual firms can directly affect prices, and firms can act strategically to affect other firms' actions. These factors mean that firms already in the market or who enter a new field early will have a powerful market position that can become unassailable.[8] The importance of first-to-market advantage will become increasingly critical in the future. Since 50 to 60 percent of the content of many new high technology products will consist of knowledge, a firm will be able to recoup the investment in creating the knowledge only by seizing significant market share by being first to market. An innovation also bestows a temporary advantage on a firm that cumulative experience can turn into an insurmountable barrier to entry.[9] Lack of experience will seriously hamper a firm's ability in the coming decades to capture market share from market leaders through reduced production costs or incremental product changes. Those competitors already established in the markets will be able to set standards and introduce innovative products that in effect create new markets of their own that will be difficult, if not virtually impossible, to enter. Here, it is important to note that many products in the high technology markets tend to be "compatible with," "complementary to," or "enhancing of" those products that are already being marketed by existing firms.

A final reason for the need for Japan to foster radical technological innovations is the present negative international climate regarding access to new technology, as evidenced by the recent American attempt to redefine the scope of patentable intellectual property. This factor will be examined more closely.

Consequently, the following examination of conditions for innovation will assume that the capacity for innovation is the most important skill Japan must nurture in order to remain an economic leader in the twenty-first century. The factors affecting innovation are government policies, organizational characteristics, and labor market conditions.

Government Policies. In recent years, Japan's industrial policy has received considerable attention. Most observers agree that in the fifties and sixties Japanese government policies were quite influential in shaping the direction and growth of Japanese industry, although these policies sometimes produced such negative results as a tendency toward overcapacity in certain industries.[10] We will attempt here, however, to determine what industrial policies the Japanese government can use to influence innovation and whether these tools are likely to be used and whether they are likely to be successful. Included in the government's policy tool kit are infant-industry-style protections—tariffs, quotas, bar-

riers to foreign investment, and nontariff barriers such as testing standards, procurements, and subsidies—and policies regarding government
R&D funding, education, and capital availability.

Many of the more overt infant-industry-style protections such as quotas
and tariffs are simply not viable industrial policy tools for the new high
technology industries. Subsidies, another potential tool to encourage investment in high technology areas, are mostly targeted to the agricultural, transportation, and mining sectors of the Japanese economy. In
comparison to other developed nations, particularly the United States,
Great Britain, and France, Japanese high technology firms receive very
few direct subsidies.[11]

In general, procurement has not been as important in Japan for fostering R&D investments as in countries such as the United States, where
a large defense industry has made government procurement an easier
tool to use. Still, government procurement has provided a considerable
impetus to the development of some Japanese high technology industries. The most striking example of government procurement is that of
Nippon Telephone and Telegraph Company (NTT), which until recently
acquired its equipment only from its family of firms. This had a tremendous impact on the development of competitive semiconductor and
computer industries in Japan. IBM holds only a 30 percent market share
in Japan as opposed to its customary 50 percent elsewhere in the world.[12]
A simple fact is that until 1975, IBM was not allowed to sell computers
to NTT.

Although used more informally than before, procurement is likely to
be one way the Japanese government attempts to foster innovation in its
high technology industries, particularly in the communications industry.
The frequently noted "buy Japanese" attitude still pervasive in Japanese
government agencies—as demonstrated in the purchase of Fujitsu supercomputers rather than allegedly superior Cray computers—can be
changed, it seems, only slowly.[13] International scrutiny and the large trade
surplus Japan enjoys today, however, will undoubtedly continue to has-
ten the pace of the change.

Formal barriers against foreign investment in Japan, which were so
important to the growth of such Japanese industries as steel and computers, have all but disappeared, and foreign direct investment in Japan
has grown somewhat in recent years. It must be pointed out, however,
that there still remain formidable obstacles to foreign direct investment
in Japan, which result in a de facto absence of strong foreign competitors
on Japan's home turf. Perhaps the most important obstacle, according to
Okimoto, is Japanese industrial organization.[14] The special way in which
Japanese firms build and maintain business relationships results in a distinctive mix of market and organization that "makes Japan such a tough
market for foreign firms to crack."[15] The upshot is that while foreign
enterprises account for only 2 percent of total economic activity in Japan,

in the United States the figure is 11 percent and in West Germany it is 20 percent.[16] Yet, because industrial organization is not easily changed by public policy, it is likely this informal barrier to foreign direct investment will shield Japanese high technology firms from foreign competition at home for some time to come.

Product standards have been used as a nontariff barrier in the high technology sectors, particularly in pharmaceuticals and telecommunications. However, under foreign pressure, the Japanese government has modified its standards, culminating in a 1985 market access package that effectively puts Japanese and foreign pharmaceutical companies on an equal footing.[17] In telecommunications, the Telecommunication Business Law of 1984 transferred the setting of standards from NTT to the Ministry of Posts and Telecommunications (MPT) and requires that MPT use a designated approval agency to certify acceptability of all telecommunication equipment. The agency initially established was in essence an inside agency of the NTT family firms, and as such it had no plans to accept foreign representation or foreign-generated technical data. Eventually, however, this was modified at the insistence of the Ministry of International Trade and Industry (MITI) and foreign governments. Yet the continuing effectiveness of the system as a nontariff barrier is evidenced by the fact that a paltry 5 percent of NTT procurements have been obtained by foreign firms. In sum, standards are still used as an effective protective device for the high technology industries.[18]

One of the seven goals of the Maekawa Report of 1986 was to improve foreign access to Japanese markets as one way of rectifying the country's lopsided trade account.[19] This private study group report marked a potential turning point in Japan's use of industrial policy to nurture growth of domestic firms at the expense of foreign competitors. Yet the report failed to specify any clear policy changes that would signal an abandonment of Japan's postprotectionist attitudes. This would seem to indicate that Japanese high technology industries can expect the government to continue to use whatever tools it can, given the present international environment, to nurture high technology innovations and the growth of high technology firms. Japan's industrial policy also includes the Japanese government involvement in R&D funding and coordination. The success of such projects as the VLSI (very large scale integrated circuit), which helped get the Japanese semiconductor industry off the ground, has brought this area of industrial policy to the attention of critics and admirers of Japan alike. Certainly the Japanese government and its various agencies such as MITI, NTT, MPT, the Science and Technology Agency (STA), and the Ministry of Agriculture, Forestry, and Fisheries are involved in a variety of well-publicized national R&D projects. Yet upon closer examination it becomes clear that (1) the level of actual government funding has been relatively small compared with that seen in other countries, such as the United States, and (2) the involvement of the government is less to produce a special competitive advantage for Japan than to overcome certain market failures, particularly low scientific labor mobility and a lack of efficient capital markets.[20] Before proceeding to a discussion of these observations, however, it is first necessary to briefly describe the actual involvement of the Japanese government in R&D.

Major ongoing Japanese national high technology R&D projects include the NTT Information Network System (1980–2000) project, numerous MITI projects, and several projects of the STA. The Japanese government has approached national R&D in several ways: direct funding of research projects in industries, universities, and government agencies; and coordination and partial funding of industry-government research projects and industry-university research projects.

MITI has three different types of R&D projects: subsidized projects, large-scale projects, and national projects.[21] Examples of MITI projects include the Fifth-Generation Computer (1979–1991), Advanced Robotics (1984–1992), Biotechnology (1981–1991), and Energy Conservation (1978–2000) projects. Most MITI projects involve only the largest companies in any field. These projects vary in type and degree of funding depending on the riskiness of the R&D undertaking. Selection of participant firms is the result of extensive consulting with trade organizations, industry representatives, and scientists, and relies on the close relations that exist between MITI and industry leaders.[22] The fact that MITI is able to organize cooperative R&D projects among the leading firms underscores the crucial differences in industrial and political structure between Japan and other developed countries. In most other countries, "the companies are not sufficiently innovative to leapfrog ahead (France), or they are too competitive to cooperate, or antitrust is too strictly enforced (the United States)."[23] Yet much of MITI's funding is rather small. The large-scale projects, for example, receive an average of only $10 million per year.

The STA, which is the creation of the Council for Science and Technology, chaired by the prime minister, has been responsible for some of the most innovative research projects organized by the Japanese government. The ERATO projects, as they are called, focus on very leading edge basic research considered prohibitively risky by industry. Examples include the Superbugs (1984–1989), Nano-Mechanisms (1985–1990), and Solid State Surfaces (1985–1990) projects. The projects are usually organized around a leading scientist. These projects will receive a total of about $70 million during the 1980s.[24]

As the foregoing shows, the sums allocated by the government to research are not particularly impressive. Indeed, the Japanese government only funded about one-fourth of the R&D carried out in Japan in 1983. The rest of the $29 billion spent that year came from the private sector. Compared with the total of $83 billion spent by the United States in

1983 on R&D, half of which was government funded, Japan's efforts in this direction seem underwhelming. Not only are the total sums relatively small, but the allocation of government R&D spending does not favor emerging fields. Forty percent of Japanese government R&D funding is directed to agriculture, while another approximately 40 percent is spent on energy research. Thus, high technology research has received relatively modest funding from the Japanese government. For example, Japanese government biotechnology research funding in 1985 was no more than $35 million, while the U.S. government funded $522.3 million.[25]

However, there are two important facts that should be noted in this regard. First, only 2 percent of Japanese R&D spending goes toward defense, while over a half of the total U.S. funds are spent on this area. Second, the trend in recent years is toward increased spending on R&D in Japan (as can be seen in table 1.8 of chap. 1). Indeed, as a percentage of GNP, combined government and private Japanese funding of non-military R&D exceeds that of the United States. Moreover, the lack of a large defense industry means that the brightest and the best scientists are not lost to firms whose products will have little commercial spillover. Firms are not crowded out of the bidding for scientific talent by defense companies. While it is difficult to measure the positive effects of these differences between the United States and Japan on the latter's high technology industries, the potential benefits of these aspects of Japanese government funding of R&D should not be ignored.

If the amount of direct Japanese government funding of R&D is not that significant, what purpose can this tool of industrial policy serve in nurturing innovation in Japan in the coming years? There are two major functions for direct government involvement. First, the nature of labor markets for scientific personnel in Japan has until recently not been amenable to the dissemination of ideas and information needed for creative activity. Japanese scientists join either company or university laboratories directly upon graduation and carry out most of their work there without outside contact. This practice, which some see as a labor market failure with regard to the dissemination of scientific information, is a serious impediment to the advancement of innovation. By creating joint national research projects such as the Fifth-Generation Computer project or the Superbugs projects, the traditional barriers separating researchers can be overcome.[26]

This is not to say that such cooperative research is undertaken with great enthusiasm by participating firms. Indeed reports abound of discord, lack of information disclosure, and the necessity of MITI strong-arming. The cutthroat competition between Japanese firms in the same industry leads to natural worries concerning loss of proprietary information, as well as concern about the usefulness of the projects themselves. However, it is an indication of the strength of the Japanese government's role in business circles and of the lax attitude toward antitrust law enforcement that a considerable number of these projects have gotten off the ground and are producing results.[27]

The second market failure that government funding helps alleviate is the lack of capital markets to fund risky R&D. In particular, the lack of venture capital and the conservatism of large corporations must be overcome by some government action. The identification of cutting-edge technologies and partial funding of research projects activate private sector funding in these areas.[28] Individual companies are not required to unilaterally undertake the costly and high-risk task of correctly targeting emerging commercially viable technologies, but rather can shift part of the burden for seeking out new technologies to the government.[29]

Before ending this examination of government R&D funding and coordination, it is useful to point out the distinctive nature of much of this research, which may be of considerable help to the future of the high-technology industries in Japan. Most research projects are long term, often up to ten years in duration. They are narrowly focused and often set development of a prototype as their goal.[30] They concentrate on seminal ideas or areas. Many of the different agencies' projects are parallel and overlapping. Most of all, the projects are commercially oriented, and very little is spent on defense research. These characteristics add up to a highly concentrated research effort that never loses sight of the ultimate aim of producing commercially viable products, even as the research in recent years has moved upstream into basic research.[31]

Education is another area in which Japanese government policies can greatly affect the capacity to innovate. Although the educational system in Japan with its well-known characteristics worked admirably for the technological catch-up period, where the abilities to pass rigorous examinations and to get along with the same group of cohorts for thirty years were most valuable, it is not a system that produces either innovative thinkers or, just as crucial, people who are supportive of individualistic behavior and ideas.[32] Besides the effect of the educational system on the supply-side characteristics of the labor market, there has been a lack of quality in university research. To a large degree this is due to the underfunding of the national university system. This underfunding results in a lack of resources for carrying out research and in inadequate academic salaries.

Finally, there is a dearth of the kind of funding support for university study that exists in the United States and Europe. Student loans, scholarships, fellowships, and tax credits for school expenses have simply not been a part of the traditional educational support system. As Japanese labor markets become more open, the burden of training will shift increasingly to individuals from corporations wary of making large human capital investments. All of the foregoing is to say that one of the most important policy areas the Japanese government must address is education. Unfortunately, probably the most conservative of all the Japanese ministries is that of education, making it unlikely that much will be done soon to create an educational system that fosters innovative thinking.

The final broad area of industrial policy at the disposal of the Japanese government in fostering innovation is capital availability. This includes financial market regulation and structure as well as tax policies such as capital gains, investment tax credits, and depreciation allowances. Government can influence the availability of capital to firms through manipulation of market regulations and through terms and conditions of access. The declining but still high dependence on debt financing by Japanese firms, as well as the large supply and low cost of capital, is in part due to a financial market still only partially internationalized. The lower cost of capital enjoyed by Japanese firms has not, as a consequence, been arbitraged away. In addition, while interest payments are deductible from corporate profits, dividend payments are not, making equity financing less attractive. These features of corporate financing have permitted greater corporate slack due to reduced pressure for high return on investments (ROI). This slack is particularly useful when high technology firms are just moving up the steep part of the learning curve, entailing high investments and low returns.

Yet although the Japanese government encourages corporate financing permitting firms to set long-term goals rather than respond to pressures for short-term profit maximization, many Japanese firms have concentrated on short-term developmental R&D projects until recently. This is one reason why MITI finds it necessary to organize national R&D projects that focus on basic R&D. This apparent contradiction between setting long-term corporate goals and short-term R&D goals is a result of the catch-up phase of Japanese technology, which precluded the necessity of basic R&D, and the inherent risk-aversiveness of large Japanese firms. However, the emptying of the world's technological storehouse is creating positive Japanese corporate attitudes toward long-term R&D projects.

In short, the easier access to low-cost capital for the high technology sectors of the Japanese economy does not necessarily lead to a definitive advantage over foreign high technology industries.[33] Indeed, the largest Japanese biotechnology firms invested only $98 million in R&D in 1981, compared with $468 million spent by the largest U.S. biotechnology firms.[34] Moreover, recent trends point to a move away from debt financing toward equity and internal financing. This may be in part a response to the internationalization of Japanese financial markets, leading to more volatile interest rates. Nevertheless, it is a trend that may possibly lead to more demand for higher short-term ROI performance—just when the availability of organizational slack may become critical to fostering innovation.

While the continuing high saving rate of the Japanese people indicates continued high capital formation, the issue of capital access will become even more important in regard to high technology firms. The lack of a venture capital market, which precludes the kind of entrepreneurial behavior common in the U.S. high technology sector, is a serious flaw. Thus Japan, which has the money, may not be allocating it to the right people. Recognizing this bottleneck, MITI set up an Office of Venture Enterprise Promotion, and in 1983 the Ministry of Finance approved the creation of three American-style over-the-counter (OTC) markets in Tokyo, Osaka, and Nagoya. There is some indication that these efforts to encourage the formation of a venture capital market are working. Venture capital investments in high technology ventures jumped from $10 million to $160 million in 1983.[35] Although this is still dwarfed by the $1.8 billion in venture capital in the United States, this development in Japan is a movement in the right direction. The problem may now be more how to foster entrepreneurs with viable projects.

The final area of industrial policy used to nurture innovation in Japan is tax incentives. Perhaps one of the most important aspects of tax policy affecting the high technology industries is the relative uniformity of the tax burden across sectors. In particular, because declining industries receive far less preferential tax treatment than in many Western countries, there is less shifting of the tax burden to the growth industries. A second major aspect is that when individual tax policies regarding high technology industries are examined, it appears that Japan does not offer significantly better tax terms to its growth industries than do other countries. For example, tax incentives for R&D investment are actually somewhat better in the United States than in Japan. Tax credits for depreciation on new equipment too are much more favorable in the United States. In this area, then, perhaps the greatest advantage derived by the Japanese high technology firms is a lower average corporate tax level than that of many other countries, with a possible exception of the United States (partially due to lower inflation), and a general fairness in sharing the tax burden with other sectors.[36]

In summary, what can be said about the role of Japanese public policy in contributing to the high technology innovations Japan needs for the future? Probably the most important contribution policy can make is to continue fostering the national consensus concerning the need to move toward the information age through such activities as well-publicized national R&D projects and resistance to providing inefficient comfort to declining industries. Policies that aid industries in bringing to market high technology products before foreign competitors can also be used as far as possible, such as encouragement of low interest rates, which permit high investment in both R&D and capital equipment.

In general, however, the state's role in the future of Japanese economic development will be quite different from that of the 1950s and 1960s. There are three reasons for this. First, international scrutiny and pressure make many of the standard policy tools (such as tariffs and quotas) unusable in today's world. Second, today most of Japanese industry is far less dependent on the government than before, particularly for capital and technology access. The internationalization of Japan has led to a decrease in government control. Finally, the government, suffering from the huge budget deficits of recent years, is less able to maintain its control.

For other reasons as well, the Japanese government's role in encouraging innovation may be somewhat different than in the past. In particular, interministerial conflicts are occurring more frequently today, thus reducing the bureaucracy's ability to devise and coordinate mutually reinforcing policies. Three principal reasons for this conflict can be cited. First, as efforts to control the budget deficit squeeze the ministries' own budgets, there is increasing conflict over other sources of funds such as the huge postal savings system.[37] Second, declining stars such as MITI are colliding with formerly less prestigious but rising agencies such as MPT. As the parent ministry for NTT and hence a central government agency in the communications industry, the power of the MPT has been growing just as MITI has been losing its influence for various reasons (including the ending of the catch-up industrialization and the liberalization of the economy that deprived MITI of much of its traditional power base). MITI's attempt to build a new role for itself as the central ministry for the new technologies has resulted in a number of skirmishes with the MPT and other agencies, such as the Ministry of Finance. Finally, just as intersectoral conflict is decreasing the ministries' ability to influence the economic decisions of Japanese firms, their power is being eroded by an increase in the role of politicians in making policy.[38] This is limiting the ministries' capability to devise policies independently of the Diet and Liberal Democratic party (LDP)—but it is also making policy-making more difficult and inefficient.[39]

The changing relationship between the Japanese ministries will probably result in a different role rather than a sharply reduced one for the government bureaucracy in the future. The central bureaucracy is still staffed by the brightest university graduates, who have extraordinary rapport with industry leaders. This provides the basis for building consensus on industrial goals and economic growth. Bureaucrats also exert strong policy-making influence, which helps keep economic goals from becoming politicized.[40] Finally, the ministries, particularly MITI, will continue to play a vital role in formulating visions of the future that, backed by national R&D projects and subsidies, reduce firm uncertainty over profitable directions for the corporation to take.

Thus, while some instruments of industrial policy, such as standards, procurement, and R&D coordination, will continue to be used, the strength or weakness of Japan as a competitor in the twenty-first century will depend more and more not on public policy but on other aspects of its society and economy. One of the most important of these is organizational structure, which is the next topic to be considered.

Organizational Structure. A relatively large amount of the R&D in Japan is carried out within corporate laboratories. In 1981, for example, the private share of R&D in Japan was 62 percent, the highest within the Organisation for Economic Cooperation and Development (OECD) group of the United States, West Germany, France, and the United Kingdom. By 1985, the private sector sponsored 70 percent of total R&D in Japan.[41] Consequently, the future of Japanese technology will be greatly affected by the organizational capability of firms to produce innovations. In this regard it is important to consider the kind of innovations that will be required of Japanese organizations before turning to an examination of the factors that will help or hinder their creation.

During the post–World War II period of catch-up economic growth, the particular strength of Japanese firms with regard to technological innovation was in creating incremental innovations. These are innovations that begin with a basic technological concept such as transistors or continuous steel casting and through a step-by-step process refine either the product or the production process. Japanese firms were especially adept at innovations in process technology geared to reducing production costs and increasing quality, to which their commanding presence in automobiles, steel, and shipbuilding bears witness. However, they have also shown great innovative capability in producing incremental product improvements, as evidenced by their lead in memory chips as well as many consumer electronics products. The decline of available technology, the present ugly international climate with regard to scientific exchange, and the pressure to cut the time to market and thus maximize R&D yield mean the Japanese must now create their own capacity to produce the basic scientific innovations that lead to technological breakthroughs.

Creating radical, rather than incremental, innovations puts pressure on firms to move upstream into basic, and hence risky, research. Radical product innovations are characterized by diverse and uncertain performance criteria. For this type of research a very different type of researcher is required, and they in turn require a different type of organization to nurture them.

What type of organizations dominate the present high technology sectors of the Japanese economy, and are they suited to fostering radical innovation? Two salient features of the top Japanese high technology firms are their size and diversification. NEC, for example, is a leader in computers, telecommunications equipment and systems, consumer electronics, and semiconductors. These firms tend to be vertically integrated, thus consuming internally a great deal of their output in another area. The dominance of large firms is exemplified by the fact that only 100 firms, mostly large, accounted for over one-half the patent applications in Japan in 1982.[42]

Many firms from declining industries, seeing the growth potential in high technology, are moving into new areas such as biotechnology and new materials. MITI has been active in helping established firms move laterally into the growth industries. For example, eleven out of the fourteen private sector participants in MITI's biotechnology projects are drawn from the declining chemical industry.[43] In addition to the features of size and the entrance of established firms, industrial structure in Japanese high technology is characterized by a high degree of interconnection. Many successful high technology firms such as Sumitomo Chemical and NEC belong to a loose group of large firms (keiretsu).

These features of Japanese high technology firms are important insofar as they influence the firms' capacity to innovate. The advantages of size and vertical integration are several. In the high technology area, where shorter product cycles, increasingly expensive R&D, and higher and higher capital investments are the norm, larger firms may be at a considerable advantage. For example, it is expected to cost $1 billion to build a new semiconductor plant by 1995.[44] Diversification allows these firms to absorb losses in one area during business downturns, which, particularly in the semiconductor industry, has been very important in the last few years. Compared with merchant semiconductor firms in the United States, Japanese firms, for whom chips represent only between 5 and 20 percent of their revenues, could afford to weather the drop in market demand.

Membership in a keiretsu also provides advantages to many high technology firms. The intra-keiretsu trading gives these large high technology firms some leverage in selling their products within the keiretsu. In addition, temporary personnel shortages can be filled by borrowing workers from less successful companies within the same keiretsu. As Nakatani points out in chapter 6, there are two distinct forms of keiretsu. Horizontal groupings are between firms operating in a wide array of markets, and vertical groupings have a core firm with major parts-suppliers and subcontractors. Both groupings lead to risk sharing, which in turn allows firms to pursue longer-term objectives and to be more flexible in responding to market changes. With regard to creating radical technological innovations, horizontal keiretsu may provide participating firms an advantage over independent competitors. This is because a wide diversity of research specialists and expertise extant in a group's many R&D laboratories can be shared to create the technological fusion characteristic of radical innovations. This sharing is particularly important in Japan, where relatively closed markets for scientific information prevail. The downside of the keiretsu phenomenon with regard to technological innovation is that the propensity to look within the keiretsu for technological expertise can result in overlooking fruitful research directions. In addition, the question of proprietary rights over new discoveries becomes difficult and can create conflicts.

In terms of creating the initial innovations that lead to new products, there is some reason to be concerned about the size of Japanese organizations. In general, large firms are large in order to be more efficient. Large organizations created to produce incrementally superior *goods* efficiently are not necessarily adept at producing radically different and superior *ideas*. A significant body of research supports this conclusion. Studies "have typically shown that while there may be certain advantages of size in exploiting the fruits of R&D, it is more efficiently done in small to medium size firms than in large ones."[45]

The people who produce the ideas are nurtured by a very different sort of environment from that conducive to efficient production. Fry and Saxberg call such people *Homo ludens* and state that "innovative organizations must provide conditions conducive to play, even though this contradicts bureaucratic efficiency: the innovation paradox."[46] There is some evidence that large Japanese corporations are finding the task of nurturing innovative behavior difficult. Some semiconductor firms, for example, have created a dual organizational structure, one for components development and the other for systems applications.[47] The problem facing these large firms is how to retain the advantages conferred by their traditional structure, which was usually a functional hierarchy, while creating a new organizational structure that fosters innovation.

What are some of the features of an organization conducive to the creation of radical innovations? A recent study by Maidique and Hayes of successful high technology firms in the United States identified six characteristics that they all have in common: (1) business focus, (2) adaptability, (3) organizational cohesion, (4) entrepreneurial culture, (5) sense of integrity, and (6) "hands-on" top management.[48] In fact, most large Japanese organizations display most of these attributes. Adaptability, for example, has been a hallmark of post–World War II Japanese firms. Japan's employment system, which minimizes the fear of change and the attendant protection of turf amongst workers and managers; the special reciprocal keiretsu relationships that allow for risk sharing; and a unique approach to new product development—all allow large Japanese firms to adapt with amazing flexibility and speed.[49] As to organizational cohesion, numerous books on Japanese management in recent years attest to their success in this area.[50]

However, two of the attributes identified by Maidique and Hayes are not necessarily present in many Japanese organizations, although both may be key to nurturing radical innovations.[51] First, business focus, which is the concentration on a single product or a closely related set of product lines, is quite opposite to the large amount of diversification that characterizes the top corporate players in Japan. As long as some cohesion is maintained across product lines, however, it is possible this will not present a significant problem. More important is the creation of an entrepreneurial climate. This entails avoiding strict hierarchical relationships, creating small divisions that allow for quick decision making, and providing a variety of funding channels to potential inventors as well as the opportunity to pursue outside projects. Today most Japanese firms are attempting to cope with these problems in various ways. One example is the creation of "project teams" that are outside the hierarchical structure. How successful such efforts will be remains to be seen.

In essence, the large Japanese firms must continue to attempt to create an environment where *ronin* (masterless samurai) scientists and engineers are not only tolerated but have access to resources and the ability to make important decisions about how they spend their time. The ideas of junior researchers must be given a fairer hearing than at present. Whether this kind of environment can best be produced by creating project teams, parallel structures, or entirely separate organizations remains to be seen. Solving the problem by creating separate subsidiaries for carrying out radical R&D must first overcome the perceived stigma of banishment that being transferred to a subsidiary carries with it in Japanese organizations.[52]

Changing patterns of employment relationships will also influence the ability of large Japanese firms to innovate.[53] In particular, the practice of permanent employment, which characterized large Japanese companies from the early fifties until recently, may provide important barriers to innovation. Permanent employment as practiced in most large Japanese firms since World War II has entailed the hiring of young male high school and college graduates with an implicit contract of providing employment to them until retirement at age fifty-five. Around this core concept has grown up a variety of reinforcing personnel practices such as extensive in-company training, cross-functional job rotations, seniority-based pay increases, and performance appraisals based on subjective criteria and used mostly for career development decisions.

For both scientific and managerial personnel, the permanent employment system is not the most suitable for the new era of high technology. With regard to scientific personnel in high technology firms, the need for individuals who are capable of producing radical innovations entails hiring and managing a very different type of individual from before. In the catch-up period, firms could hire R&D engineers with basic skills and create a local or firm-specific, rather than professional, orientation. Today, however, firms need scientists and engineers with cosmopolitan or professional orientations, who are most likely to have the depth of knowledge required for creating radical innovations. These research professionals are less useful to the firms as managers and less amenable to frequent job rotations. Their willingness to accept wages based on seniority is decreasing as they perceive their limited usefulness to the firm outside the laboratory, and hence experience anxiety about their job security once their expertise is no longer in demand. The overall effect is toward external labor market practices, with higher interfirm mobility, wider recruitment sources, more merit-based pay, less corporate training, and less job rotation. This trend is already observable: "Job changes by engineers and middle-level managers—where the turnover used to be exceptionally low—is on the increase."[54]

The same trend is becoming observable among white-collar workers in general, although for somewhat different reasons. The increasing individualism of the younger generation makes them as a group less amenable to the strict hierarchical corporate lifestyle that their fathers have adapted to so well. There is more desire for leisure time and more emphasis on family activities. The demands on managers within firms also affect the employment relationship. Whereas before an important function of managers was to accumulate and coordinate the flow of information (hence increasing the desirability of long-term employment), the increasing accessibility of information makes experience and seniority less desirable characteristics. Information technology has also increased the ability of the firm to monitor performance, which in turn decreases the role of the midlevel manager.[55]

Thus both supply-side and demand-side characteristics are changing the desirability of permanent employment in Japan for both R&D and managerial personnel. Evolving a system to replace it is a challenge that is particularly crucial to high technology firms since they will need to create environments conducive to innovation even more than firms in mature industries. The organizational upheaval that will accompany a transition to a new human resource management system must be managed carefully in view of its potential damage to the competitiveness of Japanese industry in the twenty-first century. Yet the fact is that if the transition is properly managed, Japanese firms may in fact benefit from the changing values of the younger generation. Just as firms are perceiving fewer benefits from long-term employment relationships due to the transitory nature of radical R&D expertise and a concurrent decreased need for midlevel managers as information conduits, their younger employees are becoming more amenable to leaving one firm for another and to acquiring a more professional, rather than enterprise, orientation. Properly managed, the two trends could work together to create Japanese corporations in tune with the competitive realities of the twenty-first century.

Labor Markets. The ability of organizations to make the transition to the new technological era will also be influenced by the nature of the labor market itself. There are at least three important characteristics of the Japanese labor market that will have an impact on the ability of firms to staff their organizations. First, Japan as a nation is rapidly aging. Second, women's participation is increasing, while the supply of young men is declining. Finally, the new technologies will lead to a shift in the demand for labor from secondary to tertiary industries, possibly leading to significant structural unemployment.

The influence of an aging population on Japanese organizations will be felt in decreased productivity from the effects of aging, coupled with decreased returns on investments in training. Because of the inadequate pensions and increased longevity, many older people will wish to continue working well past retirement age. Yet because of obsolete skills, employers will be reluctant to hire them as they will be unlikely to regain their investments in training.[56] Furthermore, retaining older workers past retirement age makes it difficult to continue a compensation system that rewards seniority, and hence firms, despite changes they have introduced to their compensation system during the past several years, will resist retention of older workers. In short, while a larger and larger part of the available pool of workers will be older, both productivity and labor cost considerations will make this pool unattractive to high technology firms.

Another potential pool of employees for future job needs is the growing number of Japanese women entering the labor force. At about age thirty-five, when their children reach school age, many women reenter the labor market. However, even with the Equal Employment Opportunity Act that was passed in 1985 to encourage employers to hire them, so far most women are employed in relatively low skilled jobs, often part-time. But by the year 2000 there will be a shortage of men under fifty-five. This may lead to a reevaluation of the employability of women in higher-status jobs by firms pressured by shortages. The large number of highly educated Japanese women who are presently underused represents a potential bonanza for corporations. Employing women in large numbers in career-path jobs will require a drastic change in the way Japanese corporations are managed. Flexibility with regard to working hours, as well as changes in traditional practices (such as afterwork drinking parties, where important business is discussed), will have to be made. Some firms are already moving in this direction, as evidenced by a number of recent surveys.[57] In particular, firms in the newer industries seem to be hiring more women as well as making other changes in their personnel practices, such as switching to midcareer hiring, all positive signs of the adaptability of these new technology organizations to changing labor market forces.

The most serious labor market problem facing firms is the availability of workers trained in the skills needed by both high technology firms and traditional manufacturing firms. An increasing number of blue-collar jobs will disappear due to both the revolution in mechatronics and robotics and the increasing foreign direct investment of Japanese firms. By the year 2000, for example, Japan could lose as many as 800,000 jobs to overseas investment.[58] The number of redundant workers in the declining industries is already rising rapidly.[59] At the same time as blue-collar jobs are being lost and workers displaced, it is expected that the demand for professional and technical workers will double by the year 2000.[60] While Japan is presently producing a large number of scientific personnel, particularly engineers, it is doubtful that the educational and training systems now in place can cope with this surge in demand.

Consequently, there is a strong possibility that Japan will face a serious mismatch in its labor needs and supply, particularly in the high technology areas. In order to cope with this, a variety of alternatives will be necessary, including hiring foreigners and setting up scientific research centers abroad. There is evidence that both solutions are already being put into effect. The challenge of managing both foreigners and the displacement of blue-collar workers will require organizational flexibility on the part of Japanese firms as they enter the twenty-first century.

This section has examined a broad array of conditions that will affect Japan's ability to create the innovations necessary to maintain Japan's competitiveness in the twenty-first century. This broad scope necessarily leaves out details and as such can only suggest the potential problem areas and potential solutions. The overall conclusion that can be drawn is that the internal conditions are not entirely conducive to innovation and will require a great deal of social flexibility in order to be modified. The safety of the known—in education, workplace relationships, university-government relationships, government policies—will have to be selectively discarded and replaced with uncertain practices. Working with women, high labor force mobility, highly imaginative and risky government research projects, venture capital enterprises, intrapreneurship— all of these will stretch the adaptability of the Japanese people and their institutions. The irony is that even if they are successful, there is a possibility that forces outside Japan may make the effort ineffective. We will now turn to these external conditions affecting the capability to innovate.

Changing International Environment

The single greatest threat to Japan's ability to remain a leader in the technological race in the twenty-first century is anti-Japanese protectionism. The deterioration of the international trade climate during the eighties can be seen in a multitude of events related to Japanese exports: the restriction of importation into France of Japanese videocassette recorders to the small-town bottleneck of Poitiers; the numerous "voluntary" import limits imposed on Japan by the United States; and, most recently, and ominously, the imposition of tariffs on the Japanese semiconductor industry by the United States, which in turn has "encouraged similar menacing talk from other nations."[61] While international trade in general is suffering from increasing disregard of the General Agreement on Tariffs and Trade (GATT) conventions, as evidenced by the growing number of bilateral trade agreements, much of the retaliatory action in the world market has been directed at Japan.

In essence, Japan is paying the price of success, a part of which, some believe, it owes to a variety of industrial policies employed during the 1960s and 1970s. As discussed earlier, a number of the instruments are no longer in use, especially the more overt instruments associated with infant-industry protection. However, there are still a number of nontariff barriers in place, such as very limited acceptance of the certification by foreign factories of goods imported into Japan[62] and the still lingering tendency of the Japanese bureaucracy to delay implementing various types of market-opening measures. Most important, perhaps, is the extreme slowness with which the Japanese have dismantled remaining barriers, including access to lucrative projects such as the new Kansai Airport or the huge NTT procurement process.

Perhaps more than the reality of restrictions, the perceived ill grace with which the Japanese have liberalized their market has made its trading partners less willing to tolerate Japan's growing trade surpluses. The bad feelings engendered abroad have recently reached a higher level. This has resulted in a significant negative shift in opinion among lawmakers and businessmen in the United States who normally advocate open markets.[63] Nor should it be forgotten that many of Japan's trade partners in Europe and its Asian neighbors are expressing an increasing dissatisfaction with Japan's trade practices and large trade surplus.

While some Japanese lawmakers and businessmen tend to see foreign complaints and retaliatory actions as sour grapes, they are also keenly aware that should the international climate regarding Japan deteriorate much further it could pose two major obstacles to further economic growth. First, access to new developments in science and technology could be hindered. Second, market access could be denied or severely limited.

The first concern regarding access to technological developments is of particular importance during the next five to ten years. As the first part of this paper demonstrated, for Japan to be able to remain a technological leader, it must continue to rely upon groundbreaking scientific work outside its borders. Until the various national research projects and corporate R&D laboratories begin to produce a significant number of radical innovations, Japan will continue to be dependent on the international R&D community. A new national anxiety is arising concerning securing sources of technological information, the most important input of the new high technology industries.

There is reason for concern. Recent changes in U.S. patent law are especially worrisome. In 1983 U.S. law regarding patents from U.S.-funded research was changed such that a waiver must be obtained if a government patent is purchased by a firm that is producing a substantial amount of its product outside the United States.[64] The protectionist sentiments embodied in this and other changes are largely directed against Japan, which has been a major purchaser of U.S. patents, and is partially a result of past Japanese protection of patents developed by such agencies as NTT. There has also recently been a refusal by foreign firms to license microprocessor technology to Japanese companies.[65] Protection of innovation will be an increasingly important cause of international dispute as the concept of technonationalism gains hold in the United States and other OECD countries.[66]

In response to both international pressure to make its patents accessible and as a way to undercut patent protection by other countries, MITI has instituted a number of reforms that make foreign licensing much easier.[67] Prime Minister Nakasone's proposal for a Human Frontiers Science Program to bring together Japanese and foreign researchers to work on cutting-edge life science innovations is in part an attempt to enable Japan to be seen as a contributor to the international science community.[68] The Japanese government can be expected to continue as a strong opponent of technological protectionism in arenas where such issues are discussed, such as the United Nations.

Japanese multinational firms can play a significant role in decreasing the effects of foreign protectionism of technology. As mentioned previously, most of the Japanese firms dominating the new information industries are large, vertically integrated companies. They are also multinational corporations. Their international operations give these firms a variety of avenues for accessing technological developments in other countries. These avenues include joint ventures, foreign subsidiaries, and foreign direct investment.

Forming joint ventures with foreign firms is an important strategy for Japanese firms needing access to particular kinds of technology. Multinationals in general tend to enter into such agreements with partners with strengths in the same area, and a sharing of proprietary information becomes the basis of the relationship.[69] Japanese firms have preferred this form of market entry for foreign firms entering Japan as it leads to greater diffusion of foreign technology to domestic firms than do wholly owned subsidiaries. Such coalitions also allow for easy dissolution of the relationship when it is no longer perceived as beneficial. Japanese firms are now using this long experience with joint ventures to form coalitions abroad. The small U.S. biotechnology ventures are particularly attractive targets. The American firms often gain crucial process technology, while the Japanese firms gain leading-edge R&D results in a strategic industry.

Japanese foreign subsidiaries can also serve as conduits of technological information from overseas to Japan. Subsidiaries can set up their own R&D laboratories with host country scientists. Particularly in the United States, with its relatively open labor market for scientists, the Japanese subsidiary can attract quality American scientific personnel. These subsidiaries become just one of many firms involved in a research area and blend in with American firms. Yet national technology borders are circumvented by the Japanese subsidiary when it shares the R&D results produced overseas with the home organization. The most dramatic recent example of this type of technology flow comes from an American firm, IBM, whose Swiss R&D subsidiary was responsible for the crucial breakthrough in superconductors that has given IBM a lead in this area. Even when Japanese foreign subsidiaries do not have an R&D function, the overseas operation can be an important source of technological information. It garners its information from suppliers, customers, trade fairs, and local university contacts.

Finally, Japanese multinational corporations can gain direct access to overseas R&D through purchase of foreign firms. This foreign direct investment approach is exemplified by the presence in the New York office of Kirin Brewery Company of a staff member responsible for seeking out start-up U.S. biotechnology firms for investment purposes. Japanese firms with their overflowing coffers and a strong yen have recently found this a particularly attractive avenue for gaining access to overseas R&D.

In short, the Japanese fears of being cut off from important technology at a crucial juncture in their move into twenty-first-century industries may be too extreme given the many paths by which technology can flow into Japan. Getting technology may be more difficult than before but will be far from impossible. However, caution should be exercised to avoid further exacerbating international protectionism against Japan, which could destroy avenues for technology flow.

Another important consequence of the deterioration in the world trade climate is the threat of closed markets. That is, while Japan must continue to derive a significant portion of its gross national product (GNP) from exports even as it moves into the new era, it is likely to face an increasing number of players who will challenge Japan. Japan will be, in all likelihood, able to retain a good share of markets in high technology products. However, Japanese firms can no longer assume access to global markets. Despite the fact that the R&D costs involved in development of new high technology products such as computers and advanced materials can only be recouped by obtaining a dominant global market position in that product, the recent push for "reciprocity" by American lawmakers, for example, could result in cutting off Japan's access to its most important market if Japan's bilateral trade surplus continues. England, too, frustrated over lack of access for its telecommunications industry to the lucrative Japanese market, has threatened restrictions on Japanese business activity.

Given the number of tie-ups between Japanese and foreign firms, as well as the growing number of foreign corporations operating in the Japanese market, actual implementation of severe market restrictions against Japan is probably unlikely. But Japanese businessmen are taking no chances. By 1992 Japan will be producing one-fifth of its manufacturing products abroad, as is already the case with the United States.[70] Moreover, the majority of the recent direct investment abroad by Japanese firms is going into developed countries that provide access to important markets.

Whether this strategy of producing abroad will overcome market protection has yet to be proved. On the one hand, it decreases the perception of Japan as simply an export nation selfishly keeping both jobs and profits at home. On the other hand, an increasing number of critics are pointing to the relatively low skilled jobs produced by Japanese firms in foreign countries. The jobs involved in producing the higher value for the product, such as design engineering, are kept at home. Also, a criticism being raised more frequently of late is that many Japanese firms are followed abroad by branches of their supplier firms, thus decreasing the positive effect on the host economy. These criticisms could lead to a mounting clamor for adjustments in the type of foreign direct investment by Japanese firms, or perhaps even to calls for bans on new investments.

In sum, there are serious external problems facing Japan in implementing its program to remain an important high technology nation of the twenty-first century. To some degree these problems are the results of an overly successful industrial policy now largely abandoned. At the same time, there is an unwillingness on the part of many Japanese to see the dangers of ignoring the concerns of its trading partners. While the Maekawa Report of 1986 addressed many of these concerns and called for such remedies as increasing domestic demand, changing Japan's fiscal and monetary policies, and improving foreign access to Japanese markets, the lack of teeth in the proposals makes it unlikely they will actually be carried out.[71] The fact that the report also calls for a balanced budget effectively prevents implementation of programs stimulating domestic consumption and decreasing exports (*naiju*). Perhaps the most serious obstacle to true change is the difficulty of discarding such practices as saving instead of consuming that have been validated by Japan's economic success. In short, the "shackles" preventing Japan from changing "are Japan's national experience."[72] The guile and arrogance born of the success of Japanese business leaders and lawmakers may also be great dangers for Japan.[73] The skill of the more internationalized among them will be sorely needed to steer Japan through the choppy waters of international protection during the next few years.

CONCLUSIONS

Will Japan continue to be one of the major economic players in the twenty-first century? Based on what we can readily observe today and on the evidence presented in this paper, our reply to this question must be an affirmative one, with the qualifications we have presented. The foregoing analysis has suggested at least three reasons for reaching such a conclusion.

First, both Japanese government agencies and corporations are demonstrating a serious commitment to creating an economy that will be able to compete successfully in the technological race of the next century. In particular, the conditions for creating radical innovations in science and technology are being established. Although the government is hampered by large budget deficits, it is providing important leadership roles in identifying and coordinating research into new technologies. Corporate R&D funds have grown rapidly and are directed more and more to basic research. Beyond the financial commitment to high technology research is the seeming national consensus on the need for a change in direction. Since this change also means less dependence on foreign technology, it is not difficult to understand why the consensus has developed; there can be no resistance to the public and private efforts to improve Japan's capabilities to make scientific discoveries of their own. Put differently, as a nation, Japan is agreed upon the direction it wishes to follow, and this means that government and corporate resource allocation decisions can be less subject to time-consuming contentious questioning.

Second, Japan has already achieved an important commercial presence with a variety of high technology products and hence has in place the expertise needed for commercialization of future developments. Particularly in the communications industry, Japanese corporations have concentrated on mass market products that provide both learning in production technology and large revenues. The same pattern can be seen with products such as interferon and carbon fiber. While the underlying technology is often still imported and modified, the fact is that in most areas Japanese researchers are increasingly demonstrating a capacity for creative, radical innovations. As original innovations increase, they will benefit from the expertise in production technology in high technology fields already acquired in this transition period. The union of radical innovation capability with production skills will make Japan a formidable competitor in the new economic game.

Third and last, Japan has two crucial qualities needed for the new economic game: money and a well-educated labor force. The competitive ability of nations in the twenty-first century will depend less and less on location, natural resources, or cheap labor. Due to the uncoupling of employment from production and increasingly cheap commodities and transportation, the two most important requirements for success will be financial resources and highly skilled human resources. The first is necessary just to buy into the game. The cost of R&D will undoubtedly continue to escalate as will the cost of constructing manufacturing plants for both traditional and high technology industries. Only those nations with sufficient funancial resources will be able to compete. However, the financial resources must be combined with a trained labor force capable of both producing technological innovations for further development and running the increasingly complex workplace. Thus, Japan, which has both of these assets, will remain a technological power and a strong competitor in the world markets of the next century.

The most significant barrier to Japanese success in the twenty-first century is the international climate, particularly the possibility of increasing anti-Japanese economic policies by Japan's trade partners. How Japan deals with the barrier could be the key factor determining Japan's economy in the next century. To the extent that Japan can alter the climate by internationalizing and liberalizing its economy, the future of the Japanese economy rests in its own hands.

APPENDIX

Communications

Often referred to as the information industry, communications is probably the widest field of the three industries Japan has targeted as key to its future. It encompasses such areas as office automation, CAD/CAM, communications satellites, computers, and electronic information processing. The crucial foundations of this industry are semiconductors, computer science, and telecommunications.

As attested to by the imposition of stiff retaliatory tariffs on the Japanese semiconductor industry by the United States in April 1987, the commercial strength of this sector of the Japanese information industry is beyond doubt. Japanese firms now control almost half of the world chip market. In the DRAM market, which is the most widely used chip, the Japanese now hold 90 percent of the world market. Having largely taken over the commodity chip market, Japanese firms are now turning their attention to cutting-edge microprocessors and peripheral chips such as logic and semicustom chips. Since 1984, all new Japanese semiconductor plants have been built to produce specialized chips. In optoelectronic components such as laser diodes, Japanese firms are now undisputed leaders.[74] The growth in both quantity and value of Japanese production in almost all areas of semiconductors is shown by the figures in table 2.1.

Japan's recent contributions to semiconductor developments include commercialization of the 1-megabit DRAM and active research on gallium arsenide as a replacement for silicon in transistors. Fujitsu scientists were already carrying out experiments similar to those at IBM when recent breakthroughs in this important technology were made.[75] These developments, however, are only among the most visible of the signs of broader R&D efforts now being made by the Japanese. Thus, a recent expert testimony confirms the overall strength of the Japanese semiconductor industry and points to its future competitiveness:

Quantum mechanically-based dimensionally constrained devices and integrated circuits may represent the most significant future electronics and electro-optic data and signal processing options. . . . The Japanese are aggressive in acquiring, improving, and implementing these technologies, whose conceptual aspects were developed in the U.S. In opto-electronics, in particular, the Japanese have made major, original contributions and, while their adaptive ingenuity can be expected to continue to produce market oriented products, their original creative contributions to this field are expected to increase steadily in the future.[76]

Although the semiconductor industry suffered a decline in 1985, the industry is expected to have strong future growth due to its key position in the overall information industry. By the 1990s, the semiconductor industry is expected to have a $67 billion a year market, and Japanese firms seem determined to supply a large part of that market. NEC, for example, recently announced plans to build new semiconductor manufacturing facilities.[77] In gallium arsenide transistors and chips, which are expected to account for 6.5 percent of the total semiconductor market in the 1990s, Japan "is likely to become the dominant supplier."[78] In short, the Japanese are in a good position to take a large share of the semiconductor markets; these markets are crucial to technological progress in many industries and can be expected to grow rapidly in size.

Closely related to their achieving major commercial success and competitiveness in the underlying technology is the fact that the Japanese have developed a very strong semiconductor equipment manufacturing capability. While beginning mostly in chip assembly and the less sophisticated end of semiconductor equipment, recently several Japanese firms have begun moving into more complex machinery such as steppers, the most advanced type of exposure machine used in the process of forming the electric circuits on semiconductor chips.[79] As a result, Japan's reliance on imported semiconductor equipment has declined rapidly in the past few years, and today approximately 70 percent of Japan's domestic demand is supplied by Japanese firms and foreign-owned firms operating in Japan. With a commanding lead in many important semiconductor products themselves and a rapidly increasing ability to dominate the international market in semiconductor equipment, there can be no question that this is a major area of strength in Japan's communications industry.

Computers are both an important consumer of semiconductors and a vital link in the information network of the future. Recognizing this, the Japanese government beginning in the early 1960s established a variety of institutions to help promote the growth of this industry, including the Japan Electronic Computer Company and the Information Technology Promotion Agency.[80] Although views differ as to the efficacy of the protection against international competition that was provided by the government to the computer industry, Japanese computer producers pres-

TABLE 2.1

Japan's Production of Semiconductors

	1982	1983	1984	1985	1986(p)[a]
	Value (in Millions of Yen)[b]				
Integrated circuits	834,883	1,139,523	1,973,850	1,841,790	1,780,101
Linear	176,332	222,279	331,419	350,333	338,166
For industrial equipment	41,777	45,082	68,541	70,588	83,229
For consumer goods	134,555	177,197	262,878	279,745	254,937
Digital bipolar	130,493	153,371	261,004	256,076	273,390
Logic	104,232	130,805	223,726	214,827	230,052
Memory	26,261	22,566	37,278	41,249	43,337
Digital metal oxide semiconductor	436,646	663,643	1,235,596	1,070,965	999,305
Logic	208,177	296,387	481,885	482,095	483,544
Memory	228,469	367,256	753,711	588,870	515,760
Hybrid	91,412	100,230	145,831	164,417	169,241
Discrete devices	359,687	420,651	610,389	567,913	552,420
Transistors	143,457	152,726	224,845	206,205	196,041
Diodes and rectifiers	102,129	122,004	170,763	142,752	139,900
Other	114,101	145,921	214,781	218,956	216,479
Total production	1,194,570	1,560,174	2,584,239	2,409,703	2,332,521

Quantity (in Thousands of Units)

Integrated circuits	4,351	6,230	9,516	9,350	11,144
Linear	1,641	2,252	3,463	3,624	3,972
For industrial equipment	377	443	653	646	1,026
For consumer goods	1,264	1,810	2,809	2,978	2,946
Digital bipolar	963	1,387	2,230	1,882	2,379
Logic	935	1,355	2,188	1,838	2,334
Memory	29	32	41	44	45
Digital metal oxide semiconductor	1,559	2,311	3,486	3,485	4,364
Logic	1,021	1,571	2,334	2,358	2,889
Memory	537	741	1,152	1,127	1,475
Hybrid	219	279	338	360	428
Discrete devices	21,555	28,077	42,406	38,283	43,087
Transistors	8,372	9,387	14,391	14,343	15,769
Diodes and rectifiers	10,000	14,500	22,273	18,702	20,576
Other	3,183	4,191	5,743	5,237	6,743

SOURCE: Japan, Ministry of International Trade and Industry, *Yearbook of Machinery Statistics*. Reproduced in "U.S.-Japan Competition in Semiconductors: American Makers Rethink Strategies," *Japan Economic Institute Report*, no. 16A (Washington, D.C.: Japan Economic Institute, 1987).

[a]No definition given for "(p)." It is assumed to stand for "preliminary."

[b]The following average annual exchange rates, calculated by the Ministry of Finance, can be used to convert the yen production figures into U.S. dollars: 1982, ¥249.08; 1983, ¥237.51; 1984, ¥237.52; 1985, ¥238.54; and 1986, ¥168.52.

ently control about one-half of their domestic market, which is the second largest in the world. However, Japan still lags considerably behind the United States in the international market. U.S. companies sold $110 billion in computers in 1983, whereas Japan's expected 1985 computer exports were $1.7 billion.[81] Figure 2.1 shows the relative positions of the world's major computer producers, confirming the weak market position of Japanese manufacturers in the world market.[82]

Recent developments, however, clearly point toward increased competitiveness of the Japanese. In personal computers, NEC, holding the largest percentage of the Japanese market, is rapidly becoming a world competitor, and Hitachi and Fujitsu are becoming increasingly competitive in the world market for larger machines. In 1985 Fujitsu introduced its VP-56, a supercomputer able to compete against Cray and Control Data, particularly on price. Indeed, Japanese supercomputers are expected to capture 25 percent of new supercomputer applications in the United States during the remainder of the eighties.[83] The most well-publicized computer development is the Fifth-Generation Computer, a large, long-range MITI project to develop a computer using artificial intelligence. While the ultimate aim of producing a parallel-processing computer capable of processing vast amounts of knowledge at very high speeds may not be reached soon, the spin-offs from this project with regard to artificial intelligence and software may be of benefit to the Japanese computer industry in general.[84]

While generalizations can be dangerous, the overall conclusion we reach on the basis of the above and other evidence is that Japan is catching

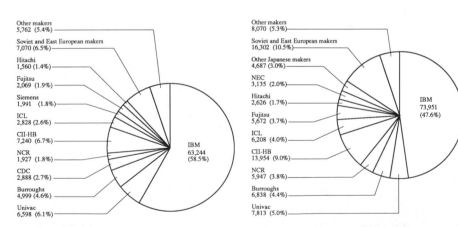

a. In units (total units installed: 155,203)

b. By value (total value of units installed: $108,176 million)

FIGURE 2.1. How computer makers share the world market. (*Source:* Long-Term Credit Bank of Japan, *Japan's High Technology Industries* [1983], p. 44.)

up in hardware but is yet severely handicapped in most areas of software. A recent assessment of Japanese computer science by a panel of experts yielded the scoreboard listed in table 2.2, which seems to support this conclusion. McClellan concluded that the best way to overcome both software problems and market and support problems was for Japanese makers to team up with overseas manufacturers.[85] Indeed, this has been and is being done, as clearly demonstrated by recent agreements among Toshiba, Olivetti of Europe, and AT&T, as well as among NEC, Honeywell, and Bull, a European manufacturer.[86]

By the end of this century, the computer industry is expected to become the world's leading business, promising both huge markets and profits. For example, the artificial intelligence market alone, encompassing such areas as expert systems and workstations, is expected to be four times the size of the present computer market in Japan by 1996.[87] Although Japan's present capability regarding this industry is mixed, there is little doubt that Japan will increasingly be a strong competitor in the international market.

The final fundamental component of the information industry is telecommunications, the network to bring together individual parts of the information system. Broadly speaking, telecommunications includes everything from phone and fiber optical cables to space satellites for relaying. In general, Japanese performance in this area has become quite competitive, especially since the early eighties. An industry developed under the protective umbrella of NTT, the recently privatized national telecommunications company, telecommunications in Japan is dominated by the NTT "family" of NEC, Hitachi, Fujitsu, and Oki Electric Industry. Taking advantage of the breakup of AT&T in the early eighties, Japanese firms moved strongly into the vast U.S. market, producing a lopsided trade picture in some telecommunications sectors. In private branch exchange (PBX) equipment, for example, NEC now holds 10 percent of the U.S. market. Overall, Japan's share of the global telecommunications market grew from 3 percent in 1978 to 11 percent in 1983.[88]

The development of computer network systems, such as the INS and CAPTAIN, by NTT points toward continued growth of the telecommunications market within Japan itself. The installation of the INS system, seen as a crucial part of the transformation of Japan into an information society, is a huge ¥30 trillion project expected to be completed by the turn of the century. The steady growth of Japan's own market is aiding Japan's efforts to gain most of the skills necessary in becoming a formidable competitor in the world market of this industry in the coming decades; the market is expected to be between $300 and $500 billion over the next twenty years. Recent contracts for large equipment orders with overseas buyers such as Thailand presage the competitiveness of Japanese telecommunications products in this large and important market. In its effort to aid Japanese firms in the global competition, the

TABLE 2.2
Assessment of Japanese Computer Science

	Basic research		Advanced development		Product engineering	
	Absolute[a]	Change[b]	Absolute	Change	Absolute	Change
Overall assessment	Far behind	Losing ground	Behind	Holding position	Even	Gaining ground
Summary assessment by field						
Software	Far behind	Slipping quickly	Behind	Losing ground	Ahead	Pulling away
Artificial intelligence	Far behind	Losing ground	Behind	Holding position	Behind	Holding position
Processor architecture and computer organization	Far behind	Losing ground	Even	Gaining ground	Ahead	Gaining ground
Communications	Far behind	Losing ground	Even	Holding position	Ahead	Gaining ground
Hardware			Even	Holding position	Ahead	Gaining ground
Software (esp. protocols and systems software)			Behind	Holding position	Far behind	Losing ground
Software						
Software engineering	Far behind	Losing ground	Behind	Catching up	Far ahead	Pulling away
Operating systems	Far behind	Slipping quickly	Far behind	Slipping quickly	Ahead	Holding position
Applications software packages	Far behind	Slipping quickly	Behind	Losing ground	Unknown	
Languages	Far behind	Slipping quickly	Behind	Losing ground	Far ahead	Holding position
Data base systems	Far behind	Slipping quickly	Far behind	Losing ground	Far behind	Slipping quickly

SOURCE: J. Albus, *Japanese Technology Assessment* (Park Ridge, N.J.: Noyes Data Corporation, 1986), pp. 17, 18, 24.
[a]Absolute comparison.
[b]Rate of change in absolute position.

Japanese government has identified this industry as one of the "targets" to be promoted.[89]

Of the three industries targeted by the Japanese government as key to future competitiveness, communications is arguably the most important in that it affects the ability of the Japanese to compete in both old and new industries. The application of information networking to traditional industries and newer industries will produce the gains in productivity needed in Japan's attempt to sustain its economic performance and to remain a major player in the technological competition.[90] It is possible that national weakness in either biotechnology or new materials could be borne without crippling Japan's ability to compete in the technological race—it is doubtful that it could stay on the field long without a strong information industry. Thus its overall strength in this area leads one to expect that Japan will maintain its competitiveness in the international markets of the twenty-first century.

Biotechnology

Compared with the communications industry, the evaluation of the commercial success of the Japanese biotechnology industry is considerably more difficult. The commercial application of biotechnology has only a fifteen-year history, while computers and transistors began to be used in industrial applications in the early fifties. Much of biotechnology is still a promise rather than a reality. Although biotechnology has potentially wide applications—pharmaceuticals, chemicals, textiles, agriculture, food processing, and energy—the full impact of the biotechnology field will probably be felt only at the beginning of the next century.

The Japanese belief in the promise of biotechnology is well known. Part of the impetus to develop their own biotechnology capability came from the 1981 grant of the Cohen/Boyer patent in the United States for the development of recombinant DNA vectors and techniques, which was seen as a potential barrier to future Japanese entry. Convinced of its future growth potential by the successful manufacture of interferon and insulin and anxious about continuing access to the world-class technology, the Japanese government targeted biotechnology as a key area of concentration.

The Japanese have their greatest strength in fermentation, and in this area they "already provide commercial sources of enzymes, synthetic amino acids, and antibiotics."[91] Indeed, Japan dominates the U.S. amino acid market.[92] Recently, Japanese industry has concentrated most heavily on the application of biotechnology to pharmaceuticals, and in the last few years they have produced various types of interferon for commercial sale. In addition, the Japanese pharmaceutical, food, chemical, textile, and pulp and paper industries have considerable expertise in bioprocess technology, which greatly benefits the development of commercially viable pharmaceutical products.[93]

A panel of experts recently undertook an evaluation of the Japanese position in the most important commercially viable areas of biotechnology: biochemical process technology, biosensors, cell culture technology, protein engineering, and recombinant DNA technology. With the exception of protein-engineering technology, where the Japanese seem content to acquire technology from abroad, the general conclusion is that the Japanese will be formidable competitors in these areas in the near future. In the very important area of recombinant DNA, for example, the evaluator concludes that he sees "no reason why the Japanese should not be able to pass us [the United States] in the commercial applications areas. I think it is likely that they will be able to produce higher quality products for less money."[94] In short, while there are various problems to be faced in reaching a dominant competitive position in biotechnology, such as an insufficient supply of technicians, the evaluation shows that Japan's future competitive capability will be substantial.

Speculation about the size of the market for biotechnology is difficult at best. The Japanese market alone is expected to grow to twenty-three times its present size by the year 2000, representing a value of ¥6 trillion.[95] Such huge growth potential makes it a natural target for entry by a large number of firms in declining industries, particularly chemical companies, which are allocating substantial research personnel and R&D funds to biotechnology research.[96] Even the recent setback suffered by the U.S. biotechnology firm Genetech, in which its approval application was rejected by the Food and Drug Administration for the first biotechnology blockbuster product (t-PA, a heart blood-clot drug), is not likely to deter the global growth of the field.[97]

New Materials

New materials include composites such as fiber-reinforced plastics, inorganic materials such as ceramics, and organic materials such as engineering plastics. This area has the potential to revolutionize not only end products such as automobile engines but also processing and production equipment such as machine tools. The many applications of new materials make them particularly important to future Japanese competitiveness.

In engineering plastics, Japanese makers are fast catching up to the total production of U.S. makers. Already in 1982, for example, Japan produced 286,000 tons of engineering plastics, while the United States, the largest engineering-plastic producer, now produces around 360,000 tons.[98] In fine ceramics the Japanese have become highly competitive in applications to tools and to industrial machinery and automobile engine parts.[99] In composite materials, the Japanese account for over half of the world output of carbon fiber.[100]

The advanced materials market both in Japan and the world is expected to grow enormously. Indeed, between 1986 and 1995, the new materials market in Japan is forecast to grow 2.7-fold, to about ¥4.5 trillion.[101] Carbon fibers and fine ceramics represent the two largest areas of production and value in the new materials field. Present Japanese strength in these areas portends a very competitive future position.

NOTES

1. Peter F. Drucker, "The Changed World Economy," *Foreign Affairs*, Spring 1986, pp. 768–91.

2. Martha Caldwell-Harris, "Japan's International Technology Transfers," in the report to the Joint Economic Committee, Congress of the United States, *Japan's Economy and Trade with the United States* (Washington, D.C.: U.S. Government Printing Office, 1985), p. 120.

3. Rodney Clark, *Aspects of Japanese Commercial Innovation* (London: Technical Change Centre, 1984), p. 38.

4. Caldwell-Harris, "Japan's International Technology Transfers," p. 118. For further data on Japanese technology trade in selected industries, see Clark, *Aspects of Japanese Commercial Innovation*, p. 24.

5. Kagaku Gijutsu Chō (Science and Technology Agency), *Kagaku Gijutsu Hakusho, 1984* (Tokyo: Science and Technology Agency, 1984). Similar data for scientists and engineers engaged in R&D are given in table 1.7, chap. 1.

6. National Science Board, *Science Indicators: The 1985 Report* (Washington, D.C.: U.S. Government Printing Office, 1985), p. 7.

7. Ibid., p. 23.

8. Paul R. Krugman, "New Thinking about Trade Policy," in Paul R. Krugman, ed., *Strategic Trade Policy and the New International Economics* (Cambridge: MIT Press, 1986).

9. Ibid.

10. Kozo Yamamura, "Success That Soured: Administrative Guidance and Cartels in Japan," in Kozo Yamamura, ed., *Policy and Trade Issues of the Japanese Economy: American and Japanese Perspectives* (Seattle: University of Washington Press, 1982).

11. Gary Saxonhouse, "Industrial Policy and Factor Markets," in Hugh Patrick, ed., *Japan's High Technology Industries* (Seattle: University of Washington Press, 1986); and Daniel I. Okimoto, "Conclusions," in Daniel I. Okimoto, Takuo Sugano, and Franklin B. Weinstein, eds., *Competitive Edge: The Semiconductor Industry in the U.S. and Japan* (Stanford: Stanford University Press, 1984), p. 216.

12. *Japan Economic Almanac, 1986* (Tokyo: Nihon Keizai Shimbun, 1986), p. 104.

13. Kozo Yamamura, "Joint Research and Antitrust: Japanese vs. American Strategies," in Patrick, *Japan's High Technology Industries*.

14. Daniel I. Okimoto, "Outsider Trading: Coping with Japanese Industrial Organization," *Journal of Japanese Studies* 13, no. 2 (Summer 1987): 383–414.

15. Ibid., p. 391.

16. Ibid., p. 402.

17. Saxonhouse, "Industrial Policy and Factor Markets," p. 103.

18. Chalmers Johnson, "MITI, MPT, and the Telecom Wars: How Japan Makes Policy for High Technology," in Chalmers Johnson, Laura Andrea Tyson, and John Zysman, eds., *Politics and Productivity: How Japan's Development Strategy Works* (New York: Ballinger, 1989).

19. Kozo Yamamura, "Shedding the Shackles of Success: Saving Less for Japan's Future," *Journal of Japanese Studies* 13, no. 2 (Summer 1987): 429–56.

20. Daniel I. Okimoto and Gary R. Saxonhouse, "Technology and the Future of the Economy," in Kozo Yamamura and Yasukichi Yasuba, eds., *The Political Economy of Japan*, vol. 1, *The Domestic Transformation* (Stanford: Stanford University Press, 1987).

21. Sheridan Tatsuno, *The Technopolis Strategy* (New York: Prentice-Hall, 1986), pp. 37–40.

22. Kozo Yamamura, "Joint Research and Antitrust: Japanese vs. American Strategies," p. 185.

23. Daniel I. Okimoto, "Regime Characteristics of Japanese Industrial Policy," in Patrick, *Japan's High Technology Industries*, p. 51.

24. Tatsuno, *Technopolis Strategy*, p. 39.

25. Saxonhouse, "Industrial Policy and Factor Markets," p. 106.

26. Okimoto and Saxonhouse, "Technology and the Future of the Economy."

27. Yamamura, "Joint Research and Antitrust."

28. Ronald Dore, *A Case Study of Technology Forecasting in Japan: The Next Generation Base Technologies Development Programme* (London: Technical Change Centre, 1983), especially his summary. Dore's study of the way the priorities of MITI's Next Generation Base Technologies Development Programme 1981–1991 were identified and set shows how the government helps channel resources toward promising R&D areas. Dore found that MITI actually uses mostly already existing information to draft an internal document that becomes the basis of recommendations of a publicly appointed and highly publicized committee. An important feature that makes this process successful is the high general quality of MITI personnel who research and write the original draft.

29. Okimoto and Saxonhouse, "Technology and the Future of the Economy."

30. Eads and Nelson, "Japanese High Technology Policy," p. 254.

31. Dore, *A Case Study of Technology Forecasting in Japan*, p. 3.

32. Thomas P. Rohlen, "The Juku Phenomenon: An Exploratory Essay," *Journal of Japanese Studies* 6, no. 2 (Summer 1980): 207–42; idem, *Japan's High Schools* (Berkeley and Los Angeles: University of California Press, 1983).

33. Ibid.

34. Saxonhouse, "Industrial Policy and Factor Markets," p. 121.

35. Tatsuno, *Technopolis Strategy*, p. 60.

36. Michiyuki Uenohara, Takuo Sugano, John G. Linvill, and Franklin B. Weinstein, "Background," in Okimoto, Sugano, and Weinstein, *Competitive Edge.*

37. Johnson, "MITI, MPT, and the Telecom Wars."

38. John O. Haley, "Governance by Negotiation: A Reappraisal of Bureau-

cratic Power in Japan," *Journal of Japanese Studies* 13, no. 2 (Summer 1987): 352.

39. George C. Eads and Kozo Yamamura, "The Future of Industrial Policy," and Michio Muramatsu and Ellis S. Krauss, "The Conservative Policy Line and the Development of Patterned Pluralism," in Yamamura and Yasuba, *Political Economy of Japan*, vol. 1; and Johnson, "MITI, MPT, and the Telecom Wars."

40. Okimoto, "Conclusions," p. 214.

41. "Japan Focuses on Basic Research to Close the Creativity Gap," *Business Week*, 25 February 1985, pp. 94–95; Noburo Makino, *Decline in Prosperity* (Tokyo: Kodansha International, 1987), pp. 161–64.

42. Caldwell-Harris, "Japan's International Technology Transfers," p. 120.

43. Yutaka Kosai, "Patterns of Change in Japan's Industrial Society," *Japan Echo* 13, Special Issue (1986): 36–37; Saxonhouse, "Industrial Policy and Factor Markets," p. 112.

44. Robert B. Reich, "The Rise of Techno-Nationalism," *Atlantic Monthly*, May 1987, pp. 63–69.

45. Morton I. Kamien and Nancy L. Schwartz, "Market Structure and Innovation: A Survey," *Journal of Economic Literature* 13, no. 1 (1975):9.

46. Louis W. Fry and Borje Saxberg, "*Homo Ludens*—Playing Man and Creativity in the Innovating Organization" (University of Washington Graduate School of Business Working Paper, 1987), p. 2.

47. Okimoto, "Conclusions," p. 195; Gifford Pinchot III, "Promoting Free Intraprise!" *Across the Board*, March 1985, pp. 32–39; Marsha Sinetar, "SMR Forum: Entrepreneurs, Chaos, and Creativity—Can Creative People Really Survive Large Company Structure?" *Sloan Management Review*, Winter 1985, pp. 57–62.

48. Modesto Maidique and Robert Hayes, "The Art of High-Technology Management," *Sloan Management Review*, Winter 1984, pp. 17–31.

49. Okimoto, "Outsider Trading," p. 393; Hirotaka Takeuchi and Ikujiro Nonaka, "The New Product Development Game," *Harvard Business Review*, January–February 1986, pp. 137–46.

50. See, for example, Richard Tanner Pascale and Anthony G. Athos, *The Art of Japanese Management* (New York: Simon and Schuster, 1981).

51. See, for example, James C. Abegglen and George Stalk, Jr., *Kaisha* (New York: Basic Books, 1985); R. C. Clark, *The Japanese Company* (New Haven: Yale University Press, 1979); and R. E. Cole, *Work, Mobility, and Participation* (Berkeley and Los Angeles: University of California Press, 1979).

52. Rodney Clark, *Aspects of Japanese Commercial Innovation*, pp. 75, 81.

53. Thomas P. Rohlen, "'Permanent Employment' Faces Recession, Slow Growth, and an Aging Work Force," *Journal of Japanese Studies* 5, no. 2 (Summer 1979): 235–72.

54. Haruo Shimada, "Human-Resource Strategies for a Creative Society," *Japan Echo* 13, Special Issue (1986): 44.

55. Katsuto Uchihashi, "Corporations Encounter the Information Revolution," *Japan Echo* 13, Special Issue (1986): 30; Yutaka Kosai, "Patterns of Change in Japan's Industrial Society," p. 39.

56. Shimada, "Human-Resource Strategies," p. 42.

57. Ibid., p. 40.

58. "A Job Crunch Jolts Japan," *New York Times*, 18 January 1987.

59. "Industries and Employment in the Year 2000," *Look Japan*, 10 October 1986.

60. Ibid.

61. "Japan's Closed Door Brings Hard Knocks," *Wall Street Journal*, 16 April 1987.

62. Ibid. The Japanese approve only a few dozen factories worldwide to certify goods imported into Japan, whereas the United States grants several thousand Japanese factories that privilege.

63. "U.S. to Press Nakasone for More Access in Japan for American Financial Firms," *Wall Street Journal*, 27 April 1987.

64. Saxonhouse, "Industrial Policy and Factor Markets," p. 130.

65. "Trying to Transcend Copycat Science," *Fortune*, 30 March 1987.

66. Caldwell-Harris, "Japan's International Technology Transfers," p. 142; Reich, "The Rise of Techno-Nationalism"; "How Japan Picks America's Brains," *Fortune*, 21 December 1987, pp. 79, 80, 84, 85, 89.

67. Saxonhouse, "Industrial Policy and Factor Markets," p. 130.

68. "Nakasone Nurtures Vision of Sponsoring Ground-Breaking Scientific Research," *Asian Wall Street Journal*, 13 October 1986.

69. Pankaj Ghemawat, Michael E. Porter, and Richard A. Rawlinson, "Patterns of International Coalition Activity," in Michael Porter, ed., *Competition in Global Industries* (Boston: Harvard Business School Press, 1986), pp. 367–404.

70. "From World Trade to World Investment," *Wall Street Journal*, 26 May 1987.

71. Yamamura, "Shackles of Success," p. 430.

72. Ibid., p. 454.

73. Masanori Moritani, "Japanese Technology: Potential and Pitfalls," *Japan Echo* 13, Special Issue (1986): 9–15; Yamamura, "Shackles of Success."

74. See, for examples, "Tariffs Please U.S. Chip Concerns; Others See Them as Necessary Evil," *Wall Street Journal*, 30 March 1987; *Japanese Economic Institute Report*, 24 April 1987; and "Fear and Trembling in the Colossus," *Fortune*, 30 March 1987.

75. "Silicon Successor?" *Wall Street Journal*, 29 May 1987.

76. James S. Albus, *Japanese Technology Assessment* (Park Ridge, N.J.: Noyes Data Corporation, 1986), p. 114.

77. *Japan Economic Journal*, 21 March 1987.

78. "Trying to Transcend Copycat Science," *Fortune*, 30 March 1987.

79. *Japan Economic Almanac, 1986*, p. 136.

80. Thomas Pepper, Merit E. Janow, and Jimmy W. Wheeler, *The Competition: Dealing with Japan* (New York: Praeger Press, 1985), p. 206.

81. Stephen McClellan, *The Coming Computer Industry Shakeout* (New York: John Wiley and Sons, 1984), p. 112.

82. *Japan Economic Almanac, 1986*, p. 105.

83. Albus, *Japanese Technology Assessment*, p. 68.

84. Larry R. Harris and Dwight B. Davis, *Artificial Intelligence Enters the Marketplace* (Toronto: Bantam Books, 1986), p. 127; "Trying to Transcend Copycat Science," *Fortune*, 30 March 1987.

85. McClellan, *The Coming Computer Industry Shakeout*, p. 116.

86. *Japan Economic Almanac, 1986*, p. 104.

87. Ibid., pp. 3, 108.

88. Ibid., p. 129; Johnson, "MITI, MPT, and the Telecom Wars," p. 68.

89. Johnson, "MITI, MPT, and the Telecom Wars," p. 13.

90. Drucker, "The Changed World Economy."

91. Albus, *Japanese Technology Assessment*, p. 474.

92. Ibid.

93. U.S. Congress, Office of Technology Assessment, *Commercial Biotechnology: An International Assessment* (Washington, D.C., 1984), p. 505.

94. Albus, *Japanese Technology Assessment*, pp. 459, 541.

95. *JETRO Business Facts and Figures* (Tokyo: Japan External Trade Organization, 1987), p. 39.

96. A total of forty-seven Japanese chemical companies expended ¥193 billion and allocated over 21,500 researchers to R&D in 1982, of which slightly more than ¥19 billion and nearly 1,600 researchers were allocated to biotechnology. See MITI, *Waga kuni sangyokai no biotekunorogi kenkyu kaihatsu e no torikumi* (MITI Working Paper, 1983); and Clark, *Aspects of Japanese Commercial Innovation*, p. 60.

97. "The Big Boys Are Joining the Biotech Party," *Fortune*, 6 July 1987, p. 59.

98. *Japan Economic Almanac, 1986*, p. 103.

99. Ibid., pp. 102–3.

100. Ibid., p. 103.

101. *JETRO Business Facts and Figures*, p. 36.

3

West German Technology in the 1980s:

Perceptions, Evidence, and Policy Issues

ERNST-JÜRGEN HORN

Over the past decades numerous studies analyzing economic growth have confirmed that, natural resources apart, the wealth of a nation is decisively determined by its technological capabilities. This is relevant to nations leading in technological capability and to relatively technologically backward, or follower, countries, although in different ways. Leading countries are defined here as countries that innovate or have innovated more than other countries (after properly adjusting for country size). No country has ever been the uncontested technological leader in all areas at any one time: not Britain at the peak of its industrial superiority in the nineteenth century nor the United States after World War II. Of course, only innovation that results in the successful commercialization of new technology counts in this respect. And as any new technology will inevitably diffuse internationally over time, a leading country can maintain its relative position only by producing a continuous flow of innovation to compensate for the gradual erosion of existing technological advantages.

Follower countries are defined here as those countries that innovate less than the leading countries and rely more heavily on technology imports to increase productivity and income. The import of technology is not without costs, although such costs can generally be expected to be lower than attempting to "reinvent the wheel." Related costs incurred include licensing fees, equipment costs, and investment in research and development (R&D) to adapt imported technology. In a sense, the leading countries carry the primary burden of creating new technology, while the benefits of their innovative activity are eventually shared by other countries as well. This is not entirely to the disadvantage of the leading countries, otherwise they would not seek to maintain a leading position. In the process of catching up with the leading countries, follower countries generally expand their indigenous R&D efforts and capabilities in order to adapt foreign technology more efficiently. In addition, as follower countries become more successful in their efforts, more and more innovative activity is required. Catching up is at no stage merely a "free ride" based on the availability of foreign technology. And the narrower the remaining technological gaps become, the less it will be so.

Within the Organisation for Economic Cooperation and Development (OECD) countries, the postwar period has been a period of convergence in economic development. After the war, the United States held an exceptional technological lead in a broad range of fields. In 1960, when postwar reconstruction had been largely accomplished in Western Europe and Japan, real per capita income (at purchasing power parity) in relation to the United States was 33 percent in Japan; 71 percent, West Germany; 72 percent, Denmark; 81 percent, Sweden; 84 percent, Switzerland; and 86 percent, Luxembourg. The incomes of these last four countries were among the highest, which also included Canada at 78 percent. By 1980 the leading follower countries attained relative real per capita income levels in relation to the United States of 72 percent in Japan; 86 percent, West Germany; 90 percent, (newly oil rich) Norway; 85 percent, Sweden; 84 percent, France; 80 percent, Switzerland and Denmark; and 93 percent, Canada.[1] OECD estimates for these countries and years show similar relations and magnitudes.

These figures indicate that the United States continues to enjoy a distinct lead in real income in the 1980s. These figures also indicate that West Germany is but one of a group of follower countries that have increasingly caught up to the United States in terms of real per capita income. It is not clear, however, to what extent remaining income gaps can be explained by the technological superiority of the United States; measurement errors could have a substantial impact on the size of statistically revealed "gaps," considering the declining lead of the United States.[2]

In any event, the catching up of Western Europe (at least until recently) and Japan is clearly not a statistical artifact but reality. So it can be expected that at the same time the United States has been faced with increasing international competition in innovation, it has also found a widening scope for technology imports from abroad. Just as in goods trade, international competition in technology is not generally a zero-sum game but rather a positive-sum game in which the overall welfare of all parties involved is enhanced.[3] It is only in metaeconomic consideration that technological leadership as such may be appreciated in terms of national prestige or national defense.

Will the observed postwar trends continue into the twenty-first century? There is widespread expectation that Japan will continue to catch up and may eventually overtake the United States. Several other Asian nations, particularly the four "young tigers" of South Korea, Hong Kong, Taiwan, and Singapore, seem to be following the same path. The twenty-first century has already been labeled the "Pacific Century" in contrast to the "American" twentieth century and the "British" nineteenth century.[4] Already by 1984, the dollar value of transpacific goods trade surpassed that of transatlantic trade for the first time,[5] although the figures may be distorted by the exchange rate relations of that year used as conversion factors.

Expectations are generally less optimistic for West European countries. The catch-up process seems to have lost its momentum. Unemployment remains persistently high and capital formation has dropped relatively low in the first half of the 1980s. Has Western Europe turned from catching up to falling behind, as the term *eurosclerosis*, coined to describe the alleged lack of economic vitality in European countries in comparison to the United States and the successful Asian countries, suggests? This question is particularly relevant for the West German economy, which appears to represent a West European success story thus far in international technological competition. Due to Germany's economic prominence, the future of the German economy is also relevant for Western Europe as a whole.

PERCEPTIONS OF GERMAN PERFORMANCE IN THE TECHNOLOGY RACE

Some years ago, in part triggered by the unfamiliar experience of a deficit in the current account between 1979 and 1981, a lively and controversial debate took place over the emerging technological inferiority of Germany compared with the United States and Japan. Not only of particular concern for Germany, this debate reflected the current concerns of all Western Europe. A study on industrial competitiveness by the European Commission, for example, resulted in a critical assessment of the ability of the European Community (EC) to stand its ground in international technological competition.[6]

The topic was not a new one, although Japan has graduated from a follower country to a technological leader. During the 1950s, the technological superiority of the U.S. economy was often used to explain the permanent "dollar shortage." The unexpected disappearance of the dollar shortage, however, rendered this argument obsolete. In the second half of the 1960s, gaps in technology once again became an important issue, this time primarily in connection with the causes and consequences of the increasing American direct investment in Europe. These perceived gaps, which had induced a lot of research at the OECD and elsewhere, seemingly disappeared in the early 1970s, and the world entered a period of "technological stalemate." This interpretation seemed to be confirmed in the following years when West European direct investment in the United States grew rapidly.

The ongoing international debate on gaps in technology has two distinct sides. In Western Europe (and Germany) much is said about the need to close technological gaps with the United States and (more recently) with Japan in key areas such as microelectronics, biotechnology, and telecommunications. The United States and Japan, on the other hand, generally view their own strength (actual or potential) in international technological competition more critically. For instance, there is widespread apprehension in the United Staes in recent years that other industrial countries that have caught up with the United States in technology might eventually overtake it.[7] A recent report on U.S. industrial competitiveness prepared when the dollar was strongly appreciated on international markets gives a rather critical assessment of declining technological leadership.[8] It is remarkable that this issue had already been raised in a similar manner in an earlier report prepared in 1980, when the value of the dollar had fallen to a postwar low. Accordingly, the technological catch-up of other industrial countries (or the declining leadership of the United States) is perceived to be a trend phenomenon unrelated to price competitiveness in the short run, which depends to a large extent on exchange rate positions.

Exchange rates, however, do matter. The drastic revaluations of the yen against dollar-zone currencies since spring 1985 may indicate the beginning of a longer period for Japan with a high-value currency. This could have repercussions on the evolution of technological capabilities, as export-led economic growth becomes more difficult to achieve. In the case of Japan, an economic success story for decades, strains of past success also seem to foreshadow prospects for future development. It has been questioned, for instance, whether the scientific base in Japan, particularly basic research, is sufficient to sustain a technological leader. The United States, Japan, and the EC have problems of their own to worry about regarding their respective positions in technological competition.

In Germany, the debate on gaps in technology has revealed some confusion about conceptual matters, as well as about the assessment of empirical evidence. In a sense, this only reflects the complexity of the issues involved. The central problem is how to define and measure the technological level of a country in international comparison.[9] In addition, a proper assessment of technological level must take into account its relevance in economic terms. That is, any assessment must take into account the real income achieved through technology.

Any single gap between countries in a particular technology is only of marginal relevance because as suggested by the theory of international trade, no country can have a comparative advantage in all areas. This means that average performance counts, which in turn is hard to assess. Questions abound concerning, for instance, the choice of appropriate indicators (e.g., R&D outlays, patents, productivity measures, production and international trade in high technology products however defined, or peer judgment of research results as in the case of Nobel Prize awards) and the method of aggregation (what weight is given to individual observations). Changes in the average position of a country in technological competition then may be an indicator of falling behind, catching up, or creating a lead. The entire concept of a country's technology has, however, inherent limits in the presence of an open international trade and investment system. A particular technology is first produced in an individual country, but it can then be licensed or sold abroad or applied through foreign affiliates. The know-how involved will become internationally diffused sooner or later.

The German debate on gaps in technology has been primarily concerned with trade performance in high technology products and with overall R&D expenditures or R&D expenditures in areas regarded as being especially important. The assertion that technological gaps exist and have been widening is primarily held to be confirmed by the fact that German shares in world exports of high technology products (measured in U.S. dollars) decreased as the dollar appreciated in the first half of the 1980s. Others argue that R&D expenditures as a percentage of gross national product (GNP) have reached high levels in international comparison over the last two decades and conclude that the innovativeness of the German economy has not suffered. Both arguments seem somehow to miss the point, and their conclusions are not necessarily backed by empirical evidence. To begin with, trade in high technology products is a questionable indicator in various respects. For instance, it is unclear what caused the decline in nominal export shares (measured at current exchange rates) and whether this decline will prove to be lasting. Note, for instance, that in terms of volume, export growth has remained above the average of industrial countries since the late 1970s. It has also been mentioned that R&D outlays are seldom an accurate indicator of results. The question remains, Where does Germany stand in the international technological race?

In the last two or three years, confidence in the German position in technological competition seems to have increased considerably. This has coincided with an export boom, triggered in part by the appreciation of the U.S. dollar that shifted the German current account from a deficit to a substantial surplus. It remains to be seen whether the strong revaluation of the deutsche mark since March 1985 will have repercussions on the perception of German technological competitiveness in the years ahead. Several newspaper articles summarized in free translation below give a fairly representative impression of the prevailing mood on these issues in the summer of 1987.

"German High Technology Maintains Lead over Japan," *Frankfurter Allgemeine Zeitung*, 20 July 1987: The federal minister for Research and Technology released the results of a study of patent applications and trade flows and interviews with leading experts performed by the Institut für Systemtechnik und Innovationsforschung to the public which ranked Germany second behind the United States in high technology. Japan leads in more sophisticated user techniques, but here too Germany ranks second, in front of the United States. The minister stresses that the findings prove that the German research system has maintained a leading international position.

"European Space Activities Become Increasingly Expensive," *Frankfurter Allgemeine Zeitung*, 29 July 1987: The federal minister for Research and Technology approved a German commitment to the European space program (involving estimated costs of DM65 billion at 1986 prices). The German contribution would be DM15 billion. Three projects make up the center of the program: an improved Ariane rocket, the space shuttle Hermes, and a contribution to the American space station, Columbus. This program is necessary for Europe for economic, research, and foreign and defense policy reasons.

"Electronics Industry Demands High Subsidies," *Frankfurter Allgemeine Zeitung*, 22 July 1987: A study called "Mikroelektronik 2000," a joint venture between industry, universities, and research institutes inspired by the Federal Ministry of Research and Technology, recommends that the R&D requirements of this industry by the year 2000 (estimated at DM21 billion) should be subsidized to a large extent by public grants. In addition, government should contribute to the costs of necessary capital investments over this period and should support basic research and relevant supplier industries. Western Europe is currently dependent on foreign suppliers for 60 percent of its semiconductors. Semiconductor imports should be reduced to avoid the threat of unstable supply due to potential foreign export controls.

"German Research behind the U.S.A. and Japan," *Die Welt*, 7 July 1987: The manager of the Frankfurter-based Batelle-Institut, K. W. Staehle, presented the study "Forschungsbudget 1987" to the public. He stressed that German R&D expenditure in the area of high-efficiency industrial materials was far behind that of the United States and Japan in this area.

"The First Scientists Come Back from America," *Frankfurter Allgemeine Zeitung*, 30 April 1987: The federal minister for Research and Technology announced that more and more first-class scientists are coming (back or for the first time) to the Federal Republic of Germany because the research climate and material preconditions for R&D have improved decisively in international comparison.

These selected newspaper articles representing the public perception of Germany's position in international technological competition reveal the following. First, it is important how much countries spend on R&D in international comparison. In a sense, R&D outlays are widely considered a measure of economic success. Second, a technological gap in any field that is held to be important becomes a national political issue; the concept that a country cannot have a comparative advantage in all areas is apparently given little attention in discussions on international technological competition. Third, making claims on government grants for technology promotion seems to have become normal behavior even in the case of prospering firms (e.g., Siemens AG) and industries (e.g., electronics). Public funding of R&D in industry and elsewhere raises much less suspicion in public debate than other forms of subsidy. To sum up, there is a widespread perception of a country's performance in techno- logical competition that tends to result in a traditional mercantilistic judgment: the more a country is leading in technology (in precious met- als reserves), the better off it is. Also, a policy decision is deemed nec- essary. Should governments intervene in markets in order to improve national performance in the international technology race?

SELECTED FACTUAL EVIDENCE

Macroeconomic Development since 1960

Since the first oil shock of 1973, economic growth and productivity increases in Western industrial economies have substantially slowed. This has been a general and persistent phenomenon. The average real gross domestic product (GDP) growth rate for OECD member countries de- clined from 4.9 percent in the 1960–73 period to 2.3 percent in the 1973–85 period.[10] Although growth has slowed in all industrial countries, development patterns continue to show some striking differences. Here I mention just a few significant differences in the cases of the United States, Japan, and West Germany, as shown in table 3.1.

Japan remains an outstanding case, although Japan experienced the sharpest absolute decline (6 percent) in its economic growth rate. Never- theless, the Japanese economy maintained an annual growth rate of al- most 4 percent in 1973–85, the rate achieved by the United States in its high-growth period of 1960–73. The economic growth rate of the United States has declined less in both absolute and relative terms than has the average for all industrial economies. In relation to Western Europe, the United States showed a slightly superior growth performance in the first half of the 1980s for the first time in the postwar period. Western Eu- rope seems to have suffered the most pronounced slowdown in economic development; the West German economy is no exception. In fact, overall West German economic performance has reflected that of the average of Western Europe over the entire 1960–85 period, and West Germany may well be a trend economy in the European context.

Since 1973, wide swings in the value of the dollar in relation to the currencies of other industrial countries have had considerable impact on macroeconomic development.[11] The instability of commodity prices, es- pecially oil prices, also had overlapping effects that in turn influenced exchange rate movements. Nevertheless, the periods of a falling dollar value (1973–80), of a rising dollar value (1980–85), and, not shown in table 3.1, of a declining dollar value since 1985 illustrate the relevance of exchange rates for international transactions in goods and services.

TABLE 3.1

Indicators of Economic Development: Comparison between the United States, Japan, and West Germany
(Average Percentage Changes at Annual Rate)

Indicator	United States 1960–73	1973–80	1980–85	Japan 1960–73	1973–80	1980–85	West Germany 1960–73	1973–80	1980–85	OECD total 1960–73	1973–80	1980–85
Volume indicators												
GDP	3.8	2.1	2.4	9.6	3.7	3.9	4.4	2.2	1.3	4.9	2.4	2.2
Private consumption	4.2	2.7	3.2	8.7	3.6	2.8	4.9	2.9	0.6	5.0	2.8	2.2
Government consumption	3.0	3.4	3.5	6.1	4.5	2.9	4.5	2.9	1.2	3.8	2.9	2.5
Gross fixed capital formation	4.8	0.4	5.0	13.9	1.2	2.7	4.0	0.8	−1.3	6.3	0.8	2.2
Exports of goods and services	6.9	5.9	−2.3	13.7	10.1	9.0	7.7	4.4	5.2	8.0	5.1	3.9
Imports of goods and services	7.7	2.8	8.9	14.2	1.7	2.1	8.7	5.0	1.5	8.6	3.4	3.9
Price indicators												
GDP	3.7	8.1	5.4	6.0	7.4	1.8	4.3	4.8	3.2	4.4	9.1	6.7
Private consumption	3.1	8.0	5.1	6.2	9.0	2.6	3.4	4.8	3.7	3.9	9.3	7.0
Government consumption	4.9	8.0	5.1	10.0	9.3	2.6	6.5	5.9	3.0	6.0	9.9	6.8
Gross fixed capital formation	3.3	9.9	2.3	3.8	7.9	0.1	4.6	5.4	2.7	5.0	9.9	4.6
Exports of goods and services	3.1	10.0	2.7	1.6	5.8	−1.5	2.3	5.2	3.5	3.0	9.7	6.4
Imports of goods and services	3.3	14.8	−2.0	1.5	15.7	−1.7	1.4	7.1	4.3	2.6	12.6	5.5
Population	1.2	1.0	1.0	1.2	1.0	0.7	0.7	−0.1	−0.2	1.1	0.8	0.7
Employment	2.0	2.2	1.6	1.3	0.7	1.1	0.1	−0.3	−0.6	0.9	—	0.6

SOURCE: Organisation for Economic Cooperation and Development, *National Accounts*, vol. 1, *Main Aggregates* (1960–85). Author's calculations.

This is most obvious for the 1980–85 period, when real exchange rate changes uniformly indicated a strong revaluation of the dollar against the currencies of other industrial countries. The current account of the United States deteriorated rapidly, while the current account of Western Europe and, in particular, Japan rapidly improved. The growth of domestic absorption of goods and services distinctly surpassed the growth of production in the United States; the opposite pattern was observed in Japan and Western Europe. Fixed capital formation in Western Europe was particularly weak, showing no growth at all. In this regard West Germany exhibited an especially poor performance even by West European standards. While the slump in capital formation was a general phenomenon for industrial countries in 1973–80, low capital formation has been a peculiar feature of economic development in Western Europe since 1980.

It is tempting to take this as a symptom of the eurosclerosis mentioned earlier. Note, however, that in terms of capital formation the Japanese experience in the 1980s is much less favorable than the GDP growth rates would suggest, not to speak of a comparison with the 1960–73 period. Both Japan and West Germany exported savings (or invested abroad) on a large scale in the 1980s. Such a tendency is also seen in the average for other West European countries, but it has generally been much less pronounced than in West Germany. For Japan, West Germany, and Western Europe as a whole, the export-led recovery of the early 1980s had "costs" in terms of forgone domestic absorption in general and in terms of forgone domestic fixed capital formation in particular. Put differently, the indigenous driving forces of economic growth have been too weak, for whatever reasons, to sustain the GDP growth rates achieved.

There is yet another important aspect of macroeconomic performance: the change in employment patterns. The United States had an outstanding record of employment expansion among industrial countries over the entire 1960–85 period. Notwithstanding the two major recessions in the aftermath of the oil price hikes of 1973–74 and 1979–80, the trend of rising employment has proved extraordinarily robust. Employment in Japan has also increased quite steadily over time, although at distinctly lower annual rates than in the United States. In Western Europe, on the other hand, employment increased only slightly in 1960–73, was stagnant in 1973–80, and even decreased distinctly in 1980–85. This difference in pattern reflects only slightly lower population growth. The high level of unemployment that has prevailed in most West European countries (including West Germany) in the 1980s is the result of stagnating or shrinking employment. Again, it is tempting to take the employment indicator as a symptom of eurosclerosis.

An intriguing puzzle, however, is posed by developments in labor productivity. The change in productivity per person employed in the overall economy is implicitly contained in the figures for GDP growth and employment change in table 3.1.[12] It is evident that the United States lags behind most industrial economies in terms of productivity advance. Productivity per person employed stagnated in 1973–80 and has risen only slowly since. On the other hand, Japan experienced the strongest absolute fall in its rate of productivity advance in the 1970s, yet Japan remained one of the industrial countries with the highest productivity advance in 1973–85. An important question is, then, why Western Europe—German performance has hardly differed from the European average—has been able to realize a considerably higher productivity increase than the United States, despite the obvious weakness in capital formation after 1973. The differences in employment patterns are certainly relevant in this context, but they do not seem to resolve the core of the problem. In any event, it does not fit into the picture of a technologically leading country that the United States has shown such a poor productivity growth over such an extended period.

Three major points can be concluded from the macroeconomic development of the three largest industrial countries with regard to their position in international technological competition. First, the U.S. lead has steadily diminished over the period of the general slowdown of growth in industrial countries. In particular, the weak productivity advance indicates an erosion of the U.S. position. Second, in the 1980s West Germany—like Western Europe as a whole—has ceased to exhibit growth superior to that of the United States. The process of catching up has apparently lost its momentum. Third, Japan has steadily continued its relative economic rise. It must be taken into account, however, that average productivity levels in the Japanese economy measured at purchasing-power parities are still significantly lower than in West Germany, not to mention the United States. Therefore, the scope for further catch-up is in general much wider for Japan than for West Germany, although this is not the case for Japan's leading-edge industries.

Input and Output of Innovative Activity

The evolution of the German research system in the postwar period must be discussed against the backdrop of the political upheavals of this century in Europe. Before World War I, and to a lesser extent in the interwar period, Germany held a leading position in research and industrial technology in many fields, such as chemistry, physics, and precision engineering. During the period of the Third Reich (1933–45), racial discrimination and the emigration of many highly qualified scientists and engineers led to a substantial erosion of the scientific base, most visibly in universities and public research institutions such as the Kaiser-Wilhelm-Gesellschaft (which after the war was renamed Max-Planck-Gesellschaft). Then war losses and destruction (and military occupation) finally led to the fragmentation and paralyzation of the research system.

Immediately after the war the prohibition of research in many important areas, the dispossession of all German patents by the Allied governments, and again the emigration of many highly qualified scientists and engineers resulted in a substantial lag in technological development.[13] It was not until the Federal Republic of Germany achieved sovereignty and joined NATO in 1955 that the federal government could once again implement an active research policy and the last restrictions on the innovative activity of private companies imposed by the Allied governments were removed. Given these initial conditions, the reconstruction of the German research system was bound to concentrate on catching up with the leading industrial countries, and it was clear from the outset that this process would take a long time. At the end of the 1950s, R&D expenditures exceeded for the first time 1 percent of GNP, compared with 2.6 percent in the United States and 2.3 percent in the United Kingdom. By the end of the 1960s, R&D expenditures had risen to 2 percent of GNP. Since the mid-1970s, Germany has been spending similar amounts on R&D in relation to GNP as the United States and has thus become a leading country according to this indicator.

Research and Development. The resources devoted to R&D—expenditures or personnel employed in R&D—are commonly used as indicators of innovative activities. According to this input criterion, the catch-up of Japan and West European countries has created a group of countries leading in R&D efforts of which the United States is but one member among several, although presumably as the primus inter pares (see tables 1.7 and 1.8). Due to the size of the American economy, however, the U.S. share was more than 45 percent of all public and private R&D funds allocated by OECD countries (calculated at purchasing-power parities) in the first half of the 1980s, although the U.S. share has steadily declined since the 1950s. It is remarkable that since about the mid-1970s the countries of Western Europe have not further increased their combined share in R&D expenditures of the OECD members. Only the rapidly rising Japanese R&D efforts have mirrored the declining share of the United States, while the share of Western Europe has remained fairly stable.[14] The individual shares of the larger European economies, including West Germany, also have not shown a distinct upward or downward trend. This suggests that the West European catch-up process lost its momentum during the last decades. There is no indication that West Germany or any other West European country is now on its way to overtaking the United States.

Some basic aggregate data on R&D activities in the major industrial countries are compiled in tables 1.7 and 1.8.[15] According to overall national R&D expenditures, the differences between countries has become rather small. A tentative ranking would presumably place the United States as the leader, Japan and West Germany as immediate followers, and the United Kingdom and France somewhat behind the first three.

Despite similarities in the level of overall national R&D activities, there are distinct structural differences between these countries, which may be significant in terms of economic efficiency. This concerns first and foremost the amount of defense R&D. If the whole R&D system is considered a "black box" with an economic valuation, then defense R&D certainly represents a special kind of box within the black box. The effects of defense R&D on overall economic performance can be calculated. Although the effects may well differ over time, between countries, and across fields of technology, the relation of defense R&D to the economy is decisive for the relative position of a country in technological competition.

If defense R&D was acting as a net drag on the economy (i.e., few spillover effects on civilian technology), Japan and West Germany would be leading, as they are not spending much on defense R&D. France, the United Kingdom, and in particular the United States would be lagging behind.[16] On the other hand, defense R&D can be regarded as an implicit industrial policy.[17] As the theory of monopolistic competition in international trade concludes (in the presence of high R&D entry costs, significant economies of scale, and a steep learning curve), government-funded defense R&D may give domestic companies a head start in civilian applications, which could prove to be a key ingredient to lasting commercial success. It is widely believed that the competitive strength of the U.S. civilian aircraft producers, for instance, has been enhanced by defense contracts. In this view, it is not as important how much governments spend on defense R&D as whether they spend on technology promotion at all.

The total contribution of government to national R&D expenditures also differs between the two country groups. In Japan and West Germany, about 60 percent of national R&D expenditures are financed by business enterprises, while government funds amounted to less than 30 and about 40 percent, respectively. In the case of the three other countries, the share of business enterprise funds is substantially lower, and the share of government funds is correspondingly higher (except for France). With respect to sector of performance, the international differences are less marked. Between 60 and 70 percent of all R&D is performed in the private sector in all countries. In France and the United Kingdom, government research institutions account for a relatively high share of national R&D activities, while in Japan, university research is of relatively high importance.[18]

To conclude, the national research systems of the five countries differ quite considerably. An open question is whether the high share of company funds in national R&D spending in Japan and West Germany is an indication of a strong commercial orientation within the system and, perhaps, also an indication of economic efficiency. As a matter of fact, the distribution of government R&D funds by industry differs more distinctly across countries than does the distribution of company R&D funds by industry.[19] This implies that governments strongly influence the allocation of R&D resources and, thus, the results of R&D activities.

International Patenting. The total number of patent applications or patents granted is a readily available indicator of the inventive output of a country, industry, or firm. Although there are several drawbacks to this measure, many empirical studies have shown that patent data can provide meaningful information if properly interpreted.

West Germany has traditionally held a leading position behind Switzerland in international patenting (patent applications or grants abroad), adjusted by population or GDP. According to the INPADOC data base, Germany contributed more than 20 percent of all international patent applications in the 1976–81 period and 16 percent of international key patents (with more than fifteen international applications), while Japan contributed just 10 percent in the same period.[20] In absolute terms, the United States is the only country that had more international patent applications. At the same time, R&D outlays in the United States in this period were almost five times larger than in Germany in purchasing-power parity terms. Measured by per capita of population, Germany's international patent applications outnumbered those of the United States by a ratio of almost three to one. In comparison with France and the United Kingdom, the frequency of neighborhood patent applications within Europe at best explains only part of the German position. It appears that West Germany is particularly strong in the area of invention (or has a relatively large share of punctilious inventors in its population). Of course, performance in innovation is another matter. And even with regard to the field of invention only, one must consider the relevance of those emerging technologies for which by their very nature patent protection is not an adequate device in the commercialization of technical expertise.

International patenting in Japan, though until recently far below the numbers reported for Germany in absolute and relative terms, has increased extremely rapidly along with the expansion of R&D activities. While the total number of international patent applications has declined significantly in most industrial economies since the late 1960s, the figures for Japan have almost doubled.[21]

Gross data on international patent applications may be somewhat distorted by international distribution and the patent regulations of the various countries. Furthermore, the success rate (ratio of applications to grants) may change over time and differ across countries. Therefore, it is tempting to review country performance in patent grants in a country where all patents are granted under uniform rules and procedures. The first choice is of course the United States, which is not only the world's largest technology market but also provides the most comprehensive data base in patent statistics. Germany, on average, had the strongest position in the United States among foreign countries in the 1963–83 period. The number of patent grants to applicants from Japan, however, has risen extraordinarily and surpassed patent grants to German applicants in absolute numbers by the mid-1970s. The data on patent grant dynamics also reveal that the share of American inventors in U.S. patent grants has been falling for decades. This is only in part a reflection of the erosion of its position in international technological competition. To a considerable extent, this trend reflects the increasing economic integration that has raised the economic incentives for foreign inventors to apply for patent protection in the United States.[22]

Technological Balance of Payments. West Germany's technological balance of payments—the receipts from and the payments abroad for technological property rights (royalty payments)—has shown a rising deficit for decades and has repeatedly become a matter of concern in the public debate. This pattern sharply contrasts with Germany's international patenting position. The technological balance of payments has several weaknesses as a measure. It only covers one facet of the network of international technological exchange; it may be distorted by such factors as hidden profit transfers; and it depends on the appropriation strategy chosen by technology owners both at home and abroad (exporting, licensing to foreigners, or production by affiliates abroad). In addition, international comparison reveals that a deficit in the technological balance of payments is almost the rule within the group of industrial countries, except for the United States, the United Kingdom, and Switzerland. This alone would suggest a rather cautious interpretation of the data.

Nevertheless, the technological balance of payments provides some meaningful information. It has, for instance, proved useful in distinguishing between companies under significant control by foreign equity holders (affiliates) and independent domestic companies. Such a breakdown is given for Germany in table 3.2. It shows that the balance of domestic firms is strongly positive and that the overall deficit is due to the payments of affiliates of foreign companies. This pattern even holds in the United States. In 1985 domestic firms accounted for 85 percent of total receipts and for 20 percent of total payments. Of course, the receipts of domestic firms to a large extent accrue from their affiliates abroad. It appears that the foreign direct investment position of a country is indicative of its technological balance of payments. In the case of West Germany there have been high annual net outflows of direct investment since the early 1970s. The overall receipts-payments ratio rose from 39 percent in 1970 to 55 percent in 1985. This seems largely to reflect that the emphasis in the appropriation strategy of German firms has shifted distinctly from exporting to foreign production.

Trade in High Technology Products. West German performance in high technology products trade has attracted considerable public attention in recent years. This issue has been investigated in a number of empirical studies. The main results are briefly summarized and discussed here.

TABLE 3.2
Technological Balance of Payments, West Germany
(in Millions of Deutsche Marks)

		Receipts		Payments	
Year	Balance	Domestic companies[a]	Affiliates of foreign companies	Domestic companies[a]	Affiliates of foreign companies
1970	−682	417	17	367	749
1975	−1,036	716	41	410	1,383
1980	−1,086	922	89	459	1,620
1985	−1,324	1,361	244	589	2,340

SOURCE: Deutsche Bundesbank.
NOTE: The technological balance of payments denotes international receipts and payments for "patents, inventions, and processes."
[a]Most of these companies have affiliates abroad and receive a large portion of the receipts from their affiliates.

First, the trade performance in high technology products, as revealed by statistical measures such as world export shares (relative to the average for industrial products) or export-import ratios, has proved highly sensitive to the definition of high technology. In addition, West Germany's position is weakest in areas where the competition is most strongly influenced by government R&D funds, that is, where the U.S. Department of Defense has set its priorities. Second, the competitive edge of West Germany—like that of Japan—has been and remains to be the exploitation of a technology field that has been pioneered by others. This means that German companies have seldom been innovators in new fields of technology; rather they follow once a significant field of technological improvement is introduced. Third, German companies have been relatively more successful in process, rather than product, innovation.[23] This is confirmed by the use of electronic technologies in manufacturing, particularly in robotics.[24]

In general, the German position in high technology competition appears to have weakened somewhat in the 1980s. But this picture should be considered in view of the emerging new source of supply, that is, Japan. If a strong new competitor is gaining an increasing market share, the market shares of old competitors are bound to decline. Finally, there remains the important question of whether Germany has lost ground in strategic fields of technology that may be decisive for future average performance. Losing ground in such "generic" technologies—the key example is presently electronics—might indeed indicate the ongoing erosion of Germany's position in international technological competition. It should be noted, however, that Germany has been quite successful in the application of key technologies to manufacturing, as in the application of electronics to machinery, despite an apparent weakness in the underlying key technology.

To sum up the discussion on trade performance in high technology products (and services), it is highly relevant to distinguish between issues of national prestige and actual performance. In the end, what counts is not the image of being first in the technology race, but the actual achievement of real incomes in international competition. The rise of Japan aside, the German economy has shown a fairly successful record thus far in international comparison.

The Institutional Framework

The empirical evidence on innovation performance in industrial countries indicates that the United States retains a dominant position. West Germany's position has improved over time, but much less so than that of Japan. West Germany, Switzerland, the Netherlands, and Sweden may be labeled (in relative terms) "high"-innovation performers. National differences with regard to economic institutions or in government policy stance, however, are of crucial importance. Ergas judges the fundamentals for innovative activity in West Germany to be only slightly less favorable than in Japan, while the conditions in the United States are in nearly every respect favorable to innovation.[25] The nine criteria applied are size (1) and sophistication (2) of demand; availability of scientists and engineers (3) and of skilled labor in general (4); quality of industry-university linkage (5); size of firms (6); rivalry among domestic firms (7); market entry (or exit) conditions (8); and mechanisms of cooperation among firms to secure external economics (9). These criteria are rather narrowly focused on the business enterprise sector. In a wider perspective, government R&D funding must be included, as well as the regulatory systems of capital and labor markets and of company law, and public procurement and procurement by public monopolies or quasi-public monopolies in utilities.

As for West Germany, it is important to note that key features of public R&D policy differ from the patterns observed in Japan and the United States. In 1985 only about 40 percent of federal R&D funds were devoted to industry, and about 30 percent accrued to nonprofit R&D institutions (universities and major self-administrating research organizations outside universities), with the Max-Planck-Gesellschaft and the Fraunhofer-Gesellschaft being the most important recipients. Federal government research institutions received a share of only 13 percent in federal R&D spending. More than half of total federal R&D expenditures served project promotion where government influence on the allocation of R&D resources is rather comprehensive. This share rose considerably in the era of social-liberal governments in 1969–82 and has been declining slightly since. The current center-right government coalition has declared a policy objective of reducing the role of project promotion in its R&D policy. Note that the above figures do not include the measure of indirect public R&D promotion, namely, tax allowances for R&D activities.

In comparison to the United States, labor and capital markets in West Germany seem to provide a less favorable environment for innovative activities. Labor in R&D, like labor in general, has the characteristics of a fixed cost. Except in the case of virtual bankruptcy, it is almost impossible for major firms to lay off a considerable portion of their R&D personnel within a short time, as has repeatedly occurred in the United States. The constitution of capital markets in West Germany also establishes obstacles to high technology entrepreneurship, particularly in regard to entry and exit costs. It is only in the European context that West Germany has shown a relatively high birthrate of high-technology-oriented firms. The venture capital markets seem to represent its key weakness. Some improvements in capital market efficiency have occurred in recent years, easing for instance the access of smaller firms to the stock market. Government has taken some relevant steps, too, including public support for risk capital and financing and the erection of "technology parks" that provide an infrastructure and consulting facilities for new firms in nearly every major city or university location. Further reforms in equity capital market regulations can be expected to be introduced. Things have been changing and will continue to change. It is too early, however, to assess the results of the ongoing changes on the objective that has been one of their central targets, namely, innovative activity.

CURRENT POLICY ISSUES

In the preceding sections a number of policy issues have been touched upon that are of relevance for decision making in public policy; they need not be repeated here. Instead, I will raise a couple of points concerning the fundamentals of policy choice in West Germany. I will not discuss the educational system, as it deserves a treatise of its own. Suffice it to mention that the educational system exhibits a considerable inertia when it comes to adding instruction in new fields (e.g., information sciences) in response to innovation trends in the business enterprise sector.

Traditional systems of regulation in service industries have become a major obstacle to a more successful innovation performance in the overall economy. The most pertinent example is the regulation of telecommunications (in particular, the Post, Telegraph, und Telekommunikationen monopoly). The winds of change are beginning to blow in this area, although developments in West Germany lag considerably behind those that have already taken place in the United States, the United Kingdom, and Japan.

It has been questioned whether an active technology policy for applied R&D in the business enterprise sector (i.e., general public R&D funding) is an efficient strategy to encourage innovative activities. For instance, reducing corporate taxes, which at present are rather high compared with other major industrial countries, or improving the efficiency of the capital market, particularly in terms of venture capital, could, it has been argued, be a more suitable instrument to foster private innovative activity than traditional public R&D.

The federal government (and state governments as well) has been preoccupied with adjustment assistance to declining industries.[26] In a sense, it is now trapped in the responsibility it took on for smokestack industries such as coal, steel, and shipbuilding. This budget burden limits government's ability to make general tax cuts and to raise public R&D funding.

Intensified technology export controls in the United States in recent years and the "return of the reciprocitarians" in U.S. trade policy have raised doubt in the reliability of an open international system of technology exchange.[27] This has added weight to the argument that some degree of autarky in technology must be maintained because sources of supply are unsecure. The revival of the theory of monopolistic competition in international trade—essentially not a new theory but one that governments engaged in an active R&D policy seem to have always believed—appears to have contributed to the resurrection of the notion of national technology.[28]

The EC connection is becoming increasingly important for the West German research system. This concerns international cooperative R&D ventures on an ad hoc basis (Europe à la carte), the emerging "federal" technology policy at the EC level, the common-competition policy, and the tensions between EC preferences and third-country relations in EC policy-making. It now seems to make good sense to locate large R&D projects at the European level. But there are some risks involved in common policy-making, at least for a country with a liberal trade policy stance such as West Germany. The decision to complete the internal market by 1992 has revealed that some member countries, France in particular, have a strong temptation to combine the internal opening up of high technology markets (including public procurement) with the raising of import barriers against third parties.[29]

The practice of federal R&D policy has so far in many instances been to support R&D in fields of technology that have also been the subject of technology policy in the other major industrial countries.[30] Such international links in the orientation of technology policies raise serious doubts because the theory of monopolistic competition in international trade views engaging in such subsidy races a worst-case scenario.

In conclusion, we must ask why the growth slowdown of industrial economies since 1973 has taken place even though these countries on average have increased the resources devoted to innovative activities. Almost certainly there has not been a similar slowdown in the output of innovative activity. Therefore, factors other than innovative activity are highly relevant for economic achievement.

NOTES

1. Robert Summers and Alan Heston, "Improved International Comparisons of Real Product and Its Composition: 1950–1980," *Review of Income and Wealth* 30, no. 2 (June 1984): 207–62.

2. One of the results of international real income comparisons that does not pass the plausibility test (and the test of tourists' experience) is the relatively high rank of some centrally planned economies. This indicates that systematic drawbacks indeed disturb the results of the computations quoted.

3. This is not to deny the possibility that a country may also suffer welfare losses (e.g., if a declining technological lead in a certain area triggers a decline in its average terms of trade). But any particular technological lead enjoyed by a firm or country, once produced, is bound to be lost to competitors over time through competition. Maintaining a leading position in the long run would require a continuous renewal of technological advantages by innovative activity.

4. Staffan Burenstam Linder, *The Pacific Century* (Stanford: Stanford University Press, 1986).

5. General Agreement on Tariffs and Trade, *International Trade, 1984/85* (Geneva: GATT, 1985).

6. Kommission der europäischen Gemeinschaften, *Die Wettbewerbsfähigkeit der Industrien der Gemeinschaft* (Luxembourg: Kommission der europäischen Gemeinschaften, 1982).

7. The so-called new technological protectionism in the United States (efforts unrelated to national defense to control or to curb technology transfer to foreigners) may also have roots in concerns over eroding technological leadership.

8. President's Commission on Industrial Competitiveness, *Global Competition: The New Reality* (Washington, D.C.: U.S. Government Printing Office, 1985).

9. Ole Börnsen, Hans H. Glismann, and Ernst-Jürgen Horn, *Der Technologietransfer zwischen den USA und der Bundesrepublik*, Kieler Studien, no. 192 (Tübingen: J. C. B. Mohr [Paul Siebeck], 1985).

10. The 1960–73, rather than the 1950–73, period is chosen as the reference period in order to exclude the impact of postwar reconstruction in Western Europe and Japan on indicators of economic performance in the 1950s. For a recent comprehensive analysis of the decline in economic growth, see Angus Maddison, "Growth and Slowdown in Advanced Capitalist Economies: Techniques of Quantitative Assessment," *Journal of Economic Literature* 25 (June 1987): 649–98.

11. Purchasing-power parities (PPP) indicate the extent to which market exchange rates deviate from what would have been predicted from economic "fundamentals" for trade in goods and services. For example, according to PPP es-

timates of the Statistical Office of the European Communities, the deutsche mark per dollar market rate was 20 percent above the PPP rate in 1973, 30 percent below in 1980, and almost 25 percent above in 1985.

12. Changes in productivity per labor-hour show a rather similar pattern across countries. The annual rate of change in 1973–85 was 3.2 percent in Japan, 3.0 percent in Germany, and 1.0 percent in the United States. See Maddison, "Growth and Slowdown in Advanced Capitalist Economies."

13. A comprehensive assessment of the reconstruction of the West German research system from 1945 to 1965 is given in Thomas Stamm, *Zwischen Staat und Selbstverwaltung: Die deutsche Forschung im Wiederaufbau, 1945–1965* (Cologne: Verlag Wissenschaft und Politik, 1981).

14. Henry Ergas, "Why Do Some Countries Innovate More than Others?" CEPS Papers, no. 5 (Brussels: Centre for European Policy Studies, 1984).

15. Some smaller countries of Western Europe (the Netherlands, Sweden, and Switzerland in particular) also belong to the group of countries leading in R&D efforts; they are omitted here only as a matter of convenience.

16. Following this line of interpretation, it could be argued that Japan and West Germany are enjoying a free ride in national security matters, because they do not bear an appropriate share of the defense R&D burden within the Western alliance.

17. As is well known, the U.S. Department of Defense also promotes the development of civilian technologies. If technologies are of a "dual" nature, which seems to be the case for a wide range of militarily relevant technologies, defense R&D implies a promotion of civilian technologies as well. It may be noted in passing that in this view public defense R&D funds raise problems regarding the proper application of subsidy rules under the international trading order of the General Agreement on Tariffs and Trade.

18. Henning Klodt, *Wettlauf um die Zukunft: Technologiepolitik im internationalen Vergleich*, Kieler Studien, no. 206 (Tübingen: J. C. B. Mohr [Paul Siebeck], 1987).

19. Ibid.

20. Wolfgang Gerstenberger, "Investitionen in die Erhaltung der Wettbewerbsfähigkeit: Ein Vergleich USA-Bundesrepublik," *Ifo-Studien* 32 (1986): 171–80.

21. This may well indicate that the relevance of patent protection as such has substantially declined. See the data for the five major industrial countries in National Science Board, *Science Indicators: The 1985 Report* (Washington, D.C.: U.S. Government Printing Office, 1985).

22. Hans H. Glismann and Ernst-Jürgen Horn, "Comparative Invention Performance of Major Industrial Countries: Patterns and Explanations" (Kiel Working Paper, no. 264, Institut für Weltwirtschaft, 1986).

23. Juergen B. Donges and Hans H. Glismann, "Industrial Adjustment in Western Europe—Retrospect and Prospect" (Kiel Working Paper, no. 280, Institut für Weltwirtschaft, 1987).

24. Margaret Sharp, ed., *Europe and the New Technologies: Six Case Studies in Innovation and Adjustment* (London: Frances Pinter Publishers, 1985).

25. Ergas, "Why Do Some Countries Innovate More than Others?" p. 32. Undoubtedly the United States has been the technological leader since World War II. But this does not necessarily imply that the institutional environment

has been particularly efficient with respect to innovative activity. To avoid such a post hoc ergo propter hoc–type fallacy, the national system of the United States cannot be applied as a yardstick in the assessment of the efficiency of other countries' institutional arrangements. It would be similarly misleading to substitute the Japanese institutional model for the American one.

26. Donges and Glismann, "Industrial Adjustment in Western Europe."

27. Jagdish N. Bhagwati and Douglas A. Irvin, "The Return of the Reciprocitarians: U.S. Trade Policy Today," *World Economy* 10, no. 2 (1987): 109–30.

28. For a recent survey of this emerging body of literature, see Leonard K. Cheng, "Optimal Trade and Technology Policies: Dynamic Linkages," *International Economic Review* 20, no. 3 (1987): 757–76.

29. Commission of the European Communities, *Completing the Internal Market* (Brussels: Commission of the European Community, 1985); idem, "Single European Act," *Bulletin of the European Communities* 2, suppl. (1986).

30. Klodt, *Wettlauf um die Zukunft.*

Part Two

ANALYTIC PERSPECTIVE

4

The Impact of Industrial Structure
and Industrial Policy on International Trade

MOTOSHIGE ITOH

Contemporary trade among the developed industrial countries is far removed from the world described by textbook, or classical, trade theory. According to textbook trade theory, comparative advantage is determined by such exogeneous factors as climatic conditions and factor endowments. In such industries as semiconductors, computers, finance, and automobiles, however, the competitiveness of individual firms and the comparative advantage of individual countries are determined largely by the firm experience and R&D activity and government regulation and industrial policies. Exogenous conditions play a relatively minor role.

The static nature of the world described by textbook trade theory also does not correspond to reality. The industrial structure and trade patterns of individual countries are changing with incredible speed, and textbook economic theory does little to help us understand these changes. Japan's postwar experience offers some valuable insight into this subject. In the process of rapid economic growth, Japan's industrial structure shifted from an emphasis on textiles and other light industries to an emphasis on heavy and chemical industries and then to machinery and other more sophisticated products following the first oil shock. Understanding rapid change in economic structure is essential for understanding the causes of Japan's rapid postwar economic growth.

All countries experience more or less similar changes in industrial structure. Today the frontier technologies are creating new products in rapid succession, and fundamental changes in older industries are predicted as well. These technological changes are altering the industrial structure of many countries, which in turn has an enormous impact on international trade and on the international economy.

Another area in which textbook trade theory diverges from real-life trade is in the matter of oligopolistic industries. Textbook trade theory posits a world of perfect competition, whereas in the real world there are several industries in which oligopolistic firm behavior is a major problem. The expanding multinational corporations, for instance, exhibit strong oligopolistic characteristics and tendencies. The importance of this issue is underlined by the fact that it is precisely such industries as aircraft, semiconductors, computers, and automobiles that tend to produce trade disputes that cannot be understood without taking into account their oligopolistic nature.

In this paper I use economic theory to explore the various trade issues faced by the major countries in the world economy—Japan, the United States, and West Germany—and the influence their trade and industrial policies will exert on other Western economies and on international trade in general. Although this topic extends over a wide range of issues, I focus here on industrial structure and oligopolistic industries.

This paper is in three parts. In the first section I examine the changes that have occurred in industrial structure and trade patterns and consider the role of R&D investment and firm experience in these changes. I then develop a simple economic model to analyze the influence that changes in industrial structure in individual countries exert on world trade patterns and the international distribution of trade benefits that arise from such changes. I also analyze the effects of industrial policies carried out by individual governments.

In the second section I examine trade and industrial policy for oligopolistic industries. In recent years there has been a great deal of research on the effects of policy toward oligopolistic industries. In addition to surveying the various studies on the topic, I discuss the implications of these studies for the policies of the three leading economies. In the final section I consider the problems of the international trade system centered on the General Agreement on Tariffs and Trade (GATT) and the positions individual governments should take toward this system in light of the economic analysis of the preceding section.

CHANGES IN INDUSTRIAL STRUCTURE:
WHAT CAUSES THEM? WHAT DIFFERENCE DO THEY MAKE?

According to textbook trade theory, trade is largely determined by such exogenous conditions as climate and factor endowment and occurs in a static world in which industrial structure does not change. It is obvious, however, that industrial structures are dynamic. Also, factor endowments are not the principal determinants of corporate competitiveness or national comparative advantage, but rather these are the results of the economic activities of individual companies, which include R&D investment and accumulated experience. That is, endogenous variables are the determining factors. I illustrate this point in terms of Japan's postwar experience.[1] Dramatic changes have occurred in the sectoral composition of Japan's exports since World War II. Immediately following the war textiles were prominent in Japan's exports; over the course of Japan's rapid growth phase until the first oil shock, however, there was an extremely rapid shift toward machinery exports such as automobiles and electronics. Even during the late 1970s, when the peak period of rapid growth had passed, exports continued a strong shift toward machinery.

Behind these changes in industrial structure was a rapid increase in productivity in the fast-growing sectors. Many point to the concentration of productivity growth in the machinery sector as the impetus for the shift in Japan's industrial structure. Japan's productivity growth has been faster than that of the United States not because of exogenous factors but rather due to the R&D activities and efforts of firms to improve production systems, as well as technological skills developed through production experience.

The Japanese experience suggests at least two important points. First, a country's industrial structure has enormous influence both on its trade patterns and on its economic welfare. Second, in most industries corporate competitiveness and national patterns of comparative advantage are not determined by factor endowment or climate but by technological factors. Moreover, these technological factors are determined by enterprise activity and government policy, which are endogenous factors. Clearly, any theory on comparative advantage must consider technological factors. I discuss both issues in more detail below.

Industrial Structure and Gains from Trade

I first consider the relationship between industrial structure and economic welfare using a simple model outlined in figure 4.1.[2] The main discussion, however, is limited to an intuitive argument. In figure 4.1 goods and services are divided into three broad categories: basic technology goods, borderline technology goods, and advanced technology goods and services. Basic technology goods are those goods in which late-developing countries have a strong comparative advantage and include textiles and other light industrial goods. Borderline technology goods are those goods in which late-developing countries are quite close to the leading countries in competitiveness and include steel and shipbuilding. Mass market automobiles might also fall into this category. Advanced technology goods and services are those that only the advanced industrial countries can offer competitively. A few examples are high technology goods such as semiconductors and aircraft and finance and communication services. When trade occurs between advanced and late-developing countries, the advanced countries export advanced technology goods, the late-developing countries export basic technology goods, and both compete in the area of borderline technology goods.

If this model represents the initial situation, what happens if changes occur in industrial structure? If the change occurs in the industrial structure of a late-developing country, two possible patterns may result. The first is a pattern of falling costs in the basic technology goods, which had

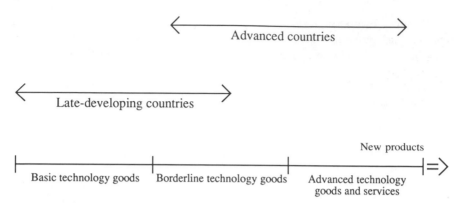

FIGURE 4.1. Technological categories of goods and services produced, by level of development.

previously established competitiveness. The second is a pattern of developing competitiveness in borderline technology industries.

A question that inevitably arises in the process of industrialization is whether more effort should be put into making existing export industries more competitive or into broadening the industrial base by establishing new export industries. In the case of Japan in the 1950s, there was serious policy debate over whether Japan should protect its automobile and steel industries, which were not internationally competitive at the time.[3] If the pattern of industrial development can be influenced by government policy, the two possible patterns of structural change outlined above become a legitimate matter for public policy consideration.

If late-developing countries choose the development path of reducing the production costs of the basic technology goods they already produce, it is not likely that great structural change will follow. In this case, both advanced and late-developing countries would receive benefits from lower production costs for basic technology goods. Improvements in the technological conditions in late-developing countries would thus provide equal benefits for the whole world in the form of lower prices.

In order to see the change in the distribution of income between the advanced and late-developing countries, let us hypothesize what would happen if the following trade balance were to develop:[4]

$$\text{Late-developing countries' imports} = \text{Advanced countries' imports} \qquad (1)$$

Here it is possible to express the imports of each country as the product of the average propensity to import and national income. Since the average propensity to import is defined as the proportion of national income spent on imports, it can be expressed in the following equation:

$$\text{Average propensity to import} = \text{Spending on imports/income} \qquad (2)$$

If we substitute equation (2) into equation (1), we have the following equation:

$$\frac{\text{Advanced countries' income}}{\text{Late-developing countries' income}} = \frac{\text{Late-developing countries' average propensity to import}}{\text{Advanced countries' average propensity to import}} \quad (3)$$

The numerator of the right-hand side of equation (3) is the late-developing countries' average propensity to import from advanced countries, and the denominator is the advanced countries' average propensity to import from late-developing countries. The ratio between the advanced and late-developing countries' incomes is equal to the ratio between their tendencies to import from one another.

This equation is simply the result of combining the definition of the average propensity to import with a condition of balanced trade and does not indicate a causal relationship between the left and right sides of the equation. Although we must use a model in which the utility function is explicitly considered in order to fully examine the welfare implications of a change in industrial structure, I choose a less rigorous approach below and give some attention to relative income.[5] The distribution of income between advanced and late-developing countries provides an important perspective on the complex economic relationships that exist between the two sets of countries. A consideration of the factors determining the late-developing and advanced countries' average propensity to import can provide insight into the factors determining the distribution of income between them.

As I have shown in an earlier study using a mathematical analytic model, the trade and industrial structures of advanced and late-developing countries are important factors behind their average propensities to import.[6] The larger the menu of export goods a country can offer, the greater other countries' propensity to import from it will be. As a country's industrial structure becomes more sophisticated, it will be able to offer a larger menu of export goods.

Let us go back and think a little further about the basic, borderline, and advanced technology goods model presented earlier. Even if late-developing countries are successful in the pattern of industrial development that reduces the production costs of basic technology export goods, they have not expanded their menu of export goods and services. Unless demand for these goods is particularly price elastic, the propensity to import in advanced or late-developing countries' will not change significantly. Thus, it will have little impact on the ratio of income between late-developing and advanced countries.

More generally, lowered production costs in established export industries in late-developing countries will result in one of the following: (1)

if the price elasticity of demand for basic technology goods is less than 1, the late-developing countries' income will decrease relative to that of advanced countries;[7] (2) when the price elasticity of demand is equal to 1, there will be no change in the income ratio between advanced and developing countries; and (3) if the price elasticity of demand for the good is greater than 1, the developing countries' income will increase relative to that of advanced countries.

It is unlikely, however, that the price elasticity of demand for basic technology goods exported by late-developing countries will be very high. Even so, it would be difficult for late-developing countries to raise their relative incomes by improving productivity in established industries. And, if the price elasticity of demand were less than 1, their relative income would actually decline. Of course, there would be the benefit of lower prices for goods, but industrialization focusing on existing export industries would actually prove injurious to the late developers' overall economic welfare if the price elasticity of demand for such goods were extremely low.[8]

In contrast, if late-developing countries are successful in developing borderline technology industries, the distribution of income between the late-developing and advanced countries will change significantly. By lowering the cost of production of borderline technology goods, the late-developing countries can expand their menu of export goods, and there will be less need to import these goods from the advanced countries, thereby reducing the late developers' propensity to import. And since the advanced countries will now import borderline technology goods from the late-developing countries, their average propensity to import from the late developers will increase. By decreasing the numerator and increasing the denominator in the right side of equation (3), this pattern of industrialization increases the late developers' income relative to that of the advanced countries.

Japan's postwar development pattern is an example of industrial development in which the industrial structure shifted toward borderline technology goods. In the period immediately following the war, the rest of the world had a low propensity to import from Japan, which could only export inexpensive textiles and other light industrial goods. Japan, which depended on foreign imports for machines, fuel, and raw materials, had potentially a very high average propensity to import. Strict import controls, however, prevented this potential demand for foreign goods from being realized. Japan's industrial structure changed dramatically, and the shipbuilding, steel, electronics, automobile, and machine tool industries were nurtured as export industries. As a result, foreign countries' average propensity to import Japanese goods increased. In comparison, Japan has been slow to increase its average propensity to import. This process of structural change has been behind the relative increase in Japan's level of income. Thus, industrial development that moves the late-developing countries into borderline technology industries raises their relative income position vis-à-vis the advanced countries, in addition to lowering prices for borderline technology goods.

When borderline technology industries are subject to dynamic economies of scale, which I discuss in more detail later, developing competitiveness in borderline technologies will have an important effect on national welfare. Since the welfare gains from the establishment of borderline technology industries benefit the entire economy (thus, there is an external economy), government has an incentive to protect them. The national gains from the development of borderline technology industries are much larger than the private gains to industry. This general equilibrium impact of infant-industry protection policy has not been discussed much in the traditional literature. However, this is one of the most important features of postwar Japanese industrial policy.[9]

This pattern of industrialization affects the welfare of the advanced countries from two directions. On the one hand, borderline technology goods from the late-developing countries become cheaper. But, on the other hand, their income declines relative to that of the late-developing countries.[10] As late-developing countries shift into borderline technology industries, trade conflicts often erupt. Borderline technology industries have figured prominently in the numerous instances of trade conflict between Japan and Western countries, particularly the United States in textiles in the 1950s, steel in the late 1960s, electronics in the 1970s, and automobiles since the late 1970s. Late-developing countries must not only lower costs in established industries but must also expand into borderline technology industries. However, this tends to create trade friction as industrialization brings changes in the distribution of income between late-developing and advanced countries.

What policies should advanced countries adopt in the face of encroachment by late-developing countries into borderline technology industries? One possibility is trade protection and various forms of subsidies aimed at maintaining domestic firms' competitiveness in affected industries. As I stated earlier, it is unclear whether the expansion of late-developing countries into borderline technology goods also improves the economic welfare of the advanced countries. It is, therefore, also unclear whether protectionist policies will benefit the advanced countries. If the late-developing countries retaliate against the protectionist policies of the advanced countries with protectionist policies of their own, total world trade may contract.

Next I consider the impact of changes in the industrial structure of advanced countries. Industrial development in the advanced countries usually means the development of new products in advanced technology industries. What effects will this have on equation (3) of the model? The development of new products will most likely lead to a shift in demand from basic and borderline technology goods to advanced technology goods, thus causing expenditures to shift from basic and borderline technology goods to advanced technology goods. The propensity to import goods produced by the advanced countries will increase and the propensity to import goods from the late-developing countries will decrease. As a result, the advanced countries' income will increase relative to that of the late-developing countries. Thus, the expansion of advanced countries into new areas and the expansion of late-developing countries into borderline technology industries will both increase the income of one set of countries relative to the other, though the former has certain aspects that the latter lacks.

First, the expansion of advanced countries into new areas contributes to the economic welfare of the late-developing countries as well as to their own by increasing the variety of goods and services available. Second, the expansion of the advanced countries into new areas will raise not only their incomes but also their factor costs. The advanced countries will become less competitive in borderline technology goods, facilitating the advance of the late-developing countries into those industries.[11]

Therefore, the expansion of advanced countries into new fields clearly also has significant benefits for the late-developing countries. It is uncertain, however, whether these benefits compensate for the decline in relative income suffered by the late-developing countries. If the new products developed by the advanced countries simply replace older products, then the decline in relative income will exceed the potential benefits. But if the new products serve new functions and provide new benefits, then these, along with new opportunities for competition in older industries, may become more important.

As I have shown, the structural changes accompanying industrial development have major effects not only on the country undergoing the development but on the economic welfare of its trading partners as well. It is imperative that the advanced countries expand into new fields to promote economic growth and international harmony to the benefit of both advanced and late-developing countries. The late-developing countries can move into the borderline technology industries without threatening the income of the advanced countries.

Determinants of Industrial Structure: Dynamic Economies of Scale

According to textbook economic theory, comparative advantage is determined by factor endowments, which are exogenous conditions. Factor endowments such as land and labor in their simplest terms do not go very far in explaining contemporary patterns of international trade in industrial goods. The technology and expertise developed by private firms are much more important. This is a very important point in explaining the competitiveness of advanced countries in new areas of production.

The two primary factors firms employ to improve technology and lower production costs are production experience and investment in research and development (R&D). Economies of scale are also important in both factors, and the combination of experience and R&D investment largely determines patterns of trade.[12]

Firms acquire expertise primarily through actual production experience. This is the so-called learning-curve effect, in which an increase in the cumulative level of production leads to a decrease in unit production costs.[13] As solutions are found for technical problems and the production process improves over time, production costs decline. The learning-curve effect can be observed to some extent in most industries and is especially marked in the frontier-technology industries such as the semiconductor industry. Although Toyota is not in a frontier-technology industry, its "just-in-time system" (*kanban* system) is an example of a production system only possible through the accumulation of a great deal of experience.

In industries where production experience can lead to dramatic cost reductions, a firm can establish a cost advantage by getting a head start on other firms in building up its production volume and thus accumulating more experience. Such economies of scale, in which timing and cumulative production over time are important, are what economists call dynamic economies of scale. In industries in which R&D investment is an important factor in developing competitiveness, the same kind of dynamic economies of scale will be relevant. R&D investment is a fixed cost; production of a larger volume of goods will reduce the R&D cost per unit.

In industries where dynamic economies of scale are important, the patterns of trade and comparative advantage are determined by R&D investments and production experience. And since these determinants of trade are heavily influenced by government policies and the market environment, they often lead to difficult international political problems. Let us assume that firms in a given industry in two countries are technological equals. What factors will determine which country's firms will develop a decisive advantage? If dynamic economies of scale are an important factor in the industry, the country whose firms build up the most production experience and invest the most in R&D will become the most competitive. If the firms in both countries face identical environmental conditions, it is possible that neither will develop a technological edge. But if the two governments adopt different policies toward the industry, significant differences in the conditions faced by firms in the two countries may arise.

Preferential policies by one government will give an advantage to domestic firms, which will be amplified by dynamic economies of scale. Differences in the market practices and market scale of the two countries can also affect the competitiveness of firms. For example, if the firms possess significant sales advantages in their own markets, the firms in the larger country will have an advantage in creating economies of scale.

Even if there is no difference in scale between the two markets, if consumers in one country have a strong preference for domestic products,
domestic firms will have an advantage.

It is essential that dynamic economies of scale be utilized to reduce
production costs to achieve an optimal worldwide allocation of resources.
The number of producers must be limited to some degree to enable
firms to achieve economies of scale. Which country's firms actually carry
out production is irrelevant from this standpoint. But, as shown above,
the presence of a computer, semiconductor, aircraft, or other high technology industry in a given country may make a big difference in its national income. Therefore, each of the advanced countries will attempt to
foster these key industries in its own country. And once an industry
becomes a target of policy-making, a scramble for market share is likely
to ensue.[14]

In industries where dynamic economies of scale are important, government policies and market practices have a great influence on the competitiveness of individual firms, and international trade friction may arise.
Of course, since the optimal size for achieving economies of scale in the
leading-technology industries is often smaller than the entire market of
a single country, it is often possible for several firms to develop within
a single country. It is also technologically feasible for a number of countries to develop production capacity in the same industry simultaneously.
The free workings of the market, however, may not lead to the development of a full set of high technology industries in all countries. Industrial policy can be used by individual countries to induce the development of these leading-technology industries, but this use of industrial
policy brings its own problems. First, industries may manipulate government to gain subsidies and other benefits (which I discuss later). Second, if each country fosters a full set of leading-technology industries,
worldwide overproduction may result.

Many might think that for the sake of fairness international agreements
should be adopted to prevent individual countries from adopting industrial policies to promote economies of scale. But industrial policy may
be necessary given that market failures are a problem in industries where
learning curves and R&D investment are important. The free market
activities of private firms in these industries will not necessarily bring
about an efficient allocation of resources. Governments devise industrial
policies to correct market failures and to facilitate a desirable allocation
of resources.[15] It would be difficult to regulate industrial policy on an
international basis, however, as the industrial policies different countries
can carry out vary for a number of reasons.

Another difficult policy question in industries where dynamic economies of scale are important concerns the appropriate response to dumping. There are various possible definitions of dumping, but here I define
dumping as selling at a price below the cost of production.[16] In industries

where dynamic economies of scale are important, sales below cost in the initial stages of production may occur. In many cases this can be justified for the sake of optimal resource allocation; a lower price in the initial stages makes it possible to expand production volume and thus greatly reduce production costs. Whether this should be regulated as dumping or not is an important issue for study.

INTERNATIONAL COMPETITION AND STRATEGIC INDUSTRIAL POLICY IN OLIGOPOLISTIC INDUSTRIES

The problem of international competition between firms in oligopolistic industries and the related issue of strategic industrial policy have attracted considerable attention in economics, as well as in the broader society, in recent years. Competition in an oligopolistic world has many fascinating facets that do not exist in a world of perfect competition. First, the forms of competition in oligopolistic industries are extremely varied and are not limited to price. Competition can take place in the area of R&D investment, plant investment, advertising and marketing, or in the development of a resource or labor base. The importance of competition and the influence of government policy depend substantially on the type of competition prevailing in a given industry. How the forms of oligopolistic competition are determined and what influence various government policies have on them are extremely important for understanding present-day trade and international competition in oligopolistic industries.[17]

Second, oligopolistic competition has many dynamic aspects. After all, competition over investment in equipment and R&D is nothing if not dynamic. Even price competition is commonly carried out in a strategic fashion based on readings of future trends. A typical example is the establishment of a "penetration price" to break into a new market. Dumping also has an important dynamic aspect. The theory of dynamic oligopoly, which has developed quickly in recent years, sheds light on a number of dynamic aspects of oligopolies and provides a valuable perspective on international competition in oligopolistic industries.[18] Dynamic oligopoly theory can help us to understand such current issues as the changes in the aircraft industry resulting from the entry of Airbus and the trade conflicts in the semiconductor and computer industries.[19]

Third, the distribution of oligopolistic rents arising from changes in international competition affects not only the benefits flowing to individual firms but the distribution of benefits among nations as well. This issue of oligopolistic rent transfer has attracted much theoretical attention and will be discussed in detail.

The fourth reason for interest in oligopolistic markets is that the policy-making process between governments and firms in this area takes on many qualities of a game. The private sector does not simply accept whatever policies government proposes but instead engages in active lobbying. And since the government policy-making process itself influences the behavior of private firms, policies can produce results completely different from those intended by government. The government-business relationship is particularly complicated in the case of oligopolies.

Monopoly and Oligopoly Rents and Strategic Industrial Policy

Rather than attempt a theoretical explanation of the transfer of rents in oligopolistic industries, I present several examples.[20] In the early 1970s, Japan and the United States negotiated over whether Japan would abolish its import quotas on color film. At that time Eastman Kodak, an American company, had an extremely large share of the world market. In the course of negotiations, it became clear that the price of Kodak color film was much higher in the United States and Australia than in Japan or West Germany. This was most likely because competition in Japan and West Germany prevented Kodak from charging a higher price. In this situation, the Japanese and West German producers challenged Kodak's international monopoly. Due to the competition represented by these companies, the rents that would have flowed to the United States as a result of a higher Kodak price remained instead in the pockets of Japanese and German consumers.

Which country will receive the profits of oligopolistic firms and how much consumers will pay for goods sold by foreign monopolies is known as the problem of international transfer of monopoly rents. As in the above example, government policy may increase international competition in an oligopolistic industry and thereby augment its own national income by transferring monopoly rents back home.[21]

This kind of analysis is an important contribution to the discussions of trade policy between advanced industrialized countries. If an oligopolistic firm's profits are an important part of national income, or if the commodities produced are extremely important to consumers, government policies may play a major role in increasing national economic welfare. If a country adopts policies that favor its own oligopolistic companies or challenge foreign oligopolies, however, policy may be reduced to a tug-of-war between governments over monopoly rents reminiscent of the debate over optimal tariff levels in traditional trade theory. A country can shift the terms of trade in its favor by adopting import taxes. But if all countries try to establish optimal tariff levels, the result would be a tariff war, a contraction in trade, and a general decline in economic welfare.

In the case of oligopolies as well, if every country adopted import tariffs to benefit its own firms, the result would be a tariff war. The effect would be quite different though if government policies consisted of production or export subsidies. As with tariffs, subsidies will lead to a transfer of monopoly rents among oligopolistic firms. As long as this happens, an international scramble for monopoly rents will ensue. Subsidies, however, have benefits for consumers, in addition to providing monopoly rents. Subsidies leading to an intensification of competition among oligopolistic firms will cause prices to fall, thus benefiting consumers.

Even if the advanced industrialized countries engage in a subsidy war, consumers will no doubt benefit. Oligopolies tend to lead to insufficient levels of production in terms of optimal resource allocation. That is, prices tend to be set at a level higher than marginal cost. Therefore, a subsidy war that drives down prices by increasing supply in an oligopolistic industry is not necessarily undesirable.[22]

Thus, the economic effects of government subsidies to domestic firms in oligopolistic industries are difficult to evaluate. If one country alone uses subsidies, it will create an international transfer of monopoly rents and cause international disputes. But if all countries establish subsidies in a balanced fashion, subsidies may lead to better resource allocation. Nevertheless, there are several reasons subsidies cannot always be justified.

First, subsidies and other domestic preference policies do not necessarily transfer monopoly rent. Eaton and Grossman showed that whether subsidies and import restrictions improve a country's economic welfare by providing monopoly rents depends entirely on the prevailing form of oligopolistic competition.[23] Thus, if a Cournot-type oligopoly prevails in a model of simple static duopoly, export subsidies increase the economic welfare of the subsidizing country. The same model applied to a Bertrand-type price-competitive oligopoly, however, leads to the conclusion that exports should actually be taxed. There are many different forms of oligopolistic competition, and subsidies do not make sense in all oligopolistic situations.

Second, trading partners may retaliate. In some situations, retaliation among trading partners in the form of subsidies can actually improve the efficiency of worldwide resource allocation. But if retaliation takes the form of import restrictions, it can distort resource allocation. Currently, restrictions on foreign imports are used more often in retaliation than domestic subsidies, as it is much easier to apply import restrictions than subsidies, given the fiscal constraints on government.

Third, subsidies can take various forms: export subsidies, production subsidies, R&D investment subsidies, and temporary subsidies for start-up costs in leading-edge industries. The effects of the various forms of subsidy vary. For example, export subsidies are generally undesirable because one of the most important effects is simply to take market share away from foreign companies. In contrast, one of the principal effects of subsidies for R&D investment is to compensate for various market failures inherent in the development of new technologies.[24] Thus, rather than draw a general conclusion about subsidies, a careful analysis of the various types of subsidy is necessary. Finally, the policy-making process itself may influence the behavior of private economic actors in unintended ways. I return to this point below.

The international competition in oligopolistic industries and the related problems of industrial policy are extremely important elements in the discussion of current and future trade problems among the advanced industrial countries. In view of the problems of market failure present in areas such as technology development, it may be legitimate for governments to carry out some kind of industrial policy. However, many issues regarding international oligopolistic competition remain unclear.

The Policy-making Process and the Response of Business

I have assumed in the discussion up to this point that private actors do not intervene in the government policy-making process. That is, private economic actors merely determine their own behavior based on conditions set down by government policy. In this sense, I have treated government policy from the point of view of private actors as simply "manna from heaven."[25] In actual practice, however, much lobbying takes place and this greatly influences policy decisions. Although lobbying is an extremely important area for study, I make no attempt to add to the numerous studies already published on this topic. Instead, I focus the discussion on the more implicit relationship between the government policy-making process and the response of business.[26]

Governments introduce policy measures in order to realize certain policy objectives. As long as private economic actors behave in a perfectly competitive manner, policy-making will be fairly straightforward. All government has to do is adopt policies to meet its policy objectives based on a certain amount of observation of private actors' behavior. But if the private economic actors form a monopoly or an oligopoly, policy-making becomes much more difficult. At the same time, private actors are also busy trying to figure out government intentions and adjusting their production and pricing decisions accordingly. In effect, a situation similar to game theory develops between government and private actors.

As in the previous section, I offer examples here rather than a model. First, consider a situation where the government policy goal is to nurture domestic industry. The industry has claimed that pressure from foreign import competition is so great that it cannot mount a sufficient response to enable it to continue domestic production without government subsidy or protection. In this case, government will most likely base its decision regarding the appropriate level of subsidies and import restrictions for an industry on various indicators of performance in the domestic industry.

If the government policymakers are extremely naive, indicators of industrial performance such as domestic production and employment levels might be chosen. Common responses to a drop in such indicators are import tariffs and increases in domestic subsidies. But since private firms themselves play a major role in determining production and employment levels, the use of these figures as a basis for government policy decisions may distort perception of the reasons behind firm behavior. For example, even if domestic firms might be able to respond to an import challenge by boosting efforts and taking on risks to increase investment, they may not bother if they know government will step in to rescue them. As a matter of fact, business people may come to depend on government aid whenever they encounter difficulties.[27]

The foreign firms that are the source of the troublesome imports will also probably respond to protective policies or subsidies. If they take an aggressive strategy and lower prices to gain a larger market share, government may intervene to adopt import restrictions. Foreign firms may also decide it is more prudent to restrain exports than risk import restrictions and to make their money by raising prices a little.[28] When foreign firms engage in such preventive actions, the result is a de facto restriction of trade, without the adoption of formal trade restrictions.

The Japanese voluntary export restraints to the United States during the 1980s are an example of trade restraint. To avoid formal import restrictions, Japanese automobile manufacturers voluntarily restricted exports. This kind of voluntary export restraint has the same effect as an international cartel, and car prices in the United States for both Japanese and American cars rose dramatically.[29] It is interesting to note that both U.S. and Japanese automobile manufacturers enjoyed enormous profit growth as a consequence of export restraint.

Thus, as long as government policy is based on economic indicators, private economic actors will have an incentive to modify their behavior to convince government to adopt policies that suit their own interests. Actual government policy-making processes, however, may be more sophisticated than the one I have outlined here. For example, government might look at production and employment figures in addition to profits, costs, price, and other indicators in deciding whether to protect a domestic industry. This will lead to an even more complicated game between government and the private sector. To make really effective policy, government must have a full grasp of the industry's situation and to what degree its information reflects the strategic response of the private sector to government policy. Until government can commit to such a painstaking, in-depth investigation, private sector response to government policy-making will continue to influence government decisions. It is not possible for government to fully grasp all the available information on a particular industry. Therefore, it is difficult for government to ascertain to what degree an industry's poor performance is due to its own lack of effort. This uncertainty often leads to the adoption of protective measures.[30]

Even when government is completely aware of an industry's situation, the firms in the industry may put pressure on government weak points to distort its policies. For example, a government that knows that poor industrial performance is the fault of domestic firms may still restrict imports. From a long-term perspective the best policy would be for government to stand firm and refuse to either grant subsidies or restrict imports. Without government protection, the threat of foreign imports would push the firms to work harder. However, when government faces a difficult reelection campaign in two years if it does not achieve more immediate economic results, government may decide to boost domestic production in the short term through import restrictions. Government in this case is constrained in the type of policies it can adopt. Private firms can easily take advantage of government vulnerability and distort policies. The political influence of oligopolistic firms is especially strong, giving them considerable control over policy-making.

POSSIBILITIES FOR AN INTERNATIONAL ACCORD ON INDUSTRIAL POLICY

Economic relationships between the advanced industrialized countries are growing ever closer and increasingly complex. As I have shown in this paper, the growth in economic ties among nations means that the policies and economic systems of individual countries can exert enormous influence on other countries and often lead to friction. The GATT-centered international trade regime, which has functioned relatively well since World War II, is no longer equipped to regulate the multitude of economic transactions that are developing within an increasingly interdependent world.

The original purpose of the GATT was to do away with restrictions on cross-border trade. GATT's activities in abolishing import quotas and cutting tariffs fell within this category. Behind the GATT was the concept that as long as restrictions were lifted at national borders, an optimal allocation of resources could be achieved even if domestic policies were left up to each country's discretion. Of course, there have also been some international agreements made within the GATT that have ventured into the territory of domestic policy. The real contribution of the GATT, however, has been limited to the removal of cross-border trade restrictions.

I have clearly indicated that the industrial policies of one country can have a great effect on the industrial structure and economic welfare of others and that so-called domestic policies have enormous significance for international trade and investment. It is becoming increasingly necessary for individual nations to adjust their domestic policies to further the development of harmonious international economic relations.

In recent years there have been some stirrings in this direction within the GATT and other international forums. Interest in trade in services and in intellectual property is increasing. In the case of trade in services, it is clear that negotiations that deal effectively in this area must extend beyond mere border controls into the realm of national economic systems and policies. Service industries such as finance and communications do not simply involve the exchange of commodities between countries; they also operate inside foreign countries in foreign subsidiaries established through foreign direct investment and international joint ventures. Therefore, as long as regulations on direct investment, immigration, and other national policies and regulations generally considered domestic are excluded from negotiations, it will be impossible to develop a meaningful international system for services trade.

For example, the United States and Great Britain have recently protested against Japanese government requirements for bank self-capitalization (the ratio of owned capital to loans). They charge that although competition between banks now takes place on a worldwide basis, Japan's loose restrictions give its banks an unfair advantage. Regardless of whether they are right or not, this case is a good example of the way in which domestic regulations can give particular countries a competitive advantage in the international arena. If real negotiations are conducted in services trade, issues such as these will have to be dealt with. The creation of a more uniform worldwide system in services differs significantly from the abolishment of trade restrictions at the border behind the original GATT. But as commodities take on more of the qualities of services, these issues will increasingly apply not only to services but to many commodities as well.

Negotiations over intellectual property present a similar problem. In the leading-technology industries, intellectual property is an extremely important factor in determining firm competitiveness in technology and product development. Patents and copyrights play an important role in protecting intellectual property rights to trademarks and technology. But patent and copyright systems vary from country to country, and some countries fail to acknowledge foreign intellectual property rights. This is a major source of international friction.

If negotiations over intellectual property rights are held, they too must go beyond border controls and deal with the domestic systems of individual countries. If intellectual property rights systems are discussed, there is no reason negotiations should not move on to address other regulations and policies with an enormous effect on trade such as antitrust policies and regulations on distribution and transportation. As a result of the diversification of trade and the internationalization of domestic economies, trade negotiations are being pushed beyond the dimension of border controls to dealing with the internal economic systems of individual countries.

Difficult questions remain, however, in how far to go in the international regulation of various domestic policies affecting trade. Inevitably, such regulations would not only reform the international economic system but would also introduce wrenching changes in domestic economic systems. Although the removal of tariffs and other trade restrictions require a certain amount of domestic adjustment, the difficulty is limited since they are only concerned with flows across national borders.

Each country has its own goals and ideas concerning its economic system and regulations, as well as sovereignty over them, which must be respected. On the other hand, there are clearly many cases now where attempts to assert sovereignty become detrimental to the beneficial flow of trade and investment. At this stage, however, there is no certainty as to how individual countries' systems should be adjusted to smooth the working of the international system. It is not even clear whether greater international homogeneity is the most desirable form of adjustment. Further study is very much needed.

NOTES

1. This paper is based on Motoshige Itoh, M. F. Okuno, K. Kiyono, and K. Suzumura, *Sangyō seisaku no keizai bunseki* (Economic analysis of industrial policy) (Tokyo: University of Tokyo Press, 1988). On postwar changes in Japanese trade policy and trade patterns, see Ryutaro Komiya and Motoshige Itoh, "International Trade and Trade Policy of Japan: 1955–1984," in Takashi Inoguchi and Daniel Okimoto, eds., *The Political Economy of Japan*, vol. 2, *The Changing International Context* (Stanford: Stanford University Press, 1988).

2. The analytical model I present here is based on Paul Krugman, "A Model of Innovation, Technology Transfer, and the World Distribution of Income," *Journal of Political Economy* 87, no. 2 (1979): 253–66. For a more technical analysis, see Motoshige Itoh and K. Kiyono, "Welfare Enhancing Export Subsidies," *Journal of Political Economy* 95, no. 1 (1987): 115–37. A similar model is used to analyze the relationship between changes in industrial structure and Japan's rapid postwar economic growth. See Itoh et al., *Sangyō seisaku no bunseki*.

3. See Motoshige Itoh and K. Kiyono, "Trade and Direct Investment," in Ryutaro Komiya, M. Okuno, and K. Suzumura, eds., *Nihon no sangyō seisaku* (Industrial policy of Japan) (Tokyo: University of Tokyo Press, 1984), with an English translation forthcoming (New York: Academic Press), for a discussion of change in Japan's postwar industrial structure and the surrounding policy debates.

4. I refer to *trade balance* here in the broad sense of the term, that is, to include trade in goods *and* services. If trade between two countries is not balanced, one party will accumulate foreign debt unless there is a transfer of aid between countries.

5. For a more rigorous analysis, see Itoh and Kiyono, "Welfare Enhancing Export Subsidies."

6. Ibid.

7. All other things being equal, a lower relative income will also result in a lower absolute income, since goods imported from the advanced countries will cost more due to higher real wages and other production costs in the advanced countries.

8. This case fits the concept of "immiserizing growth"; see Jagdish N. Bhag-

wati, "Immiserizing Growth: A Geometric Note," *Review of Economic Studies* 25, no. 3 (June 1958): 201–5.

9. See Itoh et al., *Sangyō seisaku no bunseki*, for further details.

10. It is impossible to reach a definite conclusion concerning the positive and negative effects on the economic welfare of the advanced countries. According to the model presented by Itoh and Kiyono ("Welfare Enhancing Export Subsidies"), the expansion of late-developing countries into borderline technology goods results in an overall loss in economic welfare for advanced countries.

11. It is beyond the scope of this paper to develop an analytic model on this point. The continuum-of-goods model in Itoh and Kiyono, "Welfare Enhancing Export Subsidies," does offer such an analysis.

12. See Motoshige Itoh, *Bōeki masatsu to seisakuteki taiō* (Trade friction and policy response) (Tokyo: Ministry of Finance, 1984); and Paul Krugman, "Import Protection as Export Promotion: International Competition in the Presence of Oligopoly and Economies of Scale," in H. Kierzkowski, ed., *Monopolistic Competition and International Trade* (New York: Oxford University Press, 1984), on the importance of economies of scale for learning curves and R&D investment.

13. For an economic analysis of the learning-curve effect, see A. M. Spence, "The Learning Curve and Competition," *Bell Journal of Economics* 12, no. 1 (1981).

14. See A. Panagalya, "Variable Returns to Scale in Production and Patterns of Specialization," *American Economic Review* 71 (1981): 221–30, for a discussion of the distribution of the trade benefits from economies of scale.

15. See Itoh et al., *Sangyō seisaku no bunseki*.

16. In some countries pricing export goods cheaper than those available in the domestic market is considered a form of price discrimination and dumping.

17. Here is an example that illustrates the significance such questions have for changing industrial structure and for interfirm competitiveness. If price competition in an oligopolistic industry is too stiff, each firm will either barely meet its costs or sell below cost. Since firms will not make an operating profit, funds will not be available for investment. Also, if price competition is fierce, banks will not lend to these firms, since there is no hope of high operating profits in the future. Thus, much less investment will occur in industries where there is heavy price competition.

On the other hand, competition can also take the form of investment competition. Under this mode of competition, firms are not engaged in heavy price competition and are able to earn high operating profits. These profits are then used to maximize investment in competition with other firms.

The long-term performance of an industry varies significantly depending on which pattern of competition prevails. It can be generally assumed that long-term performance will be better in an industry in which investment competition dominates. Motoshige Itoh ("Industrial Policy and Corporate Growth in the Automobile Industry: Japan's Postwar Experience," paper presented at a Ministry of International Trade and Industry conference, Tokyo, 1987) showed that the fact that competition in Japan's postwar automobile industry was investment, rather than price, competition made a great contribution to its development.

18. D. Fudenberg and J. Tirole, *Dynamic Models of Oligopoly* (Chur, Switzerland: Harwood Academic Press, 1986), provide a useful survey of dynamic oligopoly theory.

19. A. K. Dixit and A. S. Kyle, "The Use of Protection and Subsidies for Entry Promotion and Deterrence," *American Economic Review* 72 (1985): 139–52, offer an interesting analysis of the Airbus case. Krugman also touches on these issues in Paul Krugman, "The U.S. Response to Foreign Industrial Targeting," *Brooking Papers on Economic Activities* 1 (1984): 77–132.

20. For a theoretical analysis, see Motoshige Itoh, "A Theory of Imperfect Competition in International Trade and Investment" (Ph.D. diss., University of Rochester, 1978); Itoh et al., *Sangyō seisaku no bunseki;* J. A. Brander and B. J. Spencer, "Tariffs and the Extraction of Foreign Monopoly Rent under Potential Entry," *Canadian Journal of Economics* 14 (1981): 371–99; Krugman, "The U.S. Response to Foreign Industrial Targeting"; and J. Eaton and G. M. Grossman, "Optimal Trade and Industrial Policy under Oligopoly," *Quarterly Journal of Economics* 101 (1987): 383–406.

21. This point has been discussed in a number of mathematical analytic models presented in the works cited in note 20.

22. Of course, subsidies become pointless if they are provided with such abandon that they actually lead to overproduction.

23. Eaton and Grossman, "Optimal Trade and Industrial Policy under Oligopoly."

24. Much of the research has indicated that simply leaving technology development to the free workings of the market does not bring about favorable resource allocation, although it is uncertain whether the best policy to correct this is subsidy or regulation. This is because R&D investment activities in a laissez-faire environment may be either excessive or insufficient.

25. The manna metaphor is from Bhagwati, "Immiserizing Growth."

26. This subject is dealt with in more detail in Motoshige Itoh, T. Honda, and K. Kiyono, "Policy Formation and Response: The Case of Trade Policies," paper presented at National Bureau of Economic Research Summer Institute, Cambridge, Mass., 1986.

27. A similar problem is discussed in macroeconomic theory under the heading of "the problem of discretion versus rules in policy." For example, see F. E. Kydrand and E. C. Prescott, "Rules Rather than Discretion: The Inconsistency of Optimal Plans," *Journal of Political Economy* 85 (1977): 473–91. The issue is treated much differently in the macroeconomic literature, which does not deal with the problem of oligopoly. See Itoh, Honda, and Kiyono, "Policy Formation and Response," for discussion of the relationship between oligopolistic firms and government policy-making.

28. Participation by the export government in such unilateral export restrictions is described in Jagdish N. Bhagwati, J. N. Srinivasan, and T. N. Srinivasan, "Optimal Trade Policy and Compensation under Endogenous Uncertainty: The Phenomenon of Market Disruption," *Journal of International Economics* 6 (1976): 317–30.

29. Prices rise significantly when voluntary export restraints are adopted, even if the import ceiling is set at the level of export volume that had prevailed under free trade (see Motoshige Itoh and Y. Ono, "Tariffs, Quotas, and Market Structure," *Quarterly Journal of Economics* 17 [1984]: 359–73).

30. Itoh, Honda, and Kiyono ("Policy Formation and Response") use a game theory model of incomplete information to analyze this phenomenon.

5

The Agenda of the Leading Nations
for the World Economy: A Theory
of International Economic Regimes

PETER F. COWHEY

The purpose of this volume is to explore the effects of scientific and technological change on the future of the world economic order. In this chapter, I examine the role of the leading economic powers in shaping this future and argue that competition in the high technology industries is producing a very important reorganization of the general rules for international competition. This thesis reflects three recurrent themes of the other chapters in this volume. First, there is a growing parity among countries in their scientific and technological capabilities even as the speed of innovation increases. Closer parity creates competitive tensions that challenge many of the political and economic accommodations that have supported free trade and investment since 1945.

Second, contemporary experience with economic development has rekindled fundamental debates over the respective roles of governments and markets. The countries that are catching up with the United States in scientific and economic capabilities have typically relied on much more government intervention in the economy than the United States. The authors of this volume do not agree on how much credit should be given to specific government industrial and research policies, but they all acknowledge that such considerations present a puzzle for conventional economic analysis. That is, why have these countries done so well despite extensive government interference in the market? However, ever more extensive government control over markets is not the path of the future. These same countries are also experimenting with the introduction of more market-oriented policies in sectors traditionally subject to extensive government control. Deregulation is not an idiosyncratic American experiment, however; most countries look for new roles for government even as they deregulate. (Japan, for example, is introducing significant competition in telecommunications while the government is simultaneously promoting a new infrastructure for advanced communications outside Tokyo.) This reexamination of past practices necessarily raises concerns in the minds of trading partners about international conduct. This in turn both shakes confidence in the existing world trade system and opens up significant possibilities for innovation in international economic coordination.

Third, the growing parity in scientific and economic capabilities and rethinking of government policies are forcing significant experimentation by private firms. Companies are becoming more thoroughly multinational, they are experimenting with new forms of commercial alliances with other domestic or foreign firms, and they are radically redefining their lines of business (as when IBM becomes a telephone company). The experimentation and deeper internationalization of firms in all countries pose significant problems for government policies. Successful government policies implicitly depend on certain forms of firm behavior. If firms are undergoing significant transition, the perils of policy prediction increase.

In short, the broad internationalization of science and technology has prompted both more government intervention and a growing reliance on market competition. It has triggered the deeper internationalization of business and new forms of market arrangements among firms. Cumulatively, it has raised questions about the adequacy of current rules governing international economic relations. I examine in this chapter how these factors will determine the international economic order, or the international "regime," as it is called in contemporary literature on political economy.

The primary question I address concerning the future international economic regime is whether governments can preserve an "open" world economy (that is, a world economy characterized by relatively free flows of trade and investment). Many analysts worry that an era of trade wars and neomercantilism is about to begin.

Three principles anchor my analysis. First, the international economic order always rests on the leadership of one country (or a few countries), and leading countries have an interest in openness. Second, international regimes depend on more than a simple distribution of international power. Leadership by the "strong" requires "credible commitments," and credible commitments mean that international regimes must be in accord with the domestic politics of the strong. As a result, concerns over the preservation of an open world economy have been confused with questions about the form that openness can take.[1] Third, the form of openness will change if Japan and West Germany play a greater role, simply because their political approach to macroeconomic and microeconomic management differs from that of the United States. This is particularly apparent in their assumptions regarding the relationship between firms and government. Firms are vital "agents" in the management of regimes and important members of the transnational coalitions that facilitate them. Therefore, changing roles of firms alter the evolution of regimes.

More specifically, the United States promoted an open international economic order after World War II that reflected special features of the U.S. domestic political economy. The United States committed itself to policies that divorced macroeconomic management along Keynesian principles (with a commitment to social welfare policies) from the regulation of individual "micromarkets." It emphasized free trade built around the ideal of commodity auction markets and foreign investment built around the ideal of individual, vertically integrated corporations operating on a global scale. The original scope of these arrangements was largely limited to goods and not services.

As the power of Japan and West Germany increases, their special preferences for how the world economic order should be organized will become more important. This may produce a difference in the form of openness of the world economy. In particular, this new form of openness may combine classic free trade with a different form of international commerce that I term *alliances*. Alliance systems combine openness with high levels of horizontal collaboration among firms and active levels of microeconomic management by governments. The characteristics of many high technology industries and the traditions of more active microeconomic management in Japan and West Germany will combine to make such alliances more important. Meanwhile, in terms of macroeconomic policy, these two countries will push for international policies that erode the division between macroeconomic and microeconomic policies.

In the first section of this chapter I define the terms and spell out the theoretical argument of the entire chapter. In the next section I briefly recount the linkage between the political economy of the United States and the international regime after World War II. In the third section I speculate on the linkage between the German and Japanese political economies and the potential shift in the international economic regime. Finally, the last section focuses on the informatics sector, the merging of the telecommunications and information industries for both services and goods, to explore the emerging rules for the developing alliances.

A THEORY OF REGIMES

There is an elaborate literature on the political economy of international trade and monetary affairs, and it has often stumbled over two problems. First, what is the relationship between international and domestic politics in shaping the international economic order? Second, how does the international community reconcile high levels of government intervention in markets with a continued commitment to openness? This section begins with an explanation of how the distribution of international power makes regimes possible. Then it explains the relationship between international power and domestic politics. Finally, I lay out alternative options for conducting an "open" international regime.

Power and Credible Commitments

International economic cooperation takes the form of international regimes. Regimes provide principles, norms, rules, and decision-making processes to set an agenda for problem solving, reduce risks of strategic behavior, and improve communication.[2] International economic regimes have two primary dimensions: principles and rules governing the movement of international trade and investment capital, or what is called the "commerce system"; and principles and rules coordinating the management of macroeconomic policy. The latter minimally covers how monetary policy will be conducted so as to permit international commerce, but it may also include macroeconomic policy and welfare or technology policies.[3] These regimes create solutions that provide benefits to all nations, including those who do not fully contribute to their creation or continuation. In short, in important respects regimes represent international collective goods.

Given the comparatively weak network of international political institutions, it is difficult to resolve collective action problems (in the sense made famous by Mancur Olsen) when trying to create international collective goods in an anarchic world.[4] Therefore, many rules of regimes enhance the possibilities of exclusion or appropriability of economic benefits to reduce collective action problems. Nonetheless, international economic regimes depend primarily on political and economic power remaining concentrated in a relatively small number of countries.[5]

The traditional "solution" for organizing international collective goods has relied on a hegemonic power. A hegemonic power has a sufficiently large stake in the world economy to make it worth the cost of subsidizing its organization.[6] It also has the resources to offer inducements or impose penalties to encourage others to cooperate in providing the goods. More fundamentally, its overall dominance gives the hegemonic power substantial control over the setting of the international agenda. This is due in part to its general military and economic preeminence. Just as crucially, and often too little appreciated, a hegemonic power sets agendas because its firms initiate many of the key innovations in the marketplace.

Why do hegemonic powers support an open system? They do so simply because of the relative strength of their economies. They accept reciprocity in openness because it is prohibitively expensive to impose unilateral openness.[7] Moreover, international orders require bargaining between the dominant and secondary powers. This means that the international regime has to accommodate to some extent the idiosyncratic national preferences of weaker states.[8] Thus, no regime has been as open as advertised (or, conversely, as closed), as it might sometimes have seemed.

Nonetheless, the dominant power's control over the agenda has generally meant that its preferences for the specific forms of openness of the international regime have usually prevailed. Countries have an implicit intellectual ideology concerning how to interpret inherently ambiguous political and economic choices, and leading countries have always had a powerful demonstration effect on other countries.[9] Thus, Britain and the United States set the styles of their respective eras of hegemony. The nineteenth-century order was a rough version of England's laissez-faire liberalism, while the era since 1945 can be thought of as the New Deal on a global scale.[10] Such leadership often annoys the secondary powers. But they have good reasons to grant the hegemon's preferences over the form of openness. The secondary powers above all need credible commitments from the leading power if the countries are to reach an optimal agreement.[11] A credible commitment reassures other parties that it would be difficult for the dominant party to exploit its position. Otherwise, the countries will choose a less efficient contract in order to protect themselves from opportunistic behavior by the major party.

There are a variety of ways for dominant powers to establish credible commitments. One important way is to make international agreements that closely approximate what domestic political and economic interests of the dominant power naturally prefer. Then, a reversal of policy by the dominant power for the purpose of engaging in strategic bargaining with an ally would inevitably encounter powerful domestic opposition at home![12] Therefore, other countries have a vested interest in an international regime that accommodates a robust winning coalition within the hegemon's domestic borders.

The Role of Firms and Transnational Coalitions

The analysis so far has concentrated on the role of the international distribution of power in establishing international regimes. I have suggested that all countries have an incentive (the desire to win credible commitments) to allow the regime leader to shape the international regime in response to the special demands of its domestic political coalition. But there is yet another connection between domestic economic systems and the international regime. Put simply, preferences and power do not directly produce outcomes. The bargaining among actors takes place within an established institutional framework that makes some resources more valuable than others and some paths easier to follow. Theorists have dubbed this path-dependent development. That is, given that the bargaining game yields multiple equilibria, the institutional context strongly influences the outcome.[13]

Existing international organizations are an example of the institutional context for international regimes. For example, no strategy for working out reforms in world trade can ignore the General Agreement on Tariffs and Trade (GATT). But surely the most important institutional structure for international economic regimes in a capitalist system is the private market itself. The mobility of capital limits the power of government, and governments cannot easily govern the detailed conduct of markets over time.[14] This suggests that the evolution of an international regime depends significantly on the existing pattern of industrial organization. While the pattern of industrial organization itself may shift over time as a result of underlying economic conditions and government policies, it is prudent in the short- and medium-run to look at existing patterns of industrial organization in imperfect markets.[15]

The importance of firms for the conduct of the regime means that there is a strong principle-agent problem. That is, the agent may not fully conform to the desires of the principle, and therefore, the principle has to design the system to accommodate this divergence in incentives.[16] The type of firm that dominates influences the problems of "agentry" in managing the regime. A shift in the type of dominant firm (and typical interfirm relationships) will strongly influence the management of the world economy.[17] For example, the decline of the fabled Seven Sisters in the oil industry permanently changed the options for oil exporting and importing countries for organizing the world oil market. There may now be a change in the nature of multinational corporations and a resultant shift in the nature of the options for the international commercial system.[18]

The governments of the leading powers (and their companies) instinctively recognize the role of private interests in supporting international regimes. At the very least, they push for the creation of compatible national coalitions. For example, Maier has analyzed how the U.S. program for the reconstruction of the European economy required substantial efforts to reengineer the domestic political economies of European countries after World War II.[19] More ambitiously, leading powers promote transnational coalitions (coalitions of public and private actors cutting across national boundaries) in support of the international regime. The final section of this chapter argues that U.S. diplomacy in the informatics sector is currently building a new transnational coalition for that sector.[20]

The Shift from Hegemony to Oligopoly

It is possible for a single monopoly power to be replaced by a small number of oligopolistic powers. The two most important today are Japan and West Germany, and by virtue of its international financial position and size, it is Japan that is the most vital. While there is a considerable literature speculating on the consequences of a shift in economic power, the bulk of the literature is fairly optimistic, even though we are dealing with an era of diminished (but hardly vanquished) U.S. hegemony.[21] The benefits from international cooperation remain strong enough for oligopolistic leadership to surmount free rider problems in the provision of international economic cooperation.

As the leadership of the international economic system moves from hegemony to oligopoly, the central question becomes how to reorganize the international economic regime. Such a reorganization must allow greater weight to the priorities of other countries concerning the way to organize openness under the regime. Finding a new synthesis to accommodate differing national ideologies may lead to a new paradigm for problem solving.[22] These paradigms are important because they provide "focal points" (in the sense first popularized by Thomas Schelling) for bargaining in games with multiple equilibria. In the final section, I show how the trade debates concerning informatics are accomplishing this.

Leadership by oligopoly also requires more elaborate systems for monitoring cooperative arrangements and sharing costs. This probably means some movement toward more elaborate provisions for automatic retaliations.[23] These burdens also lead to greater reliance on select groups of countries rather than universal bargaining in order to reduce transaction costs. For example, Strange has argued that bilateral liberalization has greatly accelerated the growth of openness in recent years.[24]

Dimensions of International Regimes

International power, domestic politics, and transnational coalitions shape international regimes. But this does not explain what regimes do. In particular, what are the basic options for organizing an open system? As previously noted, international regimes have two components: trade and investment arrangements (the commerce system) and macroeconomic arrangements. This discussion begins with an analysis of macroeconomic arrangements but concentrates primarily on the commerce system.

Macroeconomic Coordination. Every international economic regime presupposes a system for coordinating macroeconomic policies. The system's instrumentalities often involve elements of microeconomic policy, but the logic binding it together centers on overall policies for growth and price stability. A classification of the system of macroeconomic coordination should pay special attention to the purposes and principles of the system rather than its instruments.

The leading power has traditionally set the agenda for international macroeconomic coordination. After World War II the United States helped to restore a fixed exchange rate system, but the model for macroeconomic management was Keynesian. At the international level this led to commitments to adjustment assistance through the International Monetary Fund (IMF), the World Bank, and foreign aid policies to make the costs of international openness more palatable.[25] The system also reflected a central tradition of the U.S. political economy—macroeconomic management is divorced as much as possible from microeconomic management. The Keynesian approach also considerably widened the scope of the macroeconomic regime by making the protection of the social welfare state a legitimate demand in international bargaining. There is little indication that this scope will decrease in the foreseeable future.

Both the gold standard and the early Bretton Woods system relied on the leading power to ensure the liquidity of the world economy. Portfolio investments flowed in and out of London, and a combination of foreign aid and foreign direct investment from the United States greatly facilitated international growth. Both systems ran into trouble when a single power could no longer play the pivotal role in macroeconomic coordination on its own. The transition from British to American leadership took place between World War I and II. More recently, the United States had mixed success in orchestrating the collective coordination of macroeconomic policies through the system of economic summits.[26] This occurred in part because there was a stalemate between the ability of the United States to use the international reserve role of the dollar to finance its deficits and Japan and Germany's ability to resist appreciation of their exchange rates. Only when the misalignment of currencies and budget policies threatened the international trade system did rate realignment occur.

If past history is any guide, there will be two developments in regard to international macroeconomic coordination. First, as the yen is revalued, Japan will be the co-anchor of the world financial system, and its domestic market will be vital to the functioning of the world economy. Therefore, Japan will have to open its domestic market to others and allow the rest of the world access to its capital flow. Otherwise, the world is in for hard times. (West Germany is of less importance in this game.) Second, the management of the macroeconomic system will have to reflect to a much greater degree the domestic policy preferences of Japan and West Germany. This may mean an erosion of the macroeconomic and microeconomic policy split. These preferences, however, must be understood in conjunction with the evolution of the international commerce system.

The International Commerce System. International commercial regimes have two dimensions, both of which reflect economic conditions and government policies. One dimension is the level of transaction costs; the other is the ease of entry into international trade and investment arrangements.

Transaction costs are the costs of establishing economic arrangements and include the costs of information, bargaining, the enforcement of contracts, and asset-specific investments (that is, assets not easily transferred to other uses at acceptable rates of return).[27] Even in very competitive markets, it may prove costly to establish a good reputation, share technological knowledge, or draft a satisfactory contract. Monitoring is often very difficult, and enforcement even more expensive. Moreover, Williamson has noted the need for special organizational forms whenever there are asset-specific investments, even if it is possible to monitor the performance of the players.[28] In general, a decline in international hegemony may increase transaction costs by increasing the risk that a country will renege on its commitments in international markets.[29] The level of transaction costs, however, depends more heavily on two other factors.

One factor is changing technology and economic factors. Many analysts argue that new technology is leading to the customization and specialization of systems, which often require intricate ties with both users and producers of complementary technologies. At the same time, product cycles are becoming shorter, thereby making firms more nervous about returns; this is driving them toward more teaming arrangements with other firms to speed up market penetration and to share risks. Sharing information, specialized designs, and the formation of teams all drive up transaction costs.[30] The other important factor is the rules set by national governments concerning the range of horizontal and vertical contracting permitted among firms. The United States has traditionally had much more restrictive rules than many other countries. This has driven firms in the United States to adopt more transparent agreements than those in other countries.

In summary, technology and industry structure influence transaction costs. But so does political and legal tradition. Societies can tilt the organization of markets toward standardized interchangeable goods, with an emphasis on open, transparent information under universal rules to the greatest degree possible. This is a commodity market with low transaction costs. It is the ideal underlying the free trade system. Or they can emphasize arrangements for production and distribution that favor specialized goods and distribution, with unique blends of producers and distributors tied together in ways that are not readily transparent to others. This is primarily because contracts are not easily written to cover the sharing of information and risk and there are strong incentives to cheat after reaching an agreement.[31] As a result, much of the investment by both buyers and sellers in this market tends to be asset-specific.

Entry into a market may be relatively open due to a combination of government rules and underlying economic conditions (for example, low capital investment and quick returns). The literature on the economic conditions governing the ability to enter a market ultimately rests on very market-specific conditions. In general, analysts assume each industry has stages in its life cycle when entry is either easier or more difficult. But it is becoming more difficult to judge industrial maturity as new manufacturing technologies force major innovations in even such mature industries as steel.

Government policies governing market entry vary according to national political systems and the preferences of firms. In the next two sections I discuss individual countries, but it is possible to distinguish three common dimensions of the shifting preferences of individual firms and transnational coalitions of firms. First, as firms become more internationalized (that is, more geared to international trade or more multinational in their operations), they prefer some form of openness. Therefore, to the extent that key firms in industrial countries are becoming increasingly internationalized, there is a secular trend toward a more open world economy.[32] There is some evidence of such a trend today. Second, except for firms dealing primarily in consumer goods, there is a growing trend toward the internationalization of customers (that is, their major customers are themselves global operations), and customers are tending to create new organizations to act collectively on behalf of their interests as oligopsonists. Third, the role of service firms in organizing trade and investment policy is growing significantly.

To review, the rules of the international commerce system reinforce a blend of levels of transaction costs and degrees of openness. The following analysis concentrates on only three variations of relatively open systems, of which a free trade system is only one major alternative; the more closed systems are discussed in a short note.[33]

The free trade system of open markets with low transaction costs is characterized by relatively easy entry, transparent information, and goods and sales relationships that resemble the classic auction market. Internationally, it has been associated with the principles of nondiscrimination (the most-favored-nation clause), reciprocity (equivalence in concessions in intergovernmental bargaining), and equal rights for foreign businesses engaged in local commerce once they have been granted entry.

A very large percentage of free trade involves more specialized products and assets (for example, brand names) that do not quite fit in this model of perfect commodity trading. This commerce, however, more closely resembles free trade than anything else. Moreover, although foreign investors lost their battles to hold the world to Anglo-American contract law, they have carved out a set of rules concerning investors' international rights. Thus, the dominant commerce system since World War II has been that of free trade. But it has been tempered by a secondary set of rules concerning foreign investment that involves a slightly different combination of openness and transaction costs.

Multinational vertical integration is midway between open and closed, low and high transaction cost markets. The modern multinational developed largely for two reasons. First, it was a response to politically imposed barriers to entry. Firms would invest to circumvent trade barriers or to gain reliable access to raw materials. Second, it took advantage of specialized oligopolistic advantages, many of which involved transaction cost advantages. Economists went so far as to declare that we might need a firm-specific theory of comparative advantage rather than a national one.[34]

In terms of the political economy of international commerce, the U.S. response to many of the limits on trade created by national experiments with closed markets was to encourage the expansion of U.S. multinational corporations.[35] Thus, the multinational corporation represented a critical compromise between demands for more closure and the U.S. insistence on openness and low transaction costs. The international commercial system blended free trade with vertical integration in ways that fit the traditions of U.S. domestic politics.[36] Perhaps a shift in international economic power would simply strengthen the role of multinational corporations in managing world commerce. Another possibility, however, is that the nature and role of the multinational corporation itself may change if there is a significant alteration of international economic power. The model of alliances examines this possibility.

Alliances involve high transaction costs and relatively open markets. If technology, industrial structure, and active micromanagement of markets by governments raise transaction costs while keeping markets formally open with relatively low tariffs and quotas, then alliances are very likely to develop. They are especially likely if government rules allow "ties between production units [that] are often blurred in a haze of semimarket and semiorganizational links between firms involved in different parts of the production process."[37] One might also add that the lines between buyers and sellers also begin to blur.

These alliances permit sharing risks in creating specialized assets (and the reduction of aggregate costs of managing exogenous supply and demand risks) and efforts to build special ties to customers in terms of service and in-depth knowledge of their needs. Risk sharing is one purpose of the Japanese *keiretsu*.[38] Alliance systems feature numerous incentives for horizontal and vertical coordination among firms, including a permissive legal environment.[39] There is also reason to believe that government agencies often contribute directly to the organization of these alliances when it is expected that private actors will fail to pay the costs of the initial organizational effort.[40] Moreover, although there is strong, often oligopolistic competition, governments periodically intervene to control total capacity in order to limit the risks of idle capacity.

Any discussion of alliances quickly raises the issue of the degree to which this category overlaps with the plethora of cases covered in the "strategic trade" literature. For example, much of the literature on strategic trade discusses Cournot bargains where output is the chief variable or Bertrand price setting. This in turn leads to the possibility of closing a national market in order to establish competitive advantages in a foreign market or the use of subsidies for preemptive entry to deter competitors.[41] My analysis optimistically assumes that many of the appropriate policies for discouraging strategic trading are already outlined in the literature.[42] These alliances require specialized governance structures not easily covered by standard trade policy.

The growth of teaming and alliances among international corporations in world markets seems to be increasing. Much of this is probably a result of temporary industrial restructuring that will later yield to traditional foreign investment.[43] But a combination of high transaction costs and active government roles in the market may make alliances a more permanent feature. This is significant when an international power shift occurs at the same time international trade becomes increasingly dominated by high technology and service markets.[44]

Alliances are more likely to be significant if there is a high concentration of buying power (oligopsony) in many of the most profitable segments of the services and high technology markets. For example, a leading global computer company privately estimates that 70 percent of its revenues come from fewer than twelve customers.[45] Moreover, these customers are highly internationalized themselves and so must be pursued on a global scale. Hence, the true closure of world markets is self-defeating. This dimension of global oligopolists versus global oligopsonists is a form of strategic bargaining in global markets that the scholarly literature has not yet explored persuasively.[46]

International alliances often result from a need for significant degrees of customization in services and products and a need to offer customers a flexible family of products and services. Emerging economies of scope in automated batch production and sophisticated service networks make flexibility possible. But it also requires more and more sharing of technology among companies, a particularly difficult task. This poses collective action problems for firms. Many U.S. corporations believe that Japanese firms have found superior solutions to this challenge by having a more active role for government as a catalyst for commercial research and by allowing greater freedom from antitrust restrictions.

Finally, alliances are more likely to be important if major governments play a more active role in overseeing entry and exit from the market, influence a significant degree of purchasing (as in state-owned airline companies), and actively promote joint ventures among companies in the market. Many of the forces that tear alliances apart are counterbalanced by the desire of firms to deal with active governments in partnership with other firms.

In short, these are markets that are not so easily transparent, and governments view entry into them as a matter of joining into alliances of relationships among buyers and sellers. How do governments supervise international markets characterized by alliances? I argue in the last section that U.S. trade diplomacy is experimenting with ways to set rules for markets where alliances matter.

THE UNITED STATES AND THE INTERNATIONAL ORDER

Students of the U.S. political economy point out that unique circumstances shaped its history.[47] From a comparative perspective the most important of these include the following. First, the continental size of the U.S. economy and high transoceanic shipping costs allowed U.S. firms to develop economies of scale in their home market and afforded U.S. firms some "natural" barriers to entry by foreign competition, which were reinforced by U.S. tariffs until World War I. In a significant sense the United States did not have to invent an industrial policy during its development because a general tariff policy was sufficient to nurture industry until it became globally competitive. At the same time, the early commercialization of agriculture meant that it quickly became export oriented.[48] As a result, the United States became committed to the market model of growth in all areas except the service sectors.

Second, compared with other countries the United States had few security problems and a comparatively fast consolidation of power in its central government. This meant that the growth of the state bureaucracy was less explosive in the early history of the United States. This was reinforced by the fact that Congress was an almost unique political institution—an independent legislature as the central political institution of the country and elections based on pluralities in geographic districts.

The political landscape of the United States assisted the early growth (by international standards) of large vertically integrated firms but created elaborate safeguards against horizontal cooperation among these national firms. This compromise was an effort to reduce the advantages of national firms over local regional competitors (which had powerful political support) and to ensure that the benefits of growth flowed to consumers. This led to an enormous legal effort to build transparency in market transactions in order to protect against antitrust violations, to rationalize the national capital markets, and to safeguard consumers. Ideologically, it produced a long-standing consensus opposing efforts by the U.S. government to "micromanage" individual markets.[49]

Until World War I the United States did not have to consider its potential leadership role in the world economy except in the Western Hemisphere. The history of the struggle over U.S. policy for foreign trade, investment, and money is too well known to review. But it is important to note that U.S. firms were not as involved in the world economy as is the case with their Japanese and West German counterparts today.

The disastrous U.S. choices concerning tariff and monetary policies following the economic crisis of 1929 contributed to a significant worsening of the depression. It also opened a way for a new political coalition in the United States that set the ideology guiding the creation of the international economic regime after World War II. This coalition featured a compromise between organized labor and agriculture, which agreed to support each other's policies. Joined with them were the national firms that were geared to mass consumption or the world market. "In the second New Deal . . . we see the pragmatic working out of the postwar social democratic model: a foreign economic policy, full-employment fiscal policy, social insurance transfer payments, trade-union rights in collective bargaining, high wages, and stable monetary policy."[50]

There were some other features to the U.S. domestic compromise on a Keynesian welfare state. The most fundamental was the insistence that the proper role for government was macroeconomic management (primarily by demand management), and government would not attempt to manage individual markets.[51] Meanwhile, the electoral incentives of the members of Congress after the New Deal also led to programs to subsidize consumption at the expense of savings, especially in housing. In addition, with the notable exceptions of military expenditures and some scientific research programs, the United States did not engage in much systematic steering of investments in its economy. The combination of reliance on demand management, proconsumer policies, and the absence of targeting in investment meant that the United States had a propensity to implement policies on the "demand" side of the policy ledger.[52]

When the United States emerged as the clear hegemonic power after World War II, it quickly moved to provide the necessary leadership for reorganizing the international economic regime. Its design for that regime conformed to its natural interests in openness, but the form of openness followed the logic of its own domestic order. Its overall approach favored macroeconomic cooperation while avoiding government oversight of individual international markets, thus preserving the distinction between macromanagement and micromanagement.[53]

The United States undertook a vigorous campaign to encourage political and economic compromises throughout Europe and Japan that would support constitutional democracy and open international economic policies.[54] It was particularly supportive of export-oriented growth. But it also understood that local politics would require more active government policies for economic growth than the United States. Keynesian doctrine made it easier to reconcile this activism with international openness. A principal challenge was how to save the world from a deflationary crisis by making American capital available to the rest of the world through international public institutions such as the IMF and the World Bank and a massive foreign aid program. This combination of policies plus the stimulus to aggregate demand from reopening world trade meant that the international regime would be consistent with demand stabilization.[55]

The second part of the U.S. plan for the world economy was the creation of open markets with low transaction costs for trade and investment. The GATT rules required steady movement toward nondiscrimination, reciprocity in concessions, and transparency in barriers to trade. The GATT fundamentally envisioned a world of auction commodity markets. Yet the GATT never included coverage of the investment sector, because other countries balked at formal multilateral rules as an intrusion on their sovereignty. This objection represented a real fear, but it also masked a deeper dynamic. Many countries were experimenting with formal governmental (Japan) or semiofficial (West German banks) targeting of investments.[56] The United States had to make some difficult choices. Should it seek to dismantle trade barriers and insist on reduced government controls over investments? Or should it accommodate these programs?

One response of the United States was to insist on a commitment to a progressive reduction in tariff barriers over time, although it gave up on any systematic effort to rewrite the basic domestic regulations of other countries. Its second response was more important and strongly influenced by the character of U.S. international firms. It created a dual standard for the international commerce system that basically established investment rights for U.S. firms in industrial nations (see the first section). The dual standard allowed countries to maintain trade barriers if no one actively pushed for reductions, as was the case with Japan for a long time. More importantly, it made the modern multinational corporation a central pillar of the international commerce regime. Although few formal international rules governed multinational corporations, the United States influenced many of the predominant practices through its commercial codes and tax policies.[57]

The multinational corporations represented the middle ground in terms of market openness and transaction costs. Many of their advantages were in terms of transaction costs in imperfect markets. Moreover, to the extent that there were national investment restrictions or trade barriers, a multinational that did gain entry had a further advantage—it was already "grandfathered" in the national market.

This was a classic case of "agents" (a particular form of firm fostered by a regime) skewing outcomes in a market. The U.S. policies were strongly influenced by the way in which U.S. multinationals interacted with Washington. Part of the reason was that exporting and international commerce in the U.S. economy were concentrated in a relatively small percentage of its companies. If they could gain access by means of individual bargaining and investment, the U.S. government was not inclined to press the principle of free trade.[58] And these firms actively identified selective entry privileges as a positive advantage over potential rivals.

Politically, the multinationals profited to such an extent from the comparative advantages of the United States that they rejected any form of targeting of commercial research priorities by the U.S. government. Ironically, as the rest of the world caught up with the United States, economists began to write about national comparative advantages yielding to firm-specific advantages. Even then, as long as leading multinationals believed their global operations guaranteed the necessary economies of scale and innovative research, they were content to support a minimal role for the U.S. government. Today, the active role of firms like IBM in sponsoring organizations like Sematech (a collective under-

taking by U.S. firms to improve their manufacturing skills in semiconductors) suggests that these preferences may be changing.

The result of the activity of multinationals was a double-edged sword.
On one hand, the multinationals built an impressive competitive portfolio on a global scale. Encarnation cites figures that in 1984 the Japanese
consumer purchased $215 in U.S. imports, but he or she bought an ad-
ditional $266 of goods produced in Japan by U.S. multinationals. In the
same year, a U.S. consumer bought $243 in Japanese imports and $44
in locally produced Japanese goods.[59] Moreover, despite the recent competitive problems of the United States in world trade, U.S. multinationals used their offshore activities to maintain their total share of world
markets. On the other hand, as Cohen and Zysman argue, the choices
of the U.S. multinationals raise serious questions about the research and
manufacturing skills of the U.S. economy over the long term.[60] As I argue in the last section, many prominent U.S. multinationals doubt that
they can continue to operate along traditional lines. They are now looking at new patterns of international partnerships and greater cooperation
in domestic industrial projects involving a new role for government.

During the Reagan administration the rising budget deficits, the overvalued dollar, and the mounting trade deficits finally forced a reexamination of the commercial system. Although Congress will experiment to
see if measures to "close" trade markets are politically popular, its leadership still fears the political dangers of massive international conflict.
The stock market crisis of October 1987 served to reinforce this fear.
There is a game of manners and double entendres on Capitol Hill that
only readers of the classic comedies of Feydeau could truly appreciate.
Congress seeks credit for pushing the executive branch of government
into a more aggressive trade policy, but it acts with a firm belief that it
cannot pass its more extreme trade bills. Therefore, the innovations in
trade and investment policy proposed by the executive branch are a better guide to where the United States is heading.

At one level the executive branch is being politically clever but also
very traditional. It emphasizes a new GATT round because a major multilateral negotiation gives the executive branch a bit more latitude and
deflects some protectionist claims. This is the so-called bicycle theory of
trade talks. Moreover, it is desperately rounding up new supporters for
free trade by urging its extension to the service sectors. It has made
clear that the price for helping American Express, Citicorp, or the American Insurance Group is their vigorous support of general free trade.
And, ideologically, it argues that the economic crisis of the 1970s was
partly due to the loss of market discipline and that renewed free trade
should once again assert that discipline. Meanwhile in 1985, Treasury
Secretary Baker reversed the administration's previous pleasure in a highly
valued dollar.

The more interesting message of the executive branch emerges from its bilateral trade negotiations. It is inadvertently experimenting with a new international commercial system that can combine free trade with alliance systems. I examine the central features of informatics diplomacy in the last section. These include experimenting with strategic trading rules, combining packages of services and goods in trade negotiations, building a transnational coalition of support for its services initiative by organizing international oligopsonists, internationalizing reviews of domestic regulations and interest group representation, and expanding the rights of foreign investment.

THE PREFERENCES OF WEST GERMANY AND JAPAN

This section briefly reviews how and why the preferences of West Germany and Japan differ from those of the United States. As I argued in the first section, if there is a shift in international economic power, the international economic regime will have to conform more closely to the domestic economic priorities of the secondary powers. There are many important differences between the Japanese and West German political economic orders. But in the context of the dimensions of an international economic regime, they share a number of important attributes that differ markedly from the United States. This section begins by noting the common ground and then examines the countries individually.

Similarities of the Countries

The two countries share three significant attributes. First, both stressed the merits of export-oriented growth. This priority has shaped international macroeconomic policies, especially exchange rate policies. This priority has also made the two countries far more reluctant to be agents for international growth, as the United States often proposes, even though both followed the United States in adopting more Keynesian policies in the 1960s for their domestic economies. Second, they have both emphasized the virtues of national saving and investment over proconsumer policies, although Japan has been more extreme on this point than West Germany. In addition, both countries have freely targeted investment flows in a way rarely seen in the United States. Japan has done so by direct government oversight of investment flows, while West Germany relies on a handful of oligopolistic banks in consultation with the government. Thus, they have both implemented supply-side policies at the national level. Third, each country has more actively accepted the idea of horizontal cooperation among its firms in order to build and manage economies of scale in key industries.

Japan

The literature on Japanese industrial and macroeconomic policies is so great that it would be foolish to do more than note a few features that are crucial for this analysis. There is a great deal of controversy regarding the degree to which Japan's elaborate industrial policies have succeeded. There is an equally great division over who holds political power in the Japanese system. Is it primarily guided by a group of warring elite ministries or do the Liberal Democratic party (LDP) politicians hold ultimate power? We may never know the degree to which industrial policies, as opposed to macroeconomic policies and pure luck, have accounted for Japanese success. But industrial policies certainly did far less harm than most economists would have predicted and probably have done some good.

Many North American economists argue that strategic trading may occasionally have some benefits, but it is unlikely to be used prudently. The evidence on Japan certainly shows that specific policies often failed, and industries often successfully resisted government initiatives.[61] But the long tenure of politicians, bureaucrats, and business leaders combined with the intense system of consultation and bargaining allows Japan to work out many novel cooperative bargains on how to blend public power and private markets. In short, repetitive bargaining among clearly identifiable players facilitates innovation in dealing with collective action problems.[62]

Just as importantly, the specific distributional payoffs and the political bargaining processes associated with conducting a strategic trade policy became a central feature of the domestic political economy that will not disappear in working out the future of the international economic regime. *The challenge for the international economic order is to create formulas that allow the most powerful states to easily conform to the international order; otherwise, commitments are not credible* (see the first section).

Altogether, the Japanese pattern has firmly established a strong history of government intervention in individual markets. It never accepted the U.S. distinction between macroeconomic and microeconomic management. The Japanese government engaged in both. At the macroeconomic level, as noted already, the system strongly favored supply-side policies that actively bolstered savings, penalized consumers, and targeted investment. At the microeconomic level, especially in the early years, management took the form of export oligopolies and cartels that benefited from protection from foreign competition and detailed government policies for technology transfer and investment promotion.

The classic Japanese system built elaborate ties between suppliers and subcontractors and between suppliers and customers. Foreign firms have come to recognize that these relationships run far deeper than simple arrangements to exclude foreign goods and services. Nor did such relationships eliminate competition among firms. Rather, it was a system that stressed enormous amounts of bargaining and specialized investments. In short, it was a system with very high transaction costs.[63]

With growing dissent over which firms benefit from the classic oligopolistic system and increasing pressure from other countries to open its national market, Japan is shifting its mix of policies. The maturation of Japan as a leading export power has created a constituency of important firms that are highly dependent on exports. The rising importance of services has also given other ministries an opportunity to challenge the Ministry of International Trade and Industry (MITI).

MITI is attempting to reassert its importance by becoming the spokesman for these export-dependent firms by pushing reforms in trade policies and defining a new generation of collective industrial projects in high technology, including services.[64] The government funds and selects participants in collective research projects designed to give Japan an advantage in a new generation of technologies. While these projects are far from uniformly successful, Flamm and Samuels have both concluded that they have successfully demonstrated new ways to conduct research on "generic" technologies and have avoided the tendency of such projects to select items with little likelihood of commercial success.[65] Just as characteristically, the recent introduction of competition in Japanese telecommunications networks stressed ownership of new carriers by a consortium of producers, service firms, and major users. The new networks are vehicles for bargaining on the design of services, the setting of prices, and the design and sharing of technologies of interest to all three groups of owners. The Ministry of Posts and Telecommunications oversees total capacity in the market. Thus, the Japanese approach to telecommunications combines more open entry with a continuation of alliances and government management.

Japan also continues the tradition of intensive consultation with industry associations in formulating specific trade, technology, and research policies. And there will be various attempts to form export cartels and create guidelines in order to reduce trade disputes. MITI is also encouraging leading exporters to create more aggressive multinational production systems as a way to ease trade tensions. Even in the efforts to expand multinational investment there is a strong emphasis on networking. For example, recent MITI talks with industry concerning videocassette recorder (VCR) production in the United States have considered (1) "a parts manufacturing center in the United States to be jointly owned by several Japanese VCR makers," (2) "encouraging Japanese VCR parts manufacturers to set up shop in the United States," and (3) "offering technological assistance to American firms" who supply parts for Japanese VCRs.[66]

At the same time, Japan is opening up its financial system to competition. But, characteristically, the entry of foreign stockbrokers required extensive negotiation over the number and identities of new entrants. Moreover, the government still retains strong incentives for saving, a number of ways to channel investment capital, and considerable powers of persuasion in financial markets (as witnessed by its rallying of the stock market during the October 1987 crisis). Although the Bank of Japan finally accepted the upward revaluation of the yen by the end of 1987, significant questions still remain about how Japan will perform in its role as a financial center for the world money system on a par with New York.

Perhaps most important, former Prime Minister Noboru Takeshita accepted the argument that Japan must create a more self-sufficient demand base by shifting to a slightly more proconsumer policy at home even though many worry about the size of the government budget deficit. (His stand on this issue promises to strengthen his popularity with voters.)[67] The Japanese Economic Planning Agency has linked this shift to Japan's opening its market to the outside world in order to ensure global economic stability and to avoid trade wars. It also insists the shift can occur only if Japan increases its competitiveness in the high technology industries.[68]

Even if Japan realigns its macroeconomic philosophy, it will not simply replicate the American plan for openness. Japan will retain a much more vigorous policy of microeconomic management and coordination than the United States. It also seems likely that the different relationship between macroeconomic and microeconomic policies in Japan will have important consequences.[69] Moreover, Japanese firms operate differently than their American counterparts and will draw regimes increasingly toward their practices. Thus, even if Japan is beginning to evidence some of the zeal for openness of the world economy typically found in world economic leaders, its recipe for the form for "open markets" will surely differ from the one championed by the United States.

West Germany

West Germany's political economy has several unusual features. One is the legacy of the Weimar Republic, a terrific fear of inflationary outcomes that dominates the legacy of macroeconomic policies and gives the central bank an unusual degree of freedom. Another is the legacy of the Nazi era, a rejection of active government policies to manage the industrial sectors of the economy. Yet the legacy of its early industrial history is also a tradition of oligopolistic concentration in key industries, a permissive view toward horizontal cooperation among firms in key sectors, and active intervention by a handful of banks in the "adjustment planning" of firms. More recently, this has produced a system of corporatist bargaining (well-organized associations of industry dealing with

government and well-organized federations of unions) in the private sector and between the public and private sectors. Corporatism plus a strong
social welfare state reinforced commitments to traditional leading sectors
of the economy and, some suggest, hindered a transition to new growth
sectors.[70]

As a result, the West German government engages in little formal
oversight of individual markets. There is a strong commitment to free
trade and allowing the price mechanism to work. Yet the government
actively consults with the banks, who do periodically become involved
in individual markets. Overall, this system has tended toward significant
efforts to create economies of scale for export-oriented businesses in traditional centers of German strength. Combined with a supply-side policy
for macroeconomics and a careful effort to keep the exchange rate competitive, this system produced high growth rates, low inflation, and high
employment. Only recently has growth sagged a bit (to about 2 percent
per annum) and have employment levels slipped significantly (to almost
8 percent unemployment).

West Germany has at least two problems to overcome for the future.
First, West Germany has proved slow to adapt to the revolution in services and has been much more reluctant to introduce competition. One
reason is that the leading service providers have been the pillars of strong
unions and provided a guaranteed purchasing base for the German industrial sector. Another reason is that banks have unusually close ties
with the industrial firms. Second, West Germany's efforts to strengthen
its research and educational resources for the next generation of international products cannot be applied on a national basis. To a degree
unknown in the United States or Japan, Germany has to work out its
strategy with the other members of its home markets on the European
continent.[71] Proponents of telecommunications deregulation in Europe,
for example, have carefully positioned the campaign in the context of the
prospective liberalization of the European Community's internal market
in 1992.

We cannot be certain of the future direction of West German policies.
But West Germany most likely will not drop its supply-side approach;
nor is it likely that it will be a highly cooperative participant in efforts
to synchronize demand policies through the economic summit agreements.[72] The tacit guidance of key sectors of the economy and efforts to
find European solutions to competitiveness questions also will not disappear.

Therefore, it is interesting to note the degree to which West Germany
has encouraged the growth of European corporate alliances as a vehicle
for responding to the next generation of technological challenges. In the
semiconductor business Siemens is gambling on ties to Philips and Toshiba to reestablish its credibility. In aviation it has cautiously but consistently supported Airbus. For advanced nuclear reactors and fuel cycles

it entered into elaborate consortium arrangements with other European countries. More recently, it has participated in the Esprit and Eureka programs to supplement its technological capabilities.

INFORMATICS DIPLOMACY

Three important developments have made the diplomacy of informatics a critical bellwether for the future of the international commercial system. All of these developments involve new strategic calculations by governments and corporations. First, the telecommunications and information industries are critical to organizing competitive advantages in many other service industries, such as banking. Second, services and manufacturing are becoming more interdependent. At a minimum, service companies are key customers for telecommunications and information industry manufacturers. For example, half of IBM's installed base of mainframe computers is in the financial services industry. Third, the telecommunications and computer industries are also becoming more interdependent. For example, the types of telecommunications services influence which types of equipment have advantages, and vice versa. This is particularly important because telecommunications technology is entering a new period of dynamic innovation, and networking is critical to the creation of advantages in data processing. Tyson suggests that this is a critical period for setting standards and building customer relationships that will shape enduring competitive leadership.[73]

These developments forged a coalition for reform in the telecommunications industry in the United States that produced sweeping changes.[74] Large users of telecommunications services (roughly 5 percent of all users generate half of the long-distance revenues), especially the service companies, decided that lower telecommunications costs and new services were crucial to their well-being. They concluded that competition in telecommunications would allow them to exercise their potential market power over pricing and permit more technological innovation in support of new services.

The U.S. electronics industry wanted freer entry into the telecommunications equipment market traditionally monopolized by AT&T to prevent the telecommunications network from becoming a supercomputer that could compete with traditional computer systems. Rival service suppliers in the information industry (ranging from remote computing facilities to banks wanting to offer financial information services) wanted greater freedom in the provision of telecommunications services. AT&T's political opponents consistently belittled any strategic advantages for U.S. international trade generated by the old system. No one talked about phasing in the opening of the U.S. equipment market on a schedule matched to that of U.S. rivals. No one discussed what the comparative magnitudes of the individual segments of the world informatics market were.

After deregulation the U.S. government and industry were subject to a long and painful education on the international market. After a burst of optimism government negotiators learned that it would be difficult to convert the world to American-style free trade. Even more alarmingly, government and industry learned that the United States did not necessarily have dominant advantages. More fundamentally, a new image of the world market and its organization started to emerge from the experience. Although this new image was articulated in formal policy and de facto precedents built up through case-by-case bargaining, its precise dimensions are necessarily speculative. The rest of this section presents the lessons thematically and then reflects on their meaning.

In brief, the United States is experimenting with a strategy to extend and deepen the scope of international competition, including opening up the services sector, which will in turn influence competition in goods. As explained below, part of this initiative involves rules to govern strategic trading and to curb such traditional forms of targeting as export subsidies and dumping. But even if these reforms succeed, there will be a greater role for alliances. These alliances reflect the growing internationalization and parity of power among international firms, the traditions of greater collaboration among West German and Japanese firms, the particular characteristics of the informatics industry, and the continuing active role of governments in targeting investments and micromanaging markets. High transaction costs and declining U.S. hegemony (as argued in the first section) will lead to increased monitoring of trade arrangements, fewer universal agreements, and more specialized enforcement arrangements.

The emergence of services as a critical part of the informatics industry means major firms are much more conscious of a continuing need to ensure political access to the market. On average, governments have much more tightly regulated the provision of services than of goods. The convergence of goods and services makes the political dimension of the informatics market more crucial. But how do the key actors calculate the stakes?

Governments do not devise strategies for sectors in a vacuum; rather, they seek to promote the interests of their firms. While governments differ in the degree to which they second-guess or try to direct their companies, their planning horizons invariably look a bit like those of companies. Therefore, if the purpose is to predict government sectorial policies, it is important to examine the stakes in the world market not in terms of absolute market size and trends but rather in terms of the markets that companies seek to win and control.

Customers and specialized technologies are not easily interchangeable.

But there is a substantial degree of interdependence between the core technologies and the development and manufacturing skills for a broad range of information technologies and services. Strategic planners of three global information companies estimate that the global information market for goods and services, broadly defined (for example, including robotics), will reach $2,150 billion in 1990, with the U.S. market alone accounting for $1,250 billion. The forecast suggests two things. First, the United States will continue to dominate the market. Therefore, leading firms around the world want access to the U.S. market, and they will pressure their governments to bargain for that access. Second, the market outside the United States is growing faster than that in the United States. So, leading U.S. firms will have to position themselves in those markets (as Stephen Hymer first surmised almost thirty years ago).

No firm can target all countries or technologies. So it is important to have some idea of what large firms in telecommunications and information systems might attempt. As a rule of thumb, very large firms might compete in countries and products that involve a maximum of 30 percent of these totals (the contestable market for the firm). A very large company might claim less than a 15 percent share of its contestable market, or perhaps sales of about $100 billion for a true giant, in 1990. So, there will be no "colossus" of information that will dominate the industry, although most firms believe that the gap between leading and secondary firms will continue to grow larger.

A leading firm in the informatics industry, a "major," may totally ignore television or robotics. This choice is optional. There is a core of communications, computing, and microelectronic equipment and services, however, around which it must position itself, even if it does not compete in all parts of the core. The service side of the informatics market core is much greater than the equipment side, but most of the services market is not contestable in the near term even though further liberalization is likely. Table 5.1 gives an estimate of the core market for an informatics major in 1995, provided the current round of U.S. trade diplomacy is quite successful. The calculations (optimistically) assume that all equipment markets except for telecommunications network equipment are largely contestable. But, like most corporate forecasts, the calculations assume that the company will not compete vigorously in every country.

Table 5.1 reveals three important features of the market. First, equipment and components are still the heart of the world industry. Second, the growth in services will be by far the largest new factor in the market in the next decade, and firms have to position themselves accordingly. Third, most of the services market remains uncontestable. This means that no major informatics company can operate without careful regard to the linkages between the contestable and uncontestable areas of the services market. This requires political strategies for handling the regulatory

TABLE 5.1
Core Market for an Informatics Major
in Major Industrial and Developing Nations in 1995
(in Billions of 1983 U.S. Dollars)

Telecommunications network equipment (switches, cables, satellites, etc.)[a]	35
Telecommunications customer premises equipment (office switchboards, telephones, data terminals, etc.)	40
Semiconductors and electronics components	100
Computers	130
Total equipment market	305
Information and computer services (selected software, remote computing, electronic messaging, etc.)	125
Potentially contestable basic and value-added services:[b]	
Data communications[c]	13
International long distance and telex[d]	20
Domestic	0
Total services market	158
Total market	463

SOURCE: Author estimates based on interviews with strategic planners of three global informatic companies.

[a]Assumes 50 percent of network equipment is contestable.

[b]Total global market for basic, value-added, and information services is estimated at $450 billion. Contestable is that part of the market that might be open to competition by foreign firms.

[c]Assumes data communications services will be 7 percent of market and less than half of the total may be contestable.

[d]Assumes 10 percent growth rate minimum for international services and possibility of some degree of contestability of the United States, United Kingdom, and Japanese markets.

dimension. At the same time, the ties among the market segments are driving firms to form alliances even as they try to become more international. The degree of internationalization of these firms differs substantially. Corporate reports show that IBM is a firm with a true global base, which earns about 43 percent of its revenues outside the United States, and it is increasingly moving toward teaming for "vertical segments" of the market because the need for system packages is too extensive for it to cover on its own. On the other hand, AT&T earns 95 percent of its revenues in the U.S. market. Siemens of West Germany earns 46 percent of its revenues in the domestic market, 5 percent in the United States, and the remainder primarily in other European countries. NEC, however, earns about 77 percent of its revenues in Japan, with the remainder divided equally between the U.S. and other markets.

The United States has successfully extended the scope of the free trade system during the past decade, but it has had to accept the principle of active micromanagement of sectors by other governments. It is easy to be cynical about the U.S. initiatives concerning free trade in services. In fact, the old monopoly and economies-of-scale models that dominated the major service industries are crumbling. But they have not yielded to free trade in the classic sense. Instead, a hybrid-market model for services developed that resembles the alliance system.

A new diplomatic rule of thumb is emerging for information services. It recognizes that foreign entry into the basic-services infrastructure, such as local phone calls, may be regulated or even banned. But it permits foreign firms to compete for all large national and international customers and for the segments of the market other than the basic infrastructure (for example, value-added and information services are contestable). The total number of entrants may be limited at any one time, as in international airlines or telephone networks, but it is not legitimate to fix shares for individual firms or to keep the total share fixed. It is not legitimate to exclude foreign interests, but foreign interests may, in practical terms, be expected to accept minority equity shares in an enterprise.[75]

In practical terms this approach to communications services has tremendous implications for the contestability of the equipment market. When the use of equipment entails significant joint development and sharing of technical knowledge between suppliers and users, the degree of contestability of networks influences the contestability of interconnecting manufacturing. For example, basic services, primarily telephone, remain rather strongly regulated even where provided competitively. As a result, many segments of the network equipment market remain substantially closed. However, all segments of this equipment market are more contested than ten years ago, because some areas of network services are subject to greater competition. Major phone companies are reducing their subsidies to national equipment suppliers because of competitive pressures.[76]

Data transmission and information services (remote data processing, for example) are becoming competitive. So, too, is the related field of customer premises equipment such as phone sets to private switchboards and minicomputers. This equipment requires less capital investment and its makers emphasize that sophisticated users should be able to control the communications network through their own office equipment.[77]

A significant political shift has occurred in the transnational coalition supporting free trade. The coalition for competition in the United States has not appeared uniformly across national boundaries for two reasons—industrial structures vary across countries and political processes differ sufficiently to favor varying policy options. The biggest variation in informatics in Japan, West Germany, and the United States is in the structure of the national electronics industries.

Germany's strength in informatics (except in semiconductors) is extraordinarily concentrated in Siemens.[78] Traditionally, the Bundespost garnered support by using its procurement policy to subsidize weaker electronics companies. The United States had a very competitive domestic electronics industry, and AT&T effectively discriminated against all other companies. The Japanese structure was traditionally oligopolistic, and Nippon Telephone and Telegraph Company (NTT) effectively favored four of the traditional leaders. As more companies became important in informatics, they became champions of change in Japan.[79]

The common denominator to calls for policy change is the emergence of international oligopsonists as leaders in market reform. This constitutes an important shift in the political structure of international commerce. In the informatics debate some companies (especially in the service industries) are identifying strategic opportunities to reorganize the provision of key inputs to their international operations. They control a large part of the market and are relatively few in number. Therefore, they are relatively easy to mobilize for politics.

The U.S. trade offensive since the Tokyo Round has identified these users, especially in the service industries, as a powerful transnational coalition. This coalition has proved sufficiently successful that U.S. firms now use foreign governments to promote U.S. trade policies. For example, the U.S. government encouraged large multinational firms in Europe to form a users group to influence telecommunications regulation in Europe. And a major U.S. trade association in information and computer services, ADAPSO, now turns to the European Community for support in its policy initiatives in the United States. The evidence in Japan and West Germany suggests that the style of national policy-making somewhat influences the role of service providers, but fundamentally there are complementary interests at work. The West German government's national commission on telecommunications (the Witte Commission) recommended in 1987 that the country keep a monopoly over the physical infrastructure for communications (thus pleasing the unions) but endorsed open competition in the provision of communications services over these facilities (thus pleasing the multinational firms).

The new trade negotiations are "internationalizing" domestic regulations to a degree never before contemplated. Eventually, this may influence the organization of representation in national trade associations.[80] Since the 1940s there has been a strong line drawn between international commerce and legitimate domestic regulation and policy. This line also legitimated the very powerful industrial associations in many countries that exclude foreign membership. The Tokyo Round of the GATT began the effort to reclaim jurisdiction over domestic regulation by focusing on codes for nontariff barriers related to subsidies, government procurement, and the setting of technical standards. No one was very satisfied by the outcome, but it was just a beginning when compared with negotiations in recent years, as examples below illustrate.

With a powerful boost from competitive market pressures the U.S. government is succeeding in its campaign to shift countries to technical standards of "no harm to the network" and "generic-type testing" for most customer premises equipment. The next step is likely to be standards governing how the national network may be designed in order to guarantee that foreign firms can compete, as the European Community is now attempting. In 1987 Japan's Ministry of Posts and Telecommunications ruled that NTT would have to conform its future network design much more closely to U.S. and European designs.

The United States has won battles over the pricing of leased communications channels for its companies and has established the principle that a national service monopoly must set prices for the use of its facilities in such a way that competitive entry into the domestic market by foreign firms is feasible. The U.S.-Canada free trade agreement negotiated in 1987 formalizes these requirements as a treaty obligation. The United States has also negotiated with Japan concerning how it may divide up the regional jurisdiction for companies offering cellular telephone systems in Japan. The United States argued that the proposed division effectively barred Motorola from too much of the market.

The United States is arguing that the question of which government agency has regulatory jurisdiction over the informatics market is subject to trade negotiations. The United States insists that the telecommunications authorities of the world should not have sole jurisdiction over computer and information services and that trade ministries should have a right to oversee the decisions of telecommunications authorities. The United States has challenged the exclusion of foreign firms from government-industry boards with important powers in regard to standards and regulation. In both Japan and West Germany, the United States has pressed for the right of U.S. firms to sit on national industrial boards. This has already succeeded to some extent in Japan.

The United States is formalizing the rights of investment in informatics industries far more broadly than in the past. This particular battle is more acute in Japan than in Western Europe, but it holds true in all countries. The United States is arguing that there is a functional equivalent to the right to invest, or euphemistically "the right to do business," in key service markets. The symbolic battle in informatics occurred in Japan. MITI and the procompetition coalition in Japan assisted the United States in establishing the right of foreign ownership of information and data communications services in Japan. It also won the right for minority foreign ownership of basic services and communications facilities in Japan. Britain and the United States then pressured Japan to license a new international long-distance phone company in Japan that is effectively under foreign leadership. The United States is currently pressing West Germany on value-added and information issues and is threatening potential retaliation if it does not receive satisfactory results.

Significantly, the U.S. government and U.S. companies have recognized that minority ownership in partnership with local interests not only is acceptable but in many cases is the only route to effective market entry. This leads to a situation of enormous importance for the international commercial system: governments are treating "openness" as an issue of the "right to invest" and are judging fair entry by the ability of their firms to find satisfactory national partners.

Acquiring local partners is standard practice in the world of multinational corporations, and the U.S. government yielded long ago to demands for local ownership and content. What is new is the movement toward implicitly demanding the "right" to credible local partners in the informatics industries. In effect, the U.S. government is evaluating the quality of the local commercial partners available to U.S. firms as one piece of evidence of openness in a market. This is a subtle process, in part because the government is badly equipped for the task and in part because it is supposed to shun such an explicit intrusion into business. Nonetheless, American firms actively discuss the quality of their partners in informing the government of their effective access to the market. For example, Motorola obtained Toshiba as a partner in manufacturing high-density memory chips (Toshiba technology) and microprocessors (Motorola technology), a move that many saw as a promising sign of better U.S. access. More baldly, when there are restrictions on the percentage of foreign equity (as in some telecommunications services), the U.S. government makes clear that it worries about the quality of local partners.

There is greater reliance on strategic trade policy to enforce rights to entry and define alliance rights. Although the Reagan administration rejected the congressional legislation for mandatory sanctions over a broad range of trade issues, it tended toward the use of strategic trading policy in selected segments of the informatics market. The U.S.-Japanese semiconductor agreement is the best-known case. But Washington is actively threatening use of its Section 201 and 301 powers (U.S. Trade Act of 1974) to retaliate against closure of network equipment and value-added service markets. West Germany is particularly at risk that Siemens will be penalized in the United States. The Federal Communications Commission (FCC) failed in 1987 to win the support of other government agencies and U.S. business to bolster its power to review foreign penetration of the U.S. informatics market, including purchases of foreign equipment by major phone companies. But the threat of allowing the FCC to do so has already been used in bilateral talks. The problems posed by the U.S.-Japan semiconductor agreement on market pricing suggest why bilateral pricing agreements are likely to become subject to better GATT guidelines in the future.[81] But this agreement also shows how special governance structures in informatics may emerge.

The semiconductor agreement basically conceded that it is impossible to ban all important forms of export promotion or import controls. Implicitly it says that ensuring basic good faith in international competition is very difficult unless there is informed local participation by foreign firms. Therefore, although Japan denies having made any binding commitment, the two parties set targets for minimum market shares (or sales) for U.S. firms. Most of these targets will not be met, but they provide a basis for reviewing ongoing problems and finding good allies for foreign corporations. Since the first telecommunications negotiations between the United States and Japan, the two countries have adopted a series of targets that have not been met. In short, targets are a device for exchanging information and staking claims, not realistic guides to dividing up the market.

As an example, consider that the response of MITI to the semiconductor agreement is the creation of an International Semiconductor Cooperation Center (INSEC) with membership of MITI, leading Japanese firms, and major suppliers from the United States and Europe. Public discussions stress how INSEC will facilitate marketing and research exchanges between Japanese and non-Japanese firms, while also gathering data on foreign sales in Japan. No doubt, this is in part a device employed by the Japanese to divert attention from the failure to achieve the target of a 20 percent share for U.S. firms in the Japanese market. Japanese estimates, which are higher than those of the United States, suggest that the U.S. share has grown from 10.3 to 12.7 percent.[82]

More significantly, private bargaining has focused on the need for INSEC to facilitate full disclosure of sourcing requirements by Japanese firms. U.S. firms particularly want access to the initial stages of product design, and NEC at least says that it will allow access. In return, U.S. firms in Japan will have to form stronger industry associations for group bargaining. Japanese firms and government officials have pressed INSEC to undertake broader global market analyses. Some have also urged the U.S. government to pressure U.S. firms to commit sufficient resources on a sustained basis to succeed in the Japanese market.[83]

There is growing support for pooled efforts among firms to build up the national competitive infrastructure. (European countries are doing more of this on a collective basis.) The major news in the United States is the effort by many of its leading informatics firms to undertake common research projects, set standards, and share manufacturing expertise. MCI, the Semiconductor Research Corporation, the Corporation for Open Systems (COS), and Sematech are four of the most prominent.[84]

These ventures represent a steady movement toward partnerships among firms and civilian government agencies (including local authorities) for the application of expertise, especially in manufacturing and common architectures for complex systems. COS and Sematech explicitly acknowledge that even the largest U.S. firms could not simply build individual alliances to supplement their individual capabilities (for example, IBM's temporary equity stake in Intel). There is a shared interest in creating technologies that will build a community of suppliers and designers, thus building diversity, security, and flexibility into the pool of options available for any single firm. Moreover, these ventures reflect a growing consensus that military leadership is not the best way to nurture commercial technology.

The growing reliance on joint research in Europe and the United States for commercial projects poses two important challenges to the international commercial system. The first, and conceptually simpler, is what to do about the role of foreign firms. Many of the more important ventures make significant enough demands on their members to make it imperative to permit exclusion of firms that will not contribute fully. But who should be allowed to enter? International trade rules will soon have to address what rights foreign firms have to participate in "local" research consortia. The COS bargained for access to Japanese research projects in return for Japanese membership in COS. Sematech, which is to spend $250 million (split equally between government and industry), is restricted to U.S. firms. Yet somewhat hypocritically, the United States has pressed Japan for better access to various consortia for government and industry R&D. MITI has announced plans to accommodate this demand.[85]

The second, and more subtle, issue involves the political implications of these developments for the United States and Western Europe. Implicitly, these developments represent an acknowledgment by the leading firms that their informatics sectors require further reorganization. Firms are going to become even more internationalized, including through multiple cross-national alliances. However, internationalization is going to increase, not decrease, the demand for an active government role in promoting industrial adjustment. A more active role for government is politically predictable. There is no reason why it should necessarily lead to the end of openness in the world economy.

NOTES

1. It is important to understand that openness is not the same as a total absence of controls over a market. In the context of the international economy, openness suggests that there is no discrimination between domestic and foreign suppliers or among foreign suppliers of different countries. Obviously, the world economy does not come close to this definition of openness. See the instructive essay of J. David Richardson, " 'Strategic' Trade Policy: Research and Practice

in the United States," in Richard G. Lipsey and Wendy Dobson, eds., *Shaping Comparative Advantage* (Toronto: C. D. Howe Institute, 1986), pp. 91–108.

2. Robert O. Keohane, *After Hegemony* (Princeton: Princeton University Press, 1985).

3. This definition differs from those offered by conventional approaches to the trade regime because it views foreign investment and trade as alternative ways of opening or closing the international flow of the factors of production (Peter F. Cowhey and Edward Long, "Testing Theories of Regime Change: Hegemonic Decline or Surplus Capacity," *International Organization* 37, no. 2 [Spring 1983]: 157–88).

4. Presumably, the further evolution of such international institutions could reduce the need for dominant leaders.

5. Duncan Snidal, "The Limits of Hegemonic Stability Theory," *International Organization* 39, no. 4 (Autumn 1985): 579–614; Stephen D. Krasner, *Asymmetries in Japanese-American Trade—The Case for Specific Reciprocity* (Berkeley: Institute of International Studies, 1987).

6. Robert Gilpin, *U.S. Power and the Multinational Corporation* (New York: Basic Books, 1975); Charles Kindleberger, *The World in Depression* (Berkeley and Los Angeles: University of California Press, 1973).

7. Snidal, "Limits of Hegemonic Stability Theory."

8. For example, smaller capitalist states have largely adopted relatively efficient systems of centralized bargaining among government officials, business, and labor to facilitate rapid adaptation to shifts in the international economy. They largely accept and favor open world economies as rational "price takers." These bargining systems, however, may create irregularities in some trade practices that the leading powers must accept (James E. Alt, "Party Strategies, World Demand, and Unemployment: The Political Economy of Economic Activity in Western Industrial Nations," *American Economic Review Proceedings* 75 [1985]: 57–61). My approach to the question of hegemony reflects the criticisms raised by Timothy McKeown, "Hegemonic Stability Theory and Nineteenth-Century Tariff Levels in Europe," *International Organization* 37, no. 1 (Winter 1983): 73–129; Snidal, "Limits of Hegemonic Stability Theory"; and Arthur Stein, "The Hegemon's Dilemma: Great Britain, the United States, and International Economic Order," *International Organization* 38 (1984): 355–86.

9. Waltz had made the point concerning the role of hegemons as examplars (Kenneth Waltz, *Theory of International Politics* [Reading, Mass.: Addison-Wesley, 1979]). More generally, students of international political economy have long puzzled over the degree of learning that takes place among countries on how to solve collective problems. More recently, they have recast this analysis into an inquiry of how the paradigm for understanding politics and economics is determined. This theme ties together the influential works of Robert Cox and John Ruggie, although they reach different conclusions. For samples of their work see Robert Keohane, ed., *Neorealism and Its Critics* (New York: Columbia University Press, 1986).

10. John Gerard Ruggie, "International Regimes, Transactions, and Change: Embedded Liberalism in the Postwar Economic Order," in Stephen Krasner, ed., *International Regimes* (Ithaca: Cornell University Press, 1983), pp. 195–232. Ruggie's approach stresses domestic politics much more than Yarborough and

Yarborough do in their provocative explanation of British hegemony, which stresses relatively low transaction costs as the key to its character (Elizabeth Yarborough and Robert Yarborough, "Cooperation in the Liberalization of International Trade: After Hegemony, What?" *International Organization* 41, no. 1 [Winter 1987]: 1–26). Ikenberry has done important work on linking a country's domestic order to its preferences for international regimes, although my analysis differs from his on several important counts, especially on the role of political leadership and private interests (John Ikenberry, "The State and Strategies of Adjustment," *World Politics* 39 [October 1986]: 53–77).

11. Secondary powers make commitments to economic programs based on expectations of rules generated by the leading powers. The returns from these programs may be greatly at risk if the leader varies from expectations. On the concept of credible commitments see Oliver Williamson, *The Economic Institutions of Capitalism* (New York: Free Press, 1985), pp. 167–68. For an excellent essay showing why the ability to make binding precommitments is very important for international economics, see David Currie and Paul Levine, "Macroeconomic Policy Design in an Interdependent World," in Willem H. Buiter and Richard C. Marston, eds., *International Economic Policy Coordination* (Cambridge: Cambridge University Press, 1985).

12. Another way to build credibility is for the dominant power to make specialized investments of political capital and military assets (including the creation of hostages) that cannot be easily transferred without imposing great losses on the dominant power. This is certainly true of such organizations as NATO. Larsen has also pointed out that commitments increase in credibility if the top leadership takes some political risks in making the agreement more ambitious (Deborah Welch Larsen, "Crisis Prevention and the Austrian State Treaty," *International Organization* 41, no. 1 [Winter 1987]: 27–60).

13. Krasner, *Asymmetries in Japanese-American Trade.*

14. Peter F. Cowhey, *The Problems of Plenty* (Berkeley and Los Angeles: University of California Press, 1985); Albert Hirschman, *The Passions and the Interests* (Princeton: Princeton University Press, 1977).

15. McCraw and O'Brien make a similar point concerning domestic market structures (Thomas K. McCraw and Patricia O'Brien, "Production and Distribution: Industrial Policy and Competition," in Thomas K. McCraw, ed., *America versus Japan* [Cambridge: Harvard Business School Press, 1986]).

16. Oliver Hart and Bengt Homstrom, "The Theory of Contracts" (Massachusetts Institute of Technology, Department of Economics, Working Paper no. 418, 1986).

17. Richardson has argued that the rise of the multinational corporation itself created new issues regarding strategic trading (J. David Richardson, "International Coordination of Trade Policy" [paper presented at the National Bureau of Economic Research Conference on International Coordination of Economic Policy, 1987]). Cohen has explored how the nature of U.S. commercial banks influences the workings of the international financial system (Benjamin Cohen, *In Whose Interest?* [New Haven: Yale University Press, 1986]). For the large oil firms, see Peter F. Cowhey, "The Engineers and the Price System Revisited," in Jonathan D. Aronson and Peter F. Cowhey, eds., *Profit and the Pursuit of Energy: Markets and Regulation* (Boulder: Westview, 1983). For a comparison

of nineteenth-century British and twentieth-century U.S. firms and their effect on foreign economic policy, see Charles Lipson, *Standing Guard* (Berkeley and Los Angeles: University of California Press, 1985).

18. This transformation is partially captured in Michael E. Porter, "Competition in Global Industries: A Conceptual Framework," in Michael E. Porter, ed., *Competition in Global Industries* (Cambridge: Harvard Business School Press, 1986).

19. Charles Maier, "The Politics of Productivity: Foundations of American International Economic Policy after World War II," in Peter J. Katzenstein, ed., *Between Power and Plenty* (Ithaca: Cornell University Press, 1975), pp. 23–49.

20. My approach differs from the literature on the transnational relations of the 1970s that expected complex interdependence to reduce the coherence of policy or to foster the growth of horizontal ties among social interests that would reduce the importance of loyalty to the nation-state.

21. Bruce Russett, "The Mysterious Case of Vanishing Hegemony; Or, Is Mark Twain Really Dead?" *International Organization* 39, no. 2 (Spring 1985): 207–32.

22. Modelski suggests that the agenda-setting power of the United States remains very important, and therefore, debates within the United States are vital clues to a possible new synthesis (George Modelski, *Long Cycles in World Politics* [Seattle: University of Washington Press, 1986]).

23. J. David Richardson has argued that such active dissuasionary policies can include countervailing and antidumping measures that go beyond those traditionally contemplated. However, the measures must be transparent, nondiscriminatory, and self-liquidating. This is one reason why some analysts are urging a reliance on tariffs rather than quantitative measures (Richardson, " 'Strategic' Trade Policy," pp. 100–101).

24. Susan Strange, "Protectionism and World Politics," *International Organization* 39, no. 2 (Spring 1985): 233–60.

25. Britain in the nineteenth century essentially pushed a system of fixed exchange rates set on the gold standard that favored balanced budgets and price stability. The gold standard in theory set the limits for macroeconomic and monetary policies in all major trading countries. In addition to providing adjustment assistance, the Keynesian synthesis emphasized formal international rules for prudent behavior by key actors and how to share risks in regard to key international problems. Today, for example, as international financial markets become more interdependent, each country is being urged to take responsibility for the global obligations of its national banks, and countries are standardizing certain reserve requirements for all banks in order to reduce risks of a global financial crisis. See Ruggie, "International Regimes, Transactions, and Change"; Peter Norman, "Seventeen Industrial Nations Draft Pact on Big Banks' Capital-Adequacy Needs," *Wall Street Journal*, 23 October 1987, p. 18.

26. In the early 1960s, the United States became more concerned about the level of its economic performance. It intensified its reliance on demand management by adopting more active Keynesian management techniques, and other countries soon followed. See Michael G. Rukstad, "Fiscal Policy and Business-Government Relations," in McCraw, *America versus Japan*, pp. 299–336; and Peter A. Katzenstein, "Economic Management in the Federal Republic of Germany," *German Studies Newsletter*, no. 8 (1986): 3–10. When the pressures of its IMF obligations grew very onerous under Nixon, the top political leadership

of the United States decided to shift to floating rates so that it would be easier to pursue discretionary macroeconomic policies and security objectives. See Joanne Gowa, *Closing the Gold Window* (Ithaca: Cornell University Press, 1983). Since that time, the oil shocks and stagflation have turned the United States into a champion of rather broad-ranging consultation on macroeconomic coordination among the leading powers in order to reduce its burdens. See Robert Putnam and Nicholas Bayne, *Hanging Together* (Cambridge: Harvard University Press, 1984).

27. John Joseph Wallis and Douglas C. North, "Integrating Transaction Costs into Economic History" (Washington University, Political Economy Working Papers, September 1986). Yarborough and Yarborough, in "Cooperation in Liberalization," point to transaction costs as central determinants of international regimes.

28. Williamson, *Economic Institutions of Capitalism*, p. 247.

29. Yarborough and Yarborough, "Cooperation in Liberalization."

30. Ibid.

31. A very good example of a relatively open market with high transaction costs—in part because of the legal precedents of the industry—is the making of motion pictures in the United States. Wallis and North make the crucial point that procedures seek to optimize a mix of production and transaction productivity (Wallis and North, "Integrating Transaction Costs"). Many innovations raise transaction costs but have more-than-offsetting benefits for production. This principle explains why Japanese firms may set up systems that have high transaction costs but open up unique production possibilities.

32. Millner's important new study covers both French and U.S. firms in the 1930s and the present. Despite the differences in the traditional roles of the two governments, she finds that the firms in both countries react in very similar ways. She also finds interdependence to be rising at firm level. Nowell's findings support many of Millner's points concerning the French oil industry. See Helen Millner, "Resisting the Protectionist Temptation" (Ph.D. diss., Harvard University, 1986); Gregory Nowell, "The French State and the Developing World Oil Market: Domestic, International, and Environmental Constraints, 1864–1928," *Research in Political Economy* 6 (1983): 225–76.

33. There are two types of more closed regimes: the "guild" model and cartels and national oligopolies. The "guild" model is characterized by closed markets with high transaction costs and refers to any system where specialized producers in relatively closed markets with a strong degree of domestic micromanagement dominate. International commerce is organized primarily by professional trading companies. This system dominated the early revival of the European economy and the mercantilist era of the fifteenth through eighteenth centuries in Europe. Markets were not assumed to be open; merchant houses were primarily developed to seek out bilateral opportunities (Eric R. Wolf, *Europe and the People without History* [Berkeley and Los Angeles: University of California Press, 1982], pp. 83–87, 119–20, and 268–70). Trading companies often play similar roles for countries today. See Stephen Cohen and John Zysman, *Manufacturing Matters* (New York: Basic Books, 1987), pp. 44–45, for their discussion of West Germany's Metallgesellschaft.

Cartels and national oligopolies are also characterized by closed markets but involve relatively low transaction costs. Many countries have been greatly concerned about building economies of scale in relatively small national markets. Related to these worries are concerns about surplus capacity, because the market is not allowed to "clear" automatically. In the most extreme case, concerns over achieving economies of scale in natural monopolies lead to the national utility model for providing telecommunications and airlines. This model has also shown up in such manufacturing and commodity markets as steel and energy.

If the European obsession with scale economies and static learning curves (moving along the experience curve for a single technology) dominated the future, as it did in many of the old programs for national champions, we would quickly see a world of national oligopolies where the task would be to find "nice strategies" for strategic trade (Paul R. Krugman, ed., *Strategic Trade Policy and the New International Economics* [Cambridge: MIT Press, 1985]).

34. Some of the special competitive assets were tied to technology, but many had to do with superior brand name image, close ties to major world customers, and advantages in marketing or financial know-how (Paul Krugman, "The 'New Theories' of International Trade and the Multinational Enterprise," in Charles P. Kindleberger and David B. Audretsch, eds., *The Multinational Corporation in the 1980s* [Cambridge: MIT Press, 1983], pp. 57–73).

35. Cowhey and Long, "Testing Theories."

36. McCulloch and Owen estimated that one-quarter of U.S. exports were intracorporate transfers (Rachel McCulloch and Robert F. Owen, "Linking Negotiations on Trade and Foreign Direct Investment," in Kindleberger and Audretsch, *Multinational Corporation in the 1980s*, pp. 334–58).

37. Cohen and Zysman, *Manufacturing Matters*, p. 149.

38. Masahiko Aoki, *The Co-operative Game Theory of the Firm* (New York: Oxford University Press, 1984).

39. At the national level a key to the revival of the European economy is the growth of alliances of contractors and subcontractors working collectively to create flexible production systems in order to compete in international markets (Michael Piore and Charles Sabel, *The Second Industrial Divide* [New York: Basic Books, 1984]). Friedman reports similar patterns in the Japanese machine tool industry (David Friedman, "The Misunderstood Miracle—Political and Economic Decentralization in Japan" [Ph.D. diss., Massachusetts Institute of Technology, 1984]). This also seems to be at the heart of what Dore has called "flexible rigidities" in the Japanese market (Ronald Dore, *Flexible Rigidities* [Stanford: Stanford University Press, 1986]).

40. Chalmers Johnson, *MITI and the Japanese Economic Miracle* (Stanford: Stanford University Press, 1982); McCraw and O'Brien, "Production and Distribution."

41. Barbara J. Spencer and James A. Brander, "International R&D Rivalry and Industrial Strategy," *Review of Economic Studies* 50 (October 1983): 707–22; Avinash K. Dixit and Albert S. Kyle, "On the Use of Trade Restrictions for Entry Promotion and Deterrence," *American Economic Review* 75 (1985): 139–52.

42. Brander also points out that many of the cases in strategic trade theory are welfare- and trade-creating and, therefore, require no remedy (James A. Brander, "Shaping Comparative Advantage: Trade Policy, Industrial Policy, and Economic Performance," in Lipsey and Dobson, *Shaping Comparative Advantage*, pp. 1–56).

43. David C. Mowery, *Alliance Politics and Economics* (Cambridge, Mass.: Ballinger Publishing Co., 1987).

44. This analysis does not suggest that alliances are equivalent to the pattern of global cartels that Edward Mason estimated dominated 40 to 50 percent of world trade between 1929 and 1937. This system is far more competitively organized (although it is also possible that Mason overestimated the restrictions on competition posed by the alliances of firms in that earlier period). See James A. Ruhl, "International Cartels and Their Regulation," in Oscar Schacter and Robert Hellawell, eds., *Competition in International Business* (New York: Columbia University Press, 1981), pp. 240–82.

45. Interviews held in 1987.

46. The strategic trade literature has concentrated primarily on optimal tariff policies in regard to purchasing power.

47. Ikenberry, "The State and Strategies of Adjustment"; Thomas McCraw, "Rethinking the Trust Question," in Thomas McCraw, ed., *Regulation in Perspective: Historical Essays* (Cambridge: Harvard Business School Press, 1981).

48. Nineteenth-century politics in the United States centered on a continuing battle between a coalition of industry and urban labor (which favored high tariffs) and agriculture (which favored low tariffs and easy money policies). However, both sides favored agricultural exports.

49. There was nothing to stop the government from using tax and land policies to encourage certain industries as a whole. But ideas such as creating "recession cartels" or implementing other devices of micromanagement met with strong resistance.

50. Peter A. Gourevitch, *Politics in Hard Times* (Ithaca: Cornell University Press, 1986), p. 153.

51. Given the continuing strength of conservative voters in the United States, this task was carried out primarily by automatic stabilizers (such as Social Security) until the 1960s. See Rukstad, "Fiscal Policy."

52. Piore and Sabel have called this system "Fordism" because it combines demand stabilization with an industrial system built on standardized goods on large production runs (Piore and Sabel, *Second Industrial Divide*).

53. Even when State Department and White House negotiators became interested in micromanagement in the form of the many commodity codes proposed in the International Trade Organization (ITO), Congress rejected it. This was probably fortunate for the international trade system because the domestic market arrangements in the United States made the ITO a less-than-credible commitment. Initially, the United States also stressed automatic stabilization rather than discretionary policy. In many senses the system of fixed exchange rates under the IMF was a "forgiving" gold standard.

54. Gourevitch, in *Politics in Hard Times*, is particularly enlightening on the similarity of the winning coalitions.

55. The United States also assumed that a policy commitment to fixed exchange rates, international adjustment assistance, and automatic fiscal stabilizers would control inflation and keep growth up without requiring a great amount of international fine-tuning. In short, this was a demand-side system with an emphasis on automatic policies. See Ruggie, "International Regimes, Transactions, and Change"; Herman Van der Wee, *Prosperity and Upheaval* (Berkeley and Los Angeles: University of California Press, 1986), p. 261.

56. They were also using a combination of temporary trade barriers and efforts to nurture substantial economies of scale to make their industries more competitive.

57. Gilpin, *U.S. Power and the Multinational Corporation.*

58. I have reviewed the files of one of the companies most involved in working on the early initiatives of the U.S. government on informatics trade policy. The cable traffic from U.S. embassies often showed that complaints against foreign governments were dropped after a few leading U.S. companies made private accommodations with the government.

59. Dennis Encarnation, "Cross-Investment: A Second Front of Economic Rivalry," in McCraw, ed., *America versus Japan,* pp. 117–18.

60. Cohen and Zysman, *Manufacturing Matters.*

61. Richard Samuels, *The Business of the Japanese State* (Ithaca: Cornell University Press, 1987).

62. North American economists have correctly noted that the advantages of strategic trade policies are highly sensitive to precise assumptions. But the recent work on trade constantly concedes that such policies might help some of the time if the problem of collective choice could be resolved.

63. Kozo Yamamura, "Caveat Emptor: The Industrial Policy of Japan," in Krugman, *Strategic Trade Policy,* pp. 169–210.

64. Johnson's scintillating accounts of clashing ministries with ambitious plans for their economic clients have made a crucial contribution toward showing that interministry fighting can be consistent with a "developmental state." The discussion here differs from that of Johnson because I suspect that ministries needed the license of politicians to act so independently. As long as the LDP comfortably held power and worried primarily about intraparty politics, it made sense for politicians to identify with particular ministries and to let the ministries take the lead. See Chalmers Johnson, "MITI, MPT, and the Telecom Wars: How Japan Makes Policy for High Technology," in Chalmers Johnson, Laura Andrea Tyson, and John Zysman, eds., *Politics and Productivity: How Japan's Development Strategy Works* (New York: Ballinger, 1989); Johnson, *MITI and the Japanese Miracle.*

65. Samuels notes that Saxonhouse and others argue that alliances for research are compensatory devices for the imperfections of Japan's capital markets and the lifetime employment practices of oligopolistic firms in Japan (Richard J. Samuels, "Research Collaboration in Japan" [MIT-Japan Science and Technology Program, Working Paper 87-02, 1987]; Kenneth Flamm, *Targeting the Computer—Government Support and International Competition* [Washington, D.C.: Brookings Institution, 1987]).

66. Quotes were taken from *Japan Economic Journal,* 20 June 1987, p. 4.

67. Fortunately, as electoral pressures on the LDP grow, politicians are less patient with policies that penalize consumers and are more inclined to intervene directly to fine-tune the distributional implications of progrowth policies. See Yamamura, "Caveat Emptor." They are also quite willing to engage in the same sorts of budgetary gimmicks as their U.S. counterparts. For example, Japan will fund its expansionary government budget in 1988 from the revenues it receives from selling its stock in NTT, the major Japanese telephone company.

68. "Economic Plan Drawn to Enhance Technology," *Japan Economic Journal,* 12 December 1987, p. 2.

69. It is difficult to see Japan simply trying to stimulate the world economy as the United States did by tilting the aggregate flow of capital out of Japan into the world. We should expect more emphasis on targeted investments and more detailed oversight of individual markets. A casual reading of Japanese documents finds several recurring themes about future Japanese obligations to assist global growth. They include (1) providing more assistance to regional development banks that will stimulate "real growth"; (2) creating new technological capabilities through international cooperation on research and development—these projects are linked to efforts to create new visions of social orders consistent with Japanese approaches (such as Japan's "Information Society"); and (3) repeated calls for more investment in a Pacific infrastructure for communications and transportation. See, for example, "Symposium Explores Future Asian Development," *Japan Economic Journal*, 13 June 1987, p. 7.

70. Bruno and Sachs provide interesting evidence regarding problems of wage realignments (Michael Bruno and Jeffrey D. Sachs, *The Economics of Worldwide Stagflation* [Cambridge: Harvard University Press, 1985]). Sabel suggests that more flexibility often exists at the regional level (Charles Sabel, *Work and Politics* [Cambridge: Cambridge University Press, 1982]). Some policymakers and business leaders now question any special emphasis on the electronics and information industries (see Guy de Jonquieres, "Back to Basics," *FT*, 23 July 1987, p. 12). For broader reviews of West German industrial policy, see Christian Deubner, "Change and Internationalization in Industry: Toward a Sectorial Interpretation of West German Politics," *International Organization* 38 (1984): 501–35; Jeffrey A. Hart, "West German Industrial Policy," in Claude E. Barfied and William Schambra, eds., *The Politics of Industrial Policy* (Washington, D.C.: American Enterprise Institute, 1986); and John Zysman, *Government, Markets, and Growth* (Ithaca: Cornell University Press, 1983).

71. Kenneth Dyson, "West European States and the Communications Revolution," *Western European Politics* 9 (1986): 10–55; Kevin Morgan and Douglas Webber, "Divergent Paths: Political Strategies for Telecommunications in Britain, France, and West Germany," ibid., pp. 56–79.

72. Following the October 1987 financial crisis countries severely criticized West Germany for its very modest attempts to stimulate its economy (Steven Greenhouse, "Economic Spotlight Is on Bonn," *New York Times*, 5 November 1987, p. 29).

73. Laura Tyson, "Comments on Brander's 'Shaping Comparative Advantage': Creating Advantage, an Industrial Policy Perspective," in Lipsey and Dobson, *Shaping Comparative Advantage*, pp. 65–82.

74. Peter F. Cowhey, "Trade Talks and the Informatics Sector," *International Journal* 42 (Winter 1987/88): 107–37.

75. Robert Lawrence has made a fascinating argument concerning incentives for early aggressive investment if firms expect the establishment of a system of "fair shares" that become de facto property rights. Although alliances could degenerate into fair shares, there is much greater uncertainty about the market share of any individual firm, even if some restraints on market capacity are predictable.

76. This is even true for the seemingly impregnable relationship between the West German Bundespost and Siemens.

77. This is leading some large telephone companies that have never provided

equipment to enter the customer premises equipment market in alliance with other companies. In 1987, NTT of Japan announced an alliance with Data General of the United States to make a telephone switching system for businesses (private automatic branch exchange) in Japan and the United States (David E. Sanger, "Data General–N.T.T. Alliance," *New York Times*, 8 October 1987, p. 32).

78. Nixdorf is the one truly significant rival to Siemens in computers among German firms. It is also the single sharpest critic of the Bundespost among these firms.

79. There was a similar split in regard to the broadcasting industry in the three countries. The broadcast industry is important in domestic telecommunications politics. In general, the United States has the most decentralized mass media, and West Germany has the most centralized.

80. Evidence for the following discussion can be found in Jonathan David Aronson and Peter F. Cowhey, *When Countries Talk—International Telecommunications in the 1990s* (Cambridge, Mass.: Ballinger Publishing Co., 1988).

81. For very good criticism of some U.S. positions on the bilateral talks, see Harald Malmgren, "U.S. Trade Policy—Stumbling Back to the Future," *International Economy*, October/November 1987, pp. 82–87.

82. The Japanese government has consistently denied that it agreed to the target for market share. The U.S. government began withdrawing the tariff penalties imposed to enforce the semiconductor agreement but insisted on retaining about $164 million of the $300 million total because of the shortfall in the target share. Some U.S. companies have told me that Japanese firms in the capital goods industry are more receptive to buying U.S. chips than firms primarily interested in consumer electronics ("Makers Vary Despite Chip Sale Rise," *Japan Economic Journal*, 21 November 1987, p. 1).

83. The vice-chairman of NEC, a company that will buy 23 percent of its semiconductors from foreign firms, has suggested that the U.S. government exercise oversight over its own firms ("US Remains Unhappy with Chip Market Share," *Japan Economic Journal*, 14 November 1987, p. 11; "NEC to Raise U.S. Chip Imports," *Japan Economic Journal*, 31 October 1987, p. 20).

84. Flamm notes that there were fourteen applications for antitrust waivers to the Department of Justice for joint research organizations as of early 1985 (Flamm, *Targeting the Computer*, p. 116; William H. Branson and Alvin K. Klevorick, "Strategic Behavior and Trade Policy," in Krugman, *Strategic Trade Policy*).

85. MITI announced plans to allow foreign firms to join thirty different projects under its jurisdiction as a result of U.S. pressures to expand on the 1980 bilateral accord on cooperation in high technology. Meanwhile, the new U.S. initiative on superconductivity promised to relax antitrust rules on joint domestic ventures in the field while restricting access to certain commercially valuable findings of U.S. government laboratories and making it easier for U.S. firms to sue for patent infringement in imported goods. The National Science Foundation also threatened to review Japanese patents derived from research biotechnology carried out in American universities. See James Gleick, "Reagan Outlines Steps to Promote Superconductivity Development," *International Herald Tribune*, 30

July 1987, p. 4; "Biotechnology Bumps toward Twenty-first Century," *Japan Economic Journal*, 14 November 1987, p. 15; "Foreign Firms to Join Government-Private R&D," *Japan Economic Journal*, 12 December 1987, p. 2; Michael S. Malone, "Chip Consortium: Before Congress Antes Up . . . ," *Wall Street Journal*, 17 November 1987, p. 28.

Part Three

SPECIFIC ISSUES
AND AGENDAS

6

Effectiveness in Technological Innovation:
Keiretsu versus Conglomerates

IWAO NAKATANI

One of the most interesting features of Japanese industrial structure is that the majority of Japanese firms belong to so-called corporate groups (*keiretsu*) that are linked through reciprocal shareholding, a lender-borrower relationship offering privileged financing with a "main bank," and long-term buyer-seller relations. These groupings of firms typically extend over a wide range of markets, and each keiretsu has member firms from virtually every major industry. This type of affiliation consists primarily of intermarket relationships and is termed a horizontal grouping. Another type of corporate group is the relationship formed within a given industry, such as automobiles or electronics, between a core (parent) firm and a number of parts-suppliers and subcontractors. The relationship between the core firm and its major parts-suppliers and subcontractors is usually very close and, in many cases, the former holds some equity in the latter. The relationship is essentially hierarchical and is usually characterized by a multilayered structure. This type of affiliation is termed a vertical grouping. The core firm may be a member of a keiretsu, thus linking the two different corporate groups. The combination of horizontal and vertical groupings among firms is a distinctive feature of Japan and is certainly not found so extensively in any other industrial country.

In recent years corporate groups in Japan have attracted the attention of many economists as a possible explanation for Japan's remarkable and stable economic performance after the first oil shock in 1973. Indeed, the Japanese economy adjusted to the shock quickly and with flexibility. Table 6.1 shows the coefficients of variation for several nominal and real macroeconomic variables for Japan, the United States, and the United Kingdom for the period of 1973–82. During this period, there were two oil shocks and all three countries were forced to undergo significant macroeconomic adjustment. On the one hand, the fluctuation in the growth

I am indebted to Professors Kozo Yamamura and Gary Saxonhouse, Dr. George Eads, and other participants in the Duisburg symposium for their stimulating discussion and useful comments. Nevertheless, I am solely responsible for any errors or ambiguities remaining in this chapter.

rate, nominal wage, and price level was much greater in Japan. Such dramatic changes in nominal variables are often related to changes in the money supply. As the table indicates, however, the coefficient of variation of the growth rate of money stock among these three countries was lowest in Japan. On the other hand, the degree of fluctuation in real variables such as the rate of economic growth and the unemployment rate was much smaller in Japan. Thus, if the *average* rate of economic growth and the *average* rate of unemployment approximate the *natural* rate of economic growth and the *natural* rate of unemployment, the Japanese economy came closer to its natural rates than the other two nations during this period. As seen in the last row of table 6.1, however, Japan's coefficient of variation for the rate of change in real wage relative to the unemployment rate was the largest.

These data illustrate the adjustments made in response to external shocks in these three countries. In Japan, nominal variables changed dramatically, while real variables remained relatively constant. This means that adjustment occurred primarily through changes in prices and wages. In the United States and the United Kingdom, on the other hand, adjustment was principally through changes in the size of real growth and unemployment.[1] There are many reasons for such differences in the process of macroeconomic adjustment among nations.[2] In Japan corporate groups play an important role in the performance of the Japanese economy.

In this chapter I attempt to go beyond the relationship between corporate groups and the stability of Japanese macroeconomic performance,

TABLE 6.1

Comparison of Fluctuation in Nominal and Real Variables
(Coefficients of Variation, 1973–82)

	Japan	United States	United Kingdom
Nominal rate of economic growth	0.455	0.253	0.276
Rate of change in money wage	0.771	0.117	0.385
Rate of inflation[a]	0.815	0.217	0.379
Rate of change in money supply (M2)[b]	0.246	0.338	0.411
Real rate of economic growth	0.582	1.315	2.650
Unemployment rate (A)	0.163	0.192	0.736
Rate of change in real wage (B)	1.578	0.943	3.490
Rate of change in real wage relative to unemployment rate (A/B)	9.681	4.911	4.742

SOURCE: Bank of Japan, *Kokusai hikaku tōkei*, various issues.

[a]Inflation is measured in terms of GNP deflator. Similar results are obtained if consumer price index is used.

[b]Figure for United Kingdom is for 1973–80.

which has been discussed elsewhere,[3] to examine the implications of these horizontal as well as vertical groupings among Japanese firms for research and development (R&D) activity and technological innovation. I present some background information on business groups in Japan in the first section. In the second section I outline some of the implications of group formation, and in the third section I discuss the effects of group-oriented activities on technological innovation in Japanese firms. In the fourth section I analyze the similarities and differences between horizontal and vertical groupings. The final section contains my concluding remarks.

CORPORATE GROUPS IN JAPAN

As of March 1986, 579 companies (61.4 percent) of 943 nonfinancial corporations whose shares were traded on the Tokyo Stock Exchange (First Section) belonged to one of six major financial groups (see table 6.2). These groups are Mitsui, Mitsubishi, Sumitomo, Fuji, Daiichi-Kangyō, and Sanwa. The share of sales of these groups accounts for more than 79 percent of all listed companies. The ratio of mutual shareholding by firms of the same group ranges from 25.14 percent (Mitsubishi) to 11.25 percent (Sanwa), and the ratio of borrowing from financial institutions of the same group (keiretsu financing) ranges between 22.92 percent (Mitsubishi) and 15.55 percent (Daiichi-Kangyō).

The Shachōkai (Presidents' Club) is a core group of firms within each keiretsu that are the most closely tied to each other. They total only 186 companies out of the approximately 1.8 million firms existing in Japan, but their position in the Japanese economy is overwhelming. The share of Shachōkai companies in the Japanese economy in terms of sales, net profits, total assets, paid-in capital, and current profits is around 15 percent, although the share of net profits has been somewhat higher in recent years.[4]

TABLE 6.2
Financial Corporate Groups in Japan (as of March 1986)

Group	Number of firms	Share of sales (%)	Ratio of mutual shareholding (%)	Ratio of keiretsu financing (%)
Mitsui	107	18.16	18.32	16.34
Mitsubishi	119	13.54	25.14	22.92
Sumitomo	111	15.47	24.40	22.68
Fuji	110	11.59	18.52	21.02
Daiichi-Kangyō	77	12.13	15.04	15.55
Sanwa	55	8.30	11.25	20.02

SOURCE: *Keiretsu no kenkyū* (Keizai Chōsa Kyōkai, 1987).

There is yet another type of corporate group in Japan. The leaders of these groups are the gigantic manufacturing companies such as Toyota, Matsushita, Hitachi, Shinnihon Steel, and Nissan. These groups are vertical affiliations of firms within a well-defined industry, such as the automobile, electronics, or steel industry. This type of corporate group contrasts sharply with keiretsu financial groups, because the latter are essentially intermarket groups extending to diverse industries.

The structure of group formation in Japan is diagramed in figure 6.1. Large corporations (parent companies) of different industries form intermarket financial groups (keiretsu) that are essentially horizontal affiliations of firms. Most members of the horizontal group also form and head their own vertical (and hierarchical) groups of subcontractors. The behavior of Japanese firms has been affected significantly by this industrial structure. In the following section, I discuss the implications of corporate groups for the Japanese economy as a whole as well as for participating firms.

IMPLICATIONS OF CORPORATE GROUPS

There are a number of studies advancing various hypotheses on the grouping of Japanese firms.[5] What benefits or objectives are sought in such extensive groups? Do they affect corporate behavior in any particular direction? Next I summarize my findings on these points.[6]

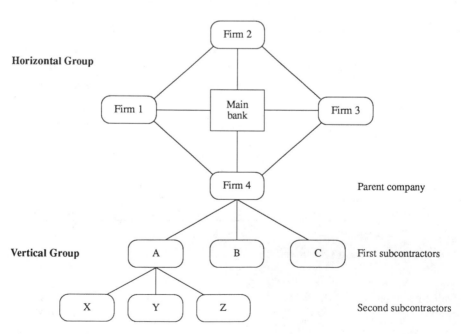

FIGURE 6.1. The dual structure of corporate groups.

First, the horizontal grouping of firms does not generally increase the rate of profits or the growth rate of a firm. However, variation in these rates over time is significantly lower for group-affiliated firms than independent firms. Figure 6.2 shows that the business performance of selected group-affiliated firms from four major keiretsu (Mitsui, Mitsubishi, Sumitomo, and Fuji) is more stable over time than that of independent firms not members of a financial corporate group in Japan. The fluctuation in business performance is measured by two indicators: variance in the rate of profit and variance in the growth rate of sales over the period of 1972–82. The smaller the variance, the more stable the performance. Elsewhere I have shown the findings to be statistically significant.[7]

The above findings imply that the formation of groups stabilizes corporate performance over time but sacrifices the level of corporate performance in profits and growth. This is made possible through an arrangement in which group-affiliated firms provide mutual aid among themselves in times of need, and it can be regarded as an implicit mutual insurance scheme among member firms and banks. This risk-sharing role of group membership is important in understanding the performance of the Japanese economy as a whole, since the majority of Japanese firms are members of some financial corporate group.

Second, the relationship between group-affiliated firms and member banks is very close and coherent. The latter, being the principal lender to member firms, acts also as insurer. When a firm is faced with financial or managerial difficulties, the member banks render necessary assistance

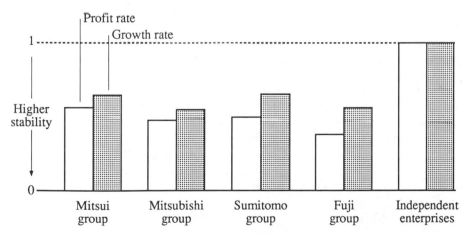

FIGURE 6.2. Stability of business performance. The variance of recurring profit rates of total liabilities and net worth and of growth rate of turnover (sales) was computed for each enterprise; then averages by group were computed. The average variance of independent firms was standardized to unity to facilitate comparison. (*Source:* Computed on the basis of Nihon Keizai Shimbunsha, *Nikkei NEEDS Financial Data File.*)

even at a far greater cost and risk than normal business reciprocity requires. The nonfinancial firms, on their part, attempt to maintain a high and stable level of outstanding debt against them.

This reciprocity between banks and keiretsu firms is the basis of long-term lender-borrower relations and indeed of financial keiretsu (keiretsu formed around a "main" bank) in Japan. According to implicit long-term contract theory, if a bank is an insurer (risk-neutral), then it is to the benefit of both the bank and the firm to fix the interest rate over all possible states of the world. Our study shows that the variability in interest rate over time is, if anything, negatively correlated to group affiliation, thus confirming (in a somewhat weak sense) that there is a long-term relationship between group-affiliated firms and banks characterized by sticky interest rates.

Due to differences in ownership patterns and long-term relationships with the bank, corporate financial policy differs considerably between member companies and independent firms. The ratio of dividends to paid-in capital is significantly lower in group-affiliated firms, and the debt-equity ratio significantly higher. It could be argued from these observations that group formation allows individual firms to insulate themselves from the imperatives of market forces, particularly of the capital market. Mutual shareholding among group firms together with keiretsu financing creates a kind of "mini" capital market within each financial corporate group. This mini capital market partially protects member firms from the pressures of normal capital markets, which tend to demand higher rates of return and in a shorter period. In the United States, capital markets tend to monitor short-term corporate performance much more closely.

These practices in the Japanese capital market allow firms to pursue their own objectives, which may differ from textbook value maximization. This is important in understanding the difference between U.S. and Japanese corporations with respect to the time horizon of investment decisions. It is often said that the managers of U.S. corporations are more concerned about short-term profits than Japanese managers due to strong pressure from myopic shareholders. (The management of some of the pension funds in the United States is an example.) Although while Japanese managers are certainly held responsible for profits in the long run, their responsibility for short-term profits is usually not so clearly perceived.

Another distinction between U.S. and Japanese investment decisions is that in Japan an investment project that produces a negative income stream in its initial phases but is expected to yield profits later is often acceptable, while a similar project is frequently rejected in the United States because management (and shareholders) prefers projects that produce positive initial returns.

These findings apply, in principle, to horizontal groupings but not necessarily to vertical groupings. The motive for vertical affiliation among firms may differ significantly from that for the horizontal grouping. It is believed that vertical affiliation is a highly efficient mode of production and is the basis of the flexible production system.[8] Asanuma shows persuasively that the relationship between the core firm and its main subcontractors in the automobile industry is far more flexible and closer in Japan than in the United States in that specifications for parts are determined jointly in the process of product improvement and customization of parts is actively pursued. He also finds that subcontractors take a more active role in both the development and the manufacturing stages.[9] In the United States, such joint efforts by a core firm and subcontractors are rare; the latter simply manufacture parts according to the drawings provided by the former.

The difference in manufacturing process and in the development of new products is significant. In the Japanese case, the risks associated with the development of a new product are seriously felt by both the core firms and the subcontractors and shared ex ante. In the U.S. case, on the other hand, risks are shared ex post; if a new product does not sell well, both parties suffer. The ex ante risk sharing by Japanese core firms and subcontractors are encouraged to utilize their own technical and market information to ensure the success of new products. In the U.S. case, information possessed by subcontractors is generally not utilized effectively in the process of product development.

CORPORATE GROUPS AND TECHNOLOGICAL INNOVATION

I have just shown that one of the major objectives of horizontal groupings is risk sharing among member firms. To the extent that this is true, one can say that firms in a group can take more risks than firms that are not members of a particular corporate group. Thus, the formation of horizontal groups will stimulate R&D investment, other things being equal.

I have also argued that corporate groups, especially horizontal groups, can insulate members from the pressure of general markets, particularly capital markets. Because of the partial insulation of Japanese keiretsu firms from capital markets, management may be able to carry out projects that are expected to produce profits only after a number of years. Because R&D activities typically require a long period before the returns on the investment become positive, Japanese firms may have an advantage.

In addition, firms in a corporate group have easier access to various sources of technological and scientific information. One of the primary characteristics of scientific research these days is technology fusion. The merging of diverse scientific knowledge from different specialties has become an important source of scientific invention and discovery. Therefore, better access to new technological developments from diverse specialties through the network of group firms may increase the productivity of R&D activities significantly.

The vertical affiliation of firms plays a different role. A typical characteristic of Japanese manufacturing is the intimate relationship between the assembler and parts-suppliers.[10] Before product details are finalized, researchers from these companies work together, often in the same place over a long period of time. They discuss ideas freely in order to improve and customize their product. The relationship between the assembler and subcontractors is two-way. It is also not as hierarchical as in the U.S. case.[11] This relationship often extends to new product development. Even at the very initial stages of new product development, the core firm and major subcontractors meet to discuss new product possibilities.

Broadly speaking, the horizontal affiliation of firms is useful for exchange of information concerning products and technological progress in different areas and ultimately for technology fusion and development of new technology. The vertical affiliation of firms is more useful in the refinement and customization of existing products and in the development of new products based on close consultation between the core firm and subcontractors in the earliest stages of product development.

It can be argued that the combination of horizontal and vertical groupings of firms in Japan provides member firms with positive stimuli and incentives to more aggressively undertake innovative activities than might otherwise be the case. The horizontal affiliation facilitates risky and long-term projects as well as technology fusion, while the vertical affiliation is effective for continuous refinements and improvements in existing products and for the development of related new products.

SIMILARITIES AND DIFFERENCES
BETWEEN KEIRETSU AND CONGLOMERATES

The preceding analysis and conclusions, particularly those concerning horizontal groupings, raise a fundamental question. How do keiretsu differ from the conglomerate arrangements typical of the United States? The effectiveness of conglomerates has been discounted significantly in recent years. Why then are the horizontal affiliations of firms in Japan successful? If these two types of affiliations of firms are as similar as they appear on the surface, their effects must be relatively similar.

The similarities between keiretsu and conglomerates are obvious. Firms belonging to keiretsu and those in conglomerates are both engaged in a horizontal relationship with firms from diverse industries and are tied together by equity participation. A crucial difference, however, is that while conglomerates are more or less fully controlled by a holding (or owner) company, keiretsu are loosely coupled affiliations of more or less independent companies. Of course, keiretsu are characterized by mutual shareholding, as well as a main bank system, but the relationship is not as tight as in conglomerate arrangements, where shareholding by the owner company is large enough to control the decision-making process of each member company.

In keiretsu arrangements, stock is *mutually* owned and decision making is carried out by each member firm under a system of "mutual recognition." Suppose company A and company B are keiretsu members and each owns a significant portion of equity in the other, and as a result, company A is the largest shareholder in company B and vice versa. In this case, company A and company B are "interlocked." It is not clear which company controls the other. Nevertheless, there is an important relationship in the sense that the management of each company requires recognition of the other on respective management policies. This is what I call a system of mutual recognition and it differs fundamentally from conglomerates. Conglomerates are hierarchical arrangements in which the stockholding company controls the entire body of conglomerate companies. Keiretsu are more democratic affiliations of firms.

In many cases, the main bank is the most influential member of a keiretsu because it is the key source of investment funds for member firms. It is not the same, however, as the stockholding company in a conglomerate. As Aoki demonstrates, the main interest of the bank is not to control management per se but rather to ensure that member companies remain stable bank borrowers.[12] Value maximization from the perspective of the main bank requires, under a plausible set of conditions, overborrowing by its members rather than value maximization of each member firm. Each company is free to choose management policies under the constraint that borrowing remain at the required level.

Another, related difference between conglomerates and keiretsu is the mode of affiliation between firms. In conglomerate arrangements each member is under the direct control of the owner company and generally must compete directly with other member firms for resources. The owner company often evaluates management based on a comparison with other companies within the conglomerate. Under such a competitive system, it may be impossible to form a cooperative relationship as seen among keiretsu companies, unless the central management of the holding company forces individual companies to cooperate. As long as they are forced to compete in the management evaluation system, it is difficult to expect a *voluntary* association among them.

In keiretsu there is neither such a management evaluation mechanism nor explicit competition among member firms, because they are scattered over a wide range of industries. Of course, since they are under a mutual insurance scheme, they are obliged to buy "insurance," and at times they are forced to buy too much. Those companies that feel they are buying too much insurance may gradually withdraw from the keiretsu. This is particularly true for companies growing fast enough to be able to dispense with their interlocking relationships with other companies. The keiretsu relationship is long-term but not permanent. Member companies can decide whether or not they want to remain within the group.

To sum up, the control mechanism differs significantly between keiretsu and conglomerates. In the former, the relationship is voluntary and the association among member companies is dynamic. For example, if they feel it would be beneficial to cooperate in the R&D process, they get together, exchange information, or organize a joint research project; they might even establish a new firm. As I discussed earlier, it is becoming more and more important to utilize knowledge from other industries for the development of new products. In many cases, internal human resources are not sufficient to meet the need for knowledge from other industries, and research activities must be jointly organized by two or more companies with diverse technology orientations.[13] It is obvious that keiretsu are highly effective and useful arrangements that extend over a wide range of industries with different knowledge bases. Member companies can participate in a joint project if they feel it is promising. Information exchange is relatively easy, and since the association is voluntary, there is no sense of control by a central authority. The situation differs significantly in the case of conglomerates. The relationship is mandatory, and the exchange of information is generally not spontaneous but must often be mediated by the owner company.

CONCLUDING REMARKS

I have argued that Japanese industrial structure, characterized by both horizontal and vertical corporate groupings, differs significantly from similar arrangements in the form of conglomerates and vertical affiliations of firms in the United States. It is not a priori easy to say which arrangement is most advantageous for technological innovation. However, the fluid nature of the Japanese organization may be more advantageous for incremental innovation, and the hierarchical nature of the American organization may be more beneficial for path-breaking innovation because the concentration of resources on a strategic project is, generally speaking, easier under the American system. Under the Japanese arrangement, information tends to be scattered, and resources are not always strategically allocated.

However, I have reached three conclusions from the above discussion. First, the risk-sharing nature of Japanese corporate groups makes it possible for each firm to pursue more risky R&D projects than would be possible in the absence of such groups. Second, the insulation of group-affiliated firms through mutual shareholding and keiretsu financing from the pressure of capital markets makes it possible for these firms to carry out long-term projects. Third, to the extent that technology fusion is a key factor for innovation, Japanese corporate groups facilitate R&D activity because the costs of collecting information on technological developments within diverse specialties can be minimized by appropriate networking among firms within horizontal as well as vertical groups. The benefits and burdens of the Japanese and U.S. arrangements are subjects for future research.

NOTES

1. For more detailed analysis, see Iwao Nakatani, "Sōtaikakaku seisaku ha naze hitsuyōka" (Why is relative price policy necessary?), *Keizai seisaku kenkyūkai* (Tokyo: Economic Planning Agency, 1984), pp. 47–55.

2. For example, see Jefferey Sachs, "Wages, Profits, and Macroeconomic Adjustment: A Comparative Study" (Brookings Papers on Economic Activity 2, Brookings Institution, Washington, D.C., 1979), pp. 269–301.

3. Iwao Nakatani, *Makuro keizaigaku nyūmon* (Introduction to macroeconomics) (Nihon keizai shimbunsha, 1982), esp. chap. 8.

4. *Kigyō keiretsu sōran* (Tokyo: Tokyo keizai, 1987).

5. For example, see Richard E. Caves and Masu Uekusa, *Industrial Organization in Japan* (Washington, D.C.: Brookings Institution, 1976); Akira Gotō, "Kigyō gurupu no keizai bunseki" (An economic analysis of firm groups), *Keizai kenkyū*, April 1978; H. Odagiri, "Kigyō-shūdan no riron" (The theory of corporate groups), *Economic Studies Quarterly*, August 1975; H. Okumura, *Shin Nihon no rokudai kigyō-shūdan* (A new look at the six major corporate groups in Japan) (Tokyo: Diamond-sha, 1983); J. Teranishi, Akira Gotō, and K. Serizawa, "Shikin shijo to kigyō gurupu" (Financial markets and corporate groups), *Keizai hyōron*, November 1975; and Y. Kobayashi, *Kigyo-shūdan no bunseki* (An analysis of corporate groups) (Sapporo: Hokkaido University Press, 1980) My own works in this area are "The Role of Intermarket Keiretsu Business Groups in Japan," *Pacific Economic Papers*, no. 97 (Australia-Japan Research Centre, Australian National University, 1982); "Risk-sharing kara mita Nihon keizai" (Risk-sharing and the role of business groups in Japan), *Osaka Economic Papers*, December 1982; "Nihon keizai no himitsu o toku kagi" (How can we find the key to the secrets of Japanese economic performance?), *Ekonomisuto*, 15 February 1983; and "The Economic Role of Financial Corporate Grouping in Japan," in Masahiko Aoki, ed., *The Economic Analysis of the Japanese Firm* (Amsterdam: North-Holland, 1984).

6. For further analysis of the motivation for group formation and its effect on corporate behavior between 1971 and 1982, see Nakatani, "Economic Role of Financial Corporate Grouping." Examining the financial and real decisions of firms, I point out that groups do not generally increase either the profit or the growth rate of firms. Rather, the major motivations for group formation are the pursuit of stability and corporate performance and the sharing of risks and profits among members in order to adjust to external shocks. For further detail see also Nakatani, "Nihon keizai no himitsu."

7. See Nakatani, "Economic Role of Financial Corporate Grouping." The inclusion of the two other groups (Daiichi-Kangyō and Sanwa) does not alter the conclusion.

8. Vertical affiliation differs significantly from vertical integration. The latter is characterized by the internalization of transactions, while the former utilizes the merits of long-term relationships among organizations and the competitive pressure of markets. Competition among Japanese subcontractors is very severe, but at the same time, the relationship between the core firm and its subcontractors is much more long term in Japan than typically found in the United States.

9. See Banri Asanuma, "Transactional Structure of Parts Supply in the Japanese Automobile and Electric Industries: A Comparative Analysis" (Socioeconomic System Research Project, Technical Report no. 3, Kyoto University, 1986.)

10. Ibid.

11. A similar point can be made for firm organization itself. U.S. firms are often more hierarchical, and the strategies of the chief executive officer play an overwhelmingly important role in the management process. In Japan, information tends to be more scattered and shared heavily by midlevel management. The information structure is more decentralized, and the management process involves more participation of mid- and high-level officers rather than being "strategic."

12. Masahiko Aoki, "Shareholders' Non-unanimity on Investment Financing: Banks vs. Individual Investors," in Aoki, *Economic Analysis of the Japanese Firm.*

13. In this connection, Aoki refers to a survey taken by the Agency for Science and Technology in 1985 (Masahiko Aoki, "A Microtheory of the Japanese Economy: Information, Incentives, and Bargaining" [Discussion Paper no. 242, Kyoto Institute of Economic Research, 1987], pp. 400–402). According to the survey, 20 percent of Japanese firms surveyed were linked with other firms in various research-related activities such as information exchange, commissioned research, and joint research projects. It should also be noted, however, that linkage between firms in the same industry has been declining in recent years. Aoki also points out that some of these joint projects are unrelated in terms of capital and are more entrepreneurial by nature. However, the majority of associations still emerge from the traditional corporate grouping if appropriate candidates for a joint project are found. The keiretsu continues to play an important role for technology fusion among its members.

7

The German Competitive Position
in Trade of Technology-Intensive Products

HARALD LEGLER

A variety of reports in the mid-1980s by such organizations as the Deutsche Bundesbank and the Organisations for Economic Cooperation and Development (OECD) found that international competitiveness of the West German economy had declined.[1] The Ministry for Research and Technology monitors the position of German industry in international trade of technology-intensive products, and partly as a result of these findings, it now produces studies to help evaluate the impact and efficiency of related policies. This essay is based on one such study made in 1986 and 1987 and offers a very different view on this subject. That is, West Germany does not have a comparative advantage in the narrowly defined sector of high technology but is extremely specialized in products of medium technology. In this respect, the structure of the German economy is similar to that of Japan and is quite different from that of the United States. And because the international division of labor in industrial research and development (R&D) is changing only slowly, the German position is not likely to change dramatically in the near future.

This study is in four sections. The first presents the economic background of international competition in technology-intensive products. The second section provides the analytical framework of this study and its assumptions. This section focuses not on technological standards but on changes in the relative position of German technological capability and structural change. Included are definitions of high, low, and no technology products as applied by economists on a macroeconomic level and methods for measuring the international competitive position of certain sectors of an economy, individual products, or product groups.

This essay is based on a short study undertaken on behalf of the West German Ministry for Research and Technology in 1986 and updated in 1987: Hariolf Grupp and Harald Legler, *Spitzentechnik, Gebrauchstechnik, Innovationspotential, und Preise* (Cologne: Verlag TÜV Rheinland, 1987), and Harald Legler, *Trends und Positionen der Bundesrepublik im internationalen Wettbewerb* (Hannover: Niedersächsisches Institut für Wirtschaftsforschung, 1987). I would like to thank those who provided invaluable assistance in preparing this paper: Dagmar Tacke and Klaus-Jürgen Hentschel, who assisted in the calculations and drawings; Christina Messer, who helped with the translation; and Irmhild Schwentke, who typed the manuscript.

The empirical findings of this analysis are presented in the third section, with special emphasis on the importance of technology-intensive products in German foreign trade; a comparison of the West German, U.S., and Japanese situations and trends; and bilateral trade relations in technology-intensive products between West Germany and both the United States and Japan. The final section of this essay offers some suggestions for assessing these findings.

ECONOMIC BACKGROUND

The need to monitor the relative competitive position in trade of technology-intensive products began to be felt in the late 1960s. At that time, the United States was said to have attained a significant technological lead, creating a "technological gap" between itself and other industrial countries. According to international trade theory, if this phenomenon had indeed occurred, the level of employment would have declined in the national economies outside the United States (with no change in relative income claims) or differences in real income (with no change in employment) would have increased between the United States and other industrial nations.

A 1970 OECD study entitled *Gaps in Technology* was the first attempt to define "technology-intensive products" and to assess the "technological intensity" of national economies as measured by activities in R&D and by foreign trade structure.[2] The results of the study did not alarm other national economies, because in the early 1970s, out-of-date (undervalued) exchange rates could still be used to ensure international competitiveness so that employment did not suffer.

Two fundamental changes in world economic conditions have once again increased interest in the subject of technological intensity. First, exchange rates can no longer be manipulated to achieve or maintain competitiveness; today they reflect international competitiveness.[3] A relatively high currency valuation, and hence high real income, combined with a high employment rate can only be realized by making optimum use of a country's comparative advantage in the endowment of factors of production. In the case of flexible exchange rates, every country can compete; it is only a question of the level of income. Second, the oil price shocks of the 1970s made industrial countries realize that they possess nothing of corresponding "value" with which to retaliate.[4] The high oil prices, which resulted in a decline in real income, could have been compensated for simply by increasing the "value" of a nation's exports.

These two changes in global economic conditions have caused a basic reassessment of what is "valuable" in terms of international trade among industrial nations, thus giving technological competition a new importance, particularly in West Germany. Because of improvement in the German balance of trade in the first half of the 1980s and the accompanying real decline in the value of the deutsche mark,[5] it became cheaper to produce in West Germany than to rely on foreign production. The German economy traditionally owed its high income to strength in competition for "quality" products; however, one must ask if the German economy has lost this competitiveness to such an extent that it is now forced to try its luck in the field of price competition. This would mean that the margin for real income increases would become even more limited, unless production costs could be reduced by strong increases in productivity, which would lead to undesirable effects on employment.

Since the spring of 1985 the deutsche mark has continued on a course of revaluation. The international sector of the German economy faced an average annual revaluation of more than 10 percent in real terms.[6] The export and import-substitution sectors have suffered some loss in their respective positions in terms of price competition and are being critically tested. Do recent successes in these sectors have a strong enough foundation in the structure and quality of West German products supplied to the world market to realize high real income as well as high employment? These issues form the background for questions about the relative position of the German economy in the competition for markets for technology-intensive products. Technology is, of course, only one facet of a successful market strategy, albeit an important one.

ANALYTICAL FRAMEWORK

Defining Technology-Intensive Products

In international comparison, it is impossible to define the technology-intensive sector of an economy objectively,[7] and thus selecting products that might be termed technology-intensive presents considerable problems. It implies a comparison between *products* as well as between *national economies* at a given point in time. Individual products are manufactured with different production factor intensities (thus diverging technologies) in accordance with the comparative advantages in the factor endowment of each economy. The differences in the technology content of a given product can be so tremendous that the products of one country (or firm) may be classified as high technology, while those of another are labeled low technology, similar to products at the end of their product cycle. For example, German industry is willing to pay DM 0.80 for an electronic microcircuit from the Philippines. However, it will pay DM 1.60 for products of the same category if they originated in France, DM 3.30 for circuits produced in Japan, and DM 3.60 for the same product from the United States.

Although electronic microcircuits are high-technology products, these price differences reflect the diverging technological content within this product group. Hitherto, there has been no method of measuring the

technology content of products that is both theoretically satisfying and
feasible for empirical research on a macroeconomic level. Various approaches have been adopted, each with its own strengths and weaknesses. The most widely used measure is the R&D intensity of industrial
branches determined at the lowest possible level of aggregation. This
approach arose from the correct assertion that a product cannot be called
technology-intensive if it is not technology-intensive in terms of the amount
of R&D invested in it.

Current R&D expenditures are related to current costs. That is, expenditures for future products are compared with the manufacturing costs
of old or newly introduced products. The basic concept is that certain
product *groups* can be considered technology-intensive and that this will
remain so until the figures prove otherwise. This approach renders a
rather rigid list whose usefulness is limited by lags in data. The division
of the relevant statistics leads to a high level of aggregation: on the one
hand, too many product groups are covered; on the other hand, some
may be excluded. For example, the limited potential to differentiate the
relevant international trade statistics does not allow one to distinguish
compact disks and related hardware from traditional records and record
players. Furthermore, one cannot distinguish robots from other lifting,
handling, and loading machines.

The example of electronic microcircuits mentioned above shows that
even if it is possible to label a certain product group as technology-
intensive, the statistics may be distorted by differences in technology
contents between economies even within a narrowly defined product
group. Therefore, in the strict sense of the international trade theory it
is possible to compare only economies very similar in their relative factor
endowments (R&D intensities). This would mean a comparison of the
bilateral trade flows between West Germany on the one side and the
United States and Japan on the other.

Even if the R&D intensity of a product group is accepted as a reasonable proxy for technology intensity, there is an additional problem.
Technical knowledge outside specialized R&D departments is not included. This particularly affects the field of mechanical engineering. Although new technologies are developed in producing a new product, the
work of the construction divisions is not registered as R&D. Practical
problems also arise from the pressure to fix a "threshold" of R&D intensity. A relatively low R&D-intensity threshold would lead to a vo-
luminous list of technology-intensive products and would include a large
volume of trade. On the other hand, a very high level of R&D intensity
would cover only a very exclusive group of products. As a result, especially within international organizations, it is difficult to reach a consensus on international reference standards, which must be determined
somewhat arbitrarily. If the definition of technology-intensive products
is very narrow, the United States leads by a wide margin. If the defi-

nition is much broader, however, Japan's share of the world market increases dramatically. As discussed below, the latter is also true to a lesser extent for West Germany.

It has been shown that some lists of technology-intensive products are biased toward national specialties.[8] This is true of the list used in European Community (EC) analyses as well as of the OECD's definition used until 1984, which refers only to R&D data for 1967 from the United States. It is evident from this tendency to favor national specialties that technology-intensive products are not always defined independently of political considerations.

My own list of technology-intensive products is based on 1980 data on the research intensities of individual product groups.[9] Enumeration of the research-intensive products alone, however, would still conceal considerable intensity differences among research-intensive products. Therefore, an additional distinction is made between "high technology" and "high commodity" product groups.[10] The high technology sector includes product groups whose R&D expenditures exceed 8 percent of total costs and which usually involve leading-edge technologies. High technology sectors are often subject to protectionism, such as in the aircraft, aerospace, and radioactive materials industries, but they also include pharmaceuticals, electronics, electronic data processing, and scientific instruments.

Data on the aircraft and aerospace industry and the fission and breeder materials industry must be analyzed separately (tables 7.1 and 7.2). These sectors are subsidized worldwide in such a way that market-related trade relations are virtually excluded, and the intensity of public R&D subsidies demonstrates that government is the true consumer of these products.[11] Furthermore, such treaties as the Nuclear Non-proliferation Treaty and the ABM Treaty operate as barriers to market entry. These "protected" areas, however, are included in data for high technology *as a whole* (tables 7.3 and 7.4).

"High commodity" is a poor translation of the German term *gehobene Gebrauchstechnologie*, which can be roughly and just as inexactly translated as "high-level consumer technology." The R&D expenditures on product groups in this category generally range from 3 to 8 percent of total costs. Some electrical, metal, and chemical products, plastic materials, office machines, and motor vehicles in particular are considered high commodity products.[12]

Lists of technology-intensive products do not cover "product cycle" goods in the true theoretical sense, because foreign trade statistics do not report data for single products but rather for *product groups* containing both old and new products. This problem is relevant for microeconomic considerations but not on a macroeconomic level.[13] On the one hand, deep disaggregation is improper, especially in cases in which process innovations cannot be attributed to a single product group. On the other

TABLE 7.1

Relative World Trade Share of Selected Countries in Trade of R&D-Intensive Products

Product group[a]	West Germany		United States		Japan	
	1978	1985	1978	1985	1978	1985
Protected industries						
Radioactive mat.	−103.9	−136.4	49.6	68.3	−430.0	−409.9
Engines and motors	−39.2	−73.2	70.8	93.2	−121.4	−237.6
Oth. power generat. m.	48.7	59.8	20.8	1.7	−1.2	−139.5
Aircraft	−75.8	−23.3	142.6	124.7	−347.8	−356.9
Average	−58.3	−33.5	116.9	110.2	−199.8	−297.8
High technology						
Other organ. chemic.	26.5	31.9	44.3	46.2	−68.8	−73.8
Medicinal products	−2.1	1.7	7.9	21.1	−168.2	−177.8
Other plastic mat.	2.6	−26.0	−2.7	67.4	−127.9	−163.3
Pesticid., disinfec.	24.7	21.7	65.8	61.7	−133.8	−138.0
Autom. data proc.	−29.4	−38.1	91.4	66.3	−91.8	21.0
Transistors, valves	−13.7	−53.5	53.1	66.0	59.6	65.8
Electrical mach.	50.6	24.5	7.6	11.2	15.2	38.2
Optical instruments	71.5	46.7	−28.2	13.8	80.7	56.7
Measurng. contr. instr.	5.1	4.7	71.5	66.9	−53.5	−48.2
Others	13.3	−6.0	47.6	51.9	−29.9	3.6
Average	−4.6	−13.5	75.4	73.3	−60.4	−30.3
High commodity						
Synthetic rubber	−39.0	−26.0	29.4	23.9	−0.1	−32.4
Synthetic fiber	37.1	22.0	−3.9	−22.1	43.3	4.4
Org.-inorg. compounds	11.8	17.7	−111.6	−145.3	−26.9	−28.0
Inorg. elem., oxides	−0.2	18.0	−4.5	7.1	−94.3	−90.3

Other inorg. chemic.	20.3	25.7	44.0	50.4	−39.4	−95.3
Synth. org. dyestuffs	82.8	83.3	−95.7	−119.0	−65.6	−63.6
Pigments, paints	52.6	49.5	−47.5	−71.0	−75.5	−78.3
Essent. oils, perfume	−85.3	−56.3	22.2	16.3	−175.1	−164.6
Prod. of condens., etc.	43.2	52.1	−52.9	−41.7	−65.0	−59.6
Prod. of polymerizg.	33.9	30.7	−44.3	−29.5	−28.4	−60.4
Cellulose derivat.	15.0	24.7	21.0	30.0	−47.4	−60.9
Misc. chemic. prods.	16.6	36.7	74.5	22.8	−109.8	−92.2
Iron stl. tubes, pipes	26.9	23.5	−68.6	−131.5	90.4	72.8
Structures and parts	−15.1	8.4	−38.5	−89.6	0.0	−39.8
Tools	36.0	37.2	0.4	−14.9	−15.4	−15.2
Tractors, nonroad	−26.7	−29.1	84.5	79.3	−36.8	6.6
Paper, etc., mill mach.	56.0	52.8	−27.3	−43.2	−107.1	−70.6
Printg. bkbindg. mach.	81.7	86.3	24.5	−22.8	−114.0	−29.7
Food mach., nondom.	47.4	12.6	0.2	−17.0	−170.0	−116.9
Oth. mach. f. spcl. ind.	64.4	52.0	−15.1	14.0	−56.0	−15.5
Mach. tools f. metal	60.0	43.8	−29.9	−46.7	14.1	47.6
Metalworking mach.	58.3	29.0	6.6	−12.0	−18.2	33.9
Heating-cooling eqpmt.	3.0	8.1	33.3	−5.0	24.2	24.3
Mech.handling eqpmt.	15.4	16.3	34.6	−10.3	−10.9	17.4
Nonelec. mach., tools	56.7	60.4	16.8	−2.5	−55.1	−46.6
Nonelec. mach., parts	41.9	46.0	−21.5	−35.7	6.7	−3.4
Office machines	−3.0	−42.0	−73.7	−72.7	110.8	134.9
Office and ADP. mach.	−25.4	−56.7	103.0	94.7	−54.1	−32.4
Television receivers	22.2	−15.5	−63.9	−134.8	105.6	133.0
Sound rec., phonogrph.	−95.8	−95.9	−100.2	−209.6	160.7	167.8
Telecom. eqpmt.	−19.5	−53.2	17.5	11.7	60.8	78.4
Switchgear, etc.	41.7	39.6	−10.1	10.8	10.2	13.6
Electro-medcl., x-ray	32.7	23.0	61.4	70.8	−80.2	12.8

Continued on next page

TABLE 7.1—Continued

Product group[a]	West Germany		United States		Japan	
	1978	1985	1978	1985	1978	1985
Household-type eqpmt.	23.7	22.2	-34.5	-74.4	5.2	47.8
Pass motor vehicles	36.9	39.7	-59.7	-71.5	59.4	68.7
Lorries, spcl.mtr.veh.	-13.0	-36.9	-12.5	-40.6	77.1	85.3
Medical instruments	21.0	60.8	44.7	130.2	-17.7	5.5
Meters, counters	50.0	54.1	-49.5	-38.2	-15.1	-23.7
Photo appar. and eqpmt.	-4.3	-9.2	10.1	-20.3	118.8	112.9
Photo cinema supply	-18.6	-18.1	68.1	-62.2	-7.7	54.0
Optical goods	19.2	10.3	-74.4	-43.1	108.0	74.0
Average	25.3	20.4	3.4	-11.6	30.3	44.3
R&D-intensive products	19.5	12.3	24.0	19.2	16.4	29.0

SOURCE: Harald Legler, *Trends und Positionen der Bundesrepublik im internationalen Wettbewerb* (Hannover: Niedersächsisches Institut für Wirtschaftsforschung, 1987).

[a]Abbreviated designations are used. For complete designations see United Nations, *Standard International Trade Classification*, rev. 2 (New York: United Nations Publications, 1975).

TABLE 7.2
Revealed Comparative Advantage of Selected Countries in Trade of R&D-Intensive Products

Product group[a]	Germany		United States		Japan	
	1978	1985	1978	1985	1978	1985
Protected industries						
Radioactive mat.	−170.4	−213.6	−8.2	47.6	−493.5	−561.5
Engines and motors	52.9	−29.5	116.6	94.1	−127.1	−282.6
Oth. power generat. m.	87.2	164.9	152.1	131.9	−43.5	−20.3
Aircraft	−74.6	−44.5	271.1	194.4	−312.9	−367.8
Average	−55.5	−48.7	176.1	150.2	−197.9	−340.4
High technology						
Other organ. chemic.	37.9	43.0	130.9	111.6	−58.2	−90.8
Medicinal products	15.3	18.6	94.6	105.3	−241.8	−233.4
Other plastic mat.	−18.2	−38.8	292.9	337.3	−167.7	−170.8
Pesticid., disinfec.	115.4	96.5	172.5	165.5	−58.9	−37.2
Autom. data proc.	−59.2	−51.1	198.4	111.4	−127.1	36.9
Transistors, valves	−68.7	−74.7	−19.9	26.6	−4.5	40.4
Electrical mach.	73.2	32.9	47.1	21.3	84.3	61.6
Optical instruments	55.3	61.4	−45.8	36.1	100.7	72.1
Measurng. contr. inst.	24.8	26.7	163.4	139.8	−61.0	−60.0
Others	14.8	−3.0	90.1	82.6	−52.3	−5.1
Average	−2.7	−16.4	123.0	106.7	−75.6	−50.5
High commodity						
Synthetic rubber	−41.3	−30.7	107.7	115.1	−148.7	−3.6
Synthetic fiber	68.0	56.5	181.3	118.8	99.7	188.6
Org.-inorg. compounds	25.0	16.4	−19.5	−37.2	−82.3	−100.9
Inorg. elem., oxides	28.0	24.8	5.9	18.0	−101.1	−142.7
Other inorg. chemic.	30.7	52.3	115.8	128.1	−16.2	−113.0

Continued on next page

TABLE 7.2—Continued

Product group[a]	Germany		United States		Japan	
	1978	1985	1978	1985	1978	1985
Synth. org. dyestuffs	146.1	136.4	-1.7	-37.9	-106.6	-74.1
Pigments, paints	78.9	77.1	134.8	67.8	-13.6	-30.4
Essent. oils, perfume	-81.5	-39.8	31.4	60.1	-251.3	-187.0
Prod. of condens., etc.	27.7	23.4	118.5	106.7	-24.4	-33.1
Prod. of polymerizg.	25.4	9.9	128.2	119.4	83.1	29.5
Cellulose derivat.	66.7	48.4	435.9	149.4	32.2	-11.7
Misc. chemic. prods.	60.3	30.8	273.4	208.2	-127.1	-131.4
Iron stl. tubes, pipes	118.6	103.7	-48.0	-108.8	384.1	330.3
Structures and parts	72.7	56.7	202.1	23.0	341.1	229.4
Tools	55.2	35.2	40.9	22.8	74.3	56.6
Tractors, nonroad	53.8	85.2	159.2	130.5	161.3	239.0
Paper, etc., mill mach.	125.9	79.6	18.0	5.1	-9.4	-41.0
Printg. bkbindg. mach.	134.5	148.6	77.4	-6.1	-107.9	34.2
Food mach., nondom.	168.0	131.3	103.0	69.3	-100.1	8.9
Oth. mach. f. spcl. ind.	150.9	115.2	78.3	69.1	43.1	60.3
Mach. tools f. metal	110.3	72.0	8.1	-36.7	96.6	104.3
Metalworking mach.	130.9	77.3	158.8	11.3	127.6	180.1
Heating-cooling eqpmt.	91.2	66.0	182.6	113.4	127.8	104.8
Mech. handling eqpmt.	96.8	100.3	139.4	35.8	136.5	166.4

Nonelec. mach., tools	118.4	115.1	83.6	42.6	-10.5	57.5
Nonelec. mach., parts	64.8	53.4	38.8	18.3	76.2	47.5
Office machines	-2.3	-26.7	-121.2	-109.9	195.2	335.9
Office and ADP. mach.	-37.7	-58.4	124.0	88.6	-23.5	29.5
Television receivers	44.9	35.0	-108.2	-153.3	399.7	469.1
Sound rec., phonogrp.	-99.7	-62.0	-182.2	-286.4	286.0	466.6
Telecom. eqpmt.	31.9	10.0	8.6	-22.3	125.8	165.8
Switchgear, etc.	68.5	48.8	59.7	48.8	72.8	53.6
Electro-medcl., x-ray	46.7	52.5	89.7	62.9	-93.4	32.2
Household-type eqpmt.	32.3	36.9	-13.1	-85.9	132.2	206.8
Pass motor vehicles	56.5	111.5	-122.1	-128.9	213.1	271.4
Lorries, spcl. mtr. veh.	148.0	125.6	18.6	-63.6	473.3	465.3
Medical instruments	41.0	55.2	90.0	172.6	-53.1	-14.9
Meters, counters	92.4	54.0	-91.5	-73.1	141.8	82.6
Photo appar. and eqpmt.	-6.7	14.6	-23.5	-27.8	131.6	117.9
Photo cinema supply	-26.7	-46.0	135.8	-21.3	-20.9	34.4
Optical goods	3.0	-8.0	-132.3	-96.9	71.4	84.2
Average	64.1	58.0	19.8	-13.2	112.1	127.5
R&D-intensive products	49.1	37.3	46.5	25.9	67.2	72.5

SOURCE: Harald Legler, *Trends und Positionen der Bundesrepublik im internationalen Wettbewerb* (Hannover: Niedersächsisches Institut für Wirtschaftsforschung, 1987).

[a]Abbreviated designations are used. For complete designation see United Nations, *Standard International Trade Classification*, rev.2 (New York: United Nations Publications, 1975).

TABLE 7.3

Relative World Trade Share of West Germany by Industrial Characteristics

Specification	1978	1979	1980	1981	1982	1983	1984	1985
R&D intensive	19.5	16.1	18.7	16.0	15.7	15.6	13.2	12.3
High technology	-4.6	-11.0	-12.3	-10.0	-8.1	-11.3	-8.4	-13.5
High commodity	25.3	22.7	26.6	23.0	22.8	23.7	20.2	20.4
Human capital intensive	9.8	9.2	8.7	7.7	6.7	6.3	5.5	5.1
Real capital intensive	-4.1	-2.7	-3.9	-0.5	-1.3	-1.6	-0.9	-0.4
Scale economics intensive	2.0	2.3	3.2	2.7	2.2	1.4	0.9	0.7
Raw material intensive	-21.9	-20.7	-19.7	-16.1	-19.4	-19.1	-14.1	-14.3
Agricultural	-53.9	-51.7	-47.4	-40.3	-39.2	-42.3	-37.4	-35.4
Mineral	-3.5	-4.4	-5.2	-1.9	-8.0	-6.1	-1.2	-2.6
Energy intensive	-1.7	-1.2	-3.5	1.6	-1.3	0.8	3.8	2.1
Environment intensive	-8.7	-9.5	-14.0	-7.7	-11.1	-9.1	-5.3	-4.4

SOURCE: Harald Legler, *Trends und Positionen der Bundesrepublik im internationalen Wettbewerb* (Hannover: Niedersächsisches Institut für Wirtschaftsforschung, 1987).

TABLE 7.4

Revealed Comparative Advantage of West Germany by Industrial Characteristics

Specification	1978	1979	1980	1981	1982	1983	1984	1985	1986
R&D intensive	49.1	44.9	7.8	43.1	44.6	41.2	39.0	37.3	33.7
High technology	−2.7	−10.1	−9.6	−21.0	−17.6	−15.0	−10.2	−16.4	−19.0
High commodity	64.1	61.3	65.5	65.7	69.0	62.2	58.6	58.0	51.9
Human capital intensive	29.3	25.0	26.4	23.1	23.8	19.3	19.3	16.8	19.8
Real capital intensive	−15.6	−13.2	−10.3	−8.5	−9.8	−10.4	−9.7	−9.2	−6.9
Scale economics intensive	8.4	7.2	10.2	5.6	4.3	4.3	5.1	3.1	5.0
Raw material intensive	−55.7	−51.0	−47.0	−47.2	−55.3	−51.3	−47.5	−49.7	−47.4
Agricultural	−97.0	−85.0	−79.4	−71.7	−76.9	−74.6	−72.5	−69.2	−73.4
Mineral	−29.7	−32.6	−29.3	−32.8	−42.4	−38.2	−33.5	−39.0	−30.5
Energy intensive	−5.5	−4.3	−8.5	−5.3	−11.4	−8.5	−7.9	−8.7	−13.4
Environment intensive	−28.4	−31.4	−28.8	−28.8	−36.0	−34.1	−31.6	−34.9	−29.2

SOURCE: Harald Legler, *Trends und Positionen der Bundesrepublik im internationalen Wettbewerb* (Hannover: Niedersächsisches Institut für Wirtschaftsforschung, 1987).

hand, this method does not attempt to identify narrowly defined product cycle goods. Rather, the aim is to define a range of old and new products characterized by innovation and technical progress and by the potential to bring high real income in international trade.

At the time our own list of technology-intensive product groups was compiled, its major advantage was its more intensive use of information available in detailed industry studies. This means a lower level of aggregation but may also mean a slight bias in favor of West Germany.

Measuring Competitive Position

The position of a country with respect to a product group on the world market is assessed by what is called a relative world trade share (RWS).[14] The RWS compares the share of a country in a particular product group with the share of all manufactured industrial goods of that country in the world market. The greater the share of a product group in the exports of the country under study relative to the share of the same product in the world market, the larger the relative world trade share.

If the world market share of the country and product group studied and its share of the whole market are equal, the RWS has a value of 0. Positive values indicate above-average export success. That is, the product group has penetrated foreign markets more successfully than other goods. The reverse is true for negative values of RWS. Hence, RWS is a measure of specialization. RWS data measuring specialization can be equated with competitiveness only if protectionist practices on exports do not differ significantly in type cr extent between product groups.

One problem with studies that emphasize export performance such as those using RWS is that the import-substitution sector is not taken into consideration. In order to assess the effects of import substitution, imports themselves must be considered. Revealed comparative advantage (RCA) shows to what extent an export surplus (deficit) for a certain product group deviates from the export position in manufactured industrial goods as a whole of the country under study.[15]

If the export-import ratio of the product group under study is equivalent to that of all product groups, the RCA has a value of 0. A high positive value indicates a comparative advantage (i.e., a strong international competitive position) in the manufacture of that product group in the country under study. The industry is considered to be particularly competitive, as foreign competitors cannot establish themselves as successfully in the domestic market as domestic producers can in foreign markets. Although the RCA measures export performance as well as the potential for import substitution through domestic production, the effects of *selective* protectionist practices are also evident here.

An Interindustrial Comparison

An examination of the German internal pattern of specialization and the role technology-intensive products play yields the following somewhat expected results. The most outstanding characteristic of West Germany's pattern of specialization is a concentration in R&D-intensive products (see tables 7.3 and 7.4). Specialization in human-capital-intensive products and the relatively small share of raw-materials-intensive and environmental-intensive products in the export supply (with simultaneously high import rates) fit the concept of relative factor endowments.

Differentiation between high technology and high commodity is useful when identifying R&D-intensive products, as West Germany does not concentrate on selected high technologies but instead specializes in supplying a wide range of products embodying high-level consumer technology. Tables 7.1 and 7.2 illustrate the distribution of West German products among individual product groups. West Germany is strong in certain electrotechnical products, measurement and control technology, optical instruments, nuclear reactors, agricultural chemicals, and pharmaceutical products. West Germany is weak, however, in high technology product groups, including aircraft and aerospace, electron tubes, radioactive materials, and data processing. The weak positions in part reflect overt political decisions (such as in regard to military research in the aerospace industry) and other factors (lack of basic raw materials and the Nuclear Non-proliferation Treaty in fission and breeder materials). While the aircraft and aerospace industry is rapidly catching up, ground was continuously lost in data processing until 1984; since then, a slight recovery has been made.

The strong German position in the high commodity sector is due primarily to mechanical engineering, some areas of electrotechnology, the motor vehicle industry, precision mechanics, steel pipes, tools, metal constructions, inorganic chemistry, synthetics (paints, plastics, fibers), and a few final chemical products. There are a few exceptions to the success in high commodity sectors, such as telecommunications, synthetic rubber, photochemicals, and office equipment, which record only moderate trade performance.

Figures 7.1 and 7.2 reveal that in the late 1970s and early 1980s, the R&D-intensive sector of the German economy suffered no significant loss in overall competitiveness. The position of high technology products improved, particularly on the international market, simultaneously with the opening of the domestic market. The high technology sector, however, is characterized by erratic variations, particularly in those markets heavily influenced by political decisions, making actual trends difficult to dis-

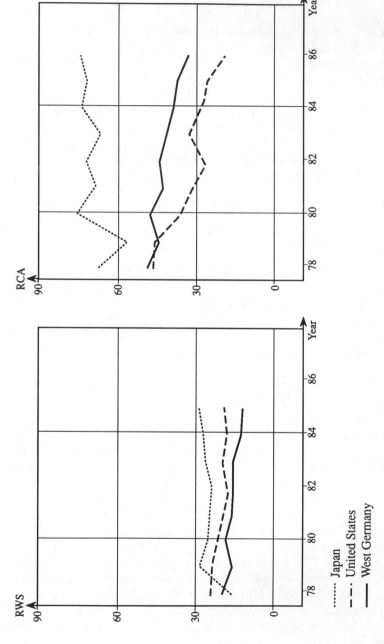

FIGURE 7.1. Specialization in trade of all R&D-intensive products. (*Source:* Harald Legler, *Trends und Positionen der Bundesrepublik im internationalen Wettbewerb* [Hannover: Niedersächsisches Institut für Wirtschaftsforschung, 1987].)

Japan
United States
West Germany

cern. In comparing the data for 1985–86 with those of 1980, it appears that the high technology sector has not held its ground. In any case, the instability of the high technology sector in international markets is clearly evident. In addition, the position of high commodity products made in West Germany is still impressive, although recent years have seen a moderate decline in the worldwide market position made worse by massive import pressure.

The developments among product groups have been very different. The R&D-intensive sectors of the machinery and electrical engineering industries, in particular, and also the chemical and chemical-linked industries have had to accept substantial losses. On the other hand, the R&D-intensive branches of automobile production and the aircraft and precision and optical goods industries have benefited from recent structural changes in international trade.

To a certain extent, the declining export performance can be attributed to shifts in the product structure and the regional structure of world demand.[16] The high technology sector enjoyed an enormous worldwide growth in demand, especially in the fields of data processing, aircraft and aerospace, electron tubes, and measurement and control instruments. On the other hand, the demand for high commodity products has expanded only slightly, especially in the area of mechanical engineering. Because of mechanical engineering's high degree of specialization, these developments have had a considerable negative structural effect on the German economy. Moreover, the demand for high technology products has increased most dramatically in those regions of the world with which West Germany traditionally has had limited trade relations, such as the Pacific region, causing a negative regional effect. Such negative structural and regional effects explain to some extent the loss of importance of the German R&D-intensive product groups on the world market. There has also been a substantial loss of international competitiveness.

A Comparison with the United States and Japan

Tables 7.1 and 7.2 compare world trade in R&D-intensive products from West Germany with those from the United States and Japan and show diverging patterns of specialization as well as diverging trends. It is useful to separate the quasi-military goods of the aircraft and aerospace industries as well as the fission and breeder products industries from high technology industries whose trade relations are permitted to form largely under market conditions. This breakdown makes it clear that the United States has achieved a high degree of specialization in high technology goods not traded under market conditions. The inclusion of these products in the high technology sector has only a minor negative impact on the relative position of West Germany, while its effect on Japan's position is substantial. The United States, however, continues to domi-

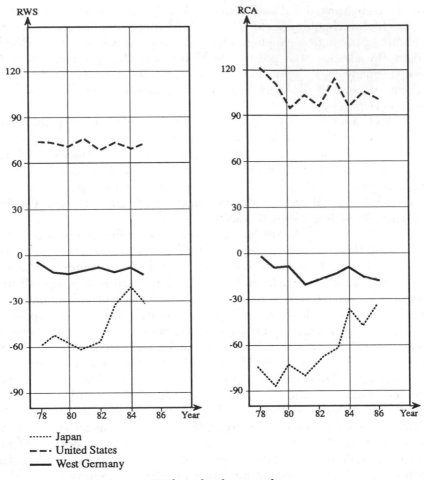

------- Japan
— —· United States
——— West Germany

a. High technology products

FIGURE 7.2. Specialization in trade of R&D-intensive products. (*Source:* Harald Legler, *Trends und Positionen der Bundesrepublik im internationalen Wettbewerb* [Hannover: Niedersächsisches Institut für Wirtschaftsforschung, 1987].)

nate the high technology sector, with a high competitive position not only in the protected areas but in every product group ranked among the leading-edge technologies.

A comparison of the RCA and RWS of these countries measures the propensity of a country to import technology-intensive products. The United States shows a strong tendency to make use, but hesitantly, of the supply of high technology from other countries. However, the import share of high commodity products is decidedly high. For West Germany and Japan, the opposite is true. The domestic market for high technology products is relatively open, and import quotas on high commodity goods

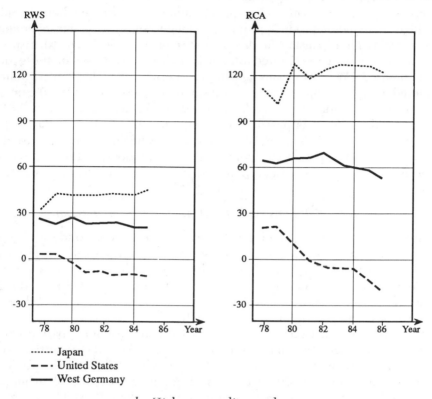

b. High commodity products

FIGURE 7.2.—*Continued*

are comparatively low. These differences could be related to comparative advantages; they could also be the result of protectionism.

Neither Japan nor West Germany concentrates exports in certain high technology areas. In contrast to the United States (and also France and Great Britain),[17] the primary domain of the Japanese and German economies is a differentiated supply of goods, part of the high commodity sector. Japan shows little specialization in chemicals and chemical-linked products, in which West Germany is particularly strong. Japanese R&D-intensive products have continually shown an upward trend on world markets. This is the result of Japan's willingness and ability to make structural changes in industries at the ends of their product cycles, such as steel, aluminum, fertilizers, and fibers. High technology areas in a narrow sense, and especially data processing, are increasingly expanding in Japan. It is interesting to note that this is largely the result of a diversification of exports without a concurrent increase in import substitution.

The success of the Japanese high technology sector, however, is not yet comparable to that of the high commodity sector. Some structural displacement in the pattern of specialization has appeared here. Trade in high commodity product groups no longer shows any improvement; the margins for expansion in this sector seem to have been exhausted.

The situation in the United States is a direct reflection of these developments in West Germany and Japan. On average, the United States suffered more distinct losses in position than West Germany, the most severe and continuous of which occurred in the high commodity area. Although the 1986 data are not yet complete, the available data for Japan, the United States, and West Germany confirm the recent trends. This is especially true of the persistent deteriorations in the high commodity sector, which has been penetrated by a host of smaller countries.

Bilateral Relations with the United States and Japan

As discussed earlier, under the theory of international trade it is possible to analyze trade flows only between economies with very similar R&D intensities. In this manner the problem of factor reversals can be avoided. Therefore, the question of how well the West German R&D-intensive sector competed with the United States and Japan in bilateral trade is also of great interest (see table 7.5).

In trade with the United States, West Germany has no apparent comparative advantage. In relative terms, however, the R&D-intensive sector of the German economy has declined since 1982 in trade with the United States. Indeed, 70 percent of all additional exports of manufactured industrial products to the United States from West Germany in that year were R&D-intensive goods. However, 110 percent of the additional imports from the United States were R&D-intensive products. That means that this sector is solely responsible for the increase of exports from the United States into West Germany; non-R&D-intensive exports from the United States into West Germany diminished not only in relative but also in absolute terms. Compared with the United States, West Germany is still a net importer of high technology goods, although this tendency appears to be diminishing. The exact opposite is true of high commodity products.

A product-group-based analysis of the division of labor between West Germany and the United States demonstrates that German industry compensates for the imbalance in R&D-intensive products predominantly through automobile exports. Exactly 50 percent of all exports of R&D-intensive goods from West Germany into the United States are automobiles. Other strong areas in German industry include mechanical engineering, precision engineering and optics, and some metal products. American industry dominates in the areas of fission and breeder products, office and data processing machines, as well as in the aircraft and aerospace industries; furthermore, the United States has a comparative advantage in electrotechnical products, synthetic materials, and various

TABLE 7.5
Revealed Comparative Advantage of West Germany in Trade of R&D-Intensive Products vis-à-vis United States and Japan

Specification	1978	1979	1980	1981	1982	1983	1984	1985	1986
United States									
High technology	−178.3	−147.4	−137.0	−142.2	−125.8	−129.3	−134.1	−149.0	−146.4
High commodity	70.3	63.4	80.5	75.3	73.6	66.2	64.1	59.5	68.0
R&D-intensive products	−0.9	0.4	15.0	1.8	11.1	5.3	3.3	−4.3	0.7
Japan									
High technology	62.7	50.8	57.4	51.2	32.4	7.3	−13.4	−23.6	−9.0
High commodity	−3.4	−6.6	−8.5	−15.8	−12.7	−11.8	−17.1	−8.5	−9.5
R&D-intensive products	11.8	3.0	2.9	−4.3	−4.2	−8.2	−16.3	−11.3	−9.4

SOURCE: Harald Legler, *Trends und Positionen der Bundesrepublik im internationalen Wettbewerb* (Hannover: Niedersächsisches Institut für Wirtschaftsforschung, 1987).

other chemical products. As demonstrated above, the United States has, on the whole, suffered large declines in its relative position in international trade of technology-intensive products. While still able to better its position relative to West Germany, the United States has lost considerable ground against other economies, mainly Japan.

West Germany has not had a positive balance of trade in R&D-intensive products with Japan in the 1980s. Nevertheless, there was a positive balance for high technology product groups until 1983. Generally, however, both categories continued to deteriorate until 1984, when German industry could improve its performance in the high commodity sector. In 1986 the German position in high technology products also improved.

A comparison of cross-sectional data for 1978 and 1986 shows that West Germany was able to increase its results only in a few groups of goods, such as fission and breeder products, precision engineering and optics, and some metal products. There has also been a focus on the chemical industry and, in relative terms, on mechanical engineering in relationship to Japan. However, the extreme deficit in the deteriorating trade balance in office and data processing machines, electrotechnology, and motor vehicles is becoming visible, as far as the R&D-intensive sector applies to these groups of goods. Deficit (but improving) balances can also be observed in precision engineering and optics and some metal products.

AN ASSESSMENT OF THE RESULTS

Two points from these results will disappoint the Ministry for Research and Technology, which commissioned the studies on which this paper is based. First, the R&D-intensive sector in West Germany has not exhibited the same brilliant results over the last few years that it has in the past. The second disappointment is that West Germany has not fared better within the narrower area of high technology products in the R&D-intensive sector. The decline in the specialization in R&D-intensive goods should, therefore, be reconsidered because R&D intensification was advocated in West Germany, especially by the Ministry for Research and Technology.

Due to its expansion of R&D capacity, German R&D intensity had surpassed Great Britain and the Netherlands by the mid-1970s and Switzerland by 1980. However, Japan, whose R&D intensity has approached that of the United States, recently surpassed West Germany (see table 7.6). Sweden and France are also in this catch-up race, and the smaller economies demonstrate the clearest success in R&D intensification. Although West Germany has consistently held third place for many years, on the whole, R&D intensification in the 1980s has not progressed as rapidly in West Germany as in the rest of the world. R&D competition has become broader, which can be interpreted to mean that West Ger-

TABLE 7.6
R&D Intensity in OECD Countries
(R&D Expenditure as a Percentage of Gross Domestic Product)

Country	1975	1980	1985
Canada	1.15	1.17	1.38
United States	2.38	2.46	2.83^b
Japan	2.01	2.22	2.81
Australia	1.0^a	1.0^a	1.14
New Zealand	0.87	0.9^a	1.1^a
Belgium-Luxembourg	1.30	1.4^a	1.4^a
Denmark	1.08	1.04	1.26^b
France	1.80	1.84	2.31^b
West Germany	2.24	2.4^a	2.66^b
Greece	0.20	0.2^a	0.34^b
Ireland	0.86	0.7^a	0.80^b
Italy	0.93	0.86	1.33
Netherlands	2.02	1.89	1.99^b
United Kingdom	2.03	2.3^a	2.33^b
Austria	0.92	1.1^a	1.27^b
Finland	0.91	1.1^a	1.53^b
Iceland	0.94	0.7^a	0.83^b
Norway	1.34	1.27	1.53
Portugal	0.3^a	0.33	0.4^a
Spain	0.35	0.40	0.4^a
Sweden	1.80	2.0^a	2.79^b
Switzerland	2.40	2.3^a	2.3^a
Turkey	0.2^a	0.6^a	0.2^a

SOURCE: Harald Legler, *Trends und Positionen der Bundesrepublik im internationalen Wettbewerb* (Hannover: Niedersächsisches Institut für Wirtschaftsforschung, 1987).
[a] Estimation.
[b] Preliminary results.

many does indeed possess considerable advantages in R&D endowment. In relative terms, however, these advantages have diminished. West Germany's high but declining specialization in technology-intensive goods is accurately portrayed in foreign trade statistics. Smaller economies have reduced the gaps, especially in the high commodity markets. The United States and Japan have had the same experiences.

Furthermore, developments in real exchange rates in the 1980s have tended to favor those sectors that are not highly R&D-intensive. Since the end of the 1970s, West Germany has supplied its products at relatively favorable prices as compared with the late 1960s. The price-elastic sector of industry, which makes little demand on R&D as well as on the quality of personnel, has benefited from this development. Those sectors that depend more heavily on qualitative competition than price competition have had only a marginal advantage. There might be an additional explanation: industries in these sectors could expand trade on the world market or substitute imports protected by above-average tariffs or nontariff trade barriers or subsidies. The structural effects of subsidies, protectionism, and changes in real exchange rates must also be considered. If all these factors are taken into account, the relative loss in importance of the R&D-intensive sector is not unexpected.

A similar situation exists for the second disillusionment mentioned, the low rank of high technology products in the hierarchy of specialization. Because West Germany ranks high in R&D, it is often concluded that if the R&D system is efficient, high technology products should be prominent in West Germany's international trade. However, this overlooks the importance of the international division of labor in R&D, in which distribution of R&D within product areas differs considerably among economies.

Table 7.7 very clearly illustrates the leading role the United States is playing in the high technology sector. It exhibits above-average R&D intensities in every branch of high technology as defined by the OECD. This record is surpassed only by Great Britain in electronics and pharmaceuticals. Great Britain is the only other country that has achieved the average 11 percent value in R&D intensity in the high technology sector, a value all but "prescribed" by the United States. Japan, with 5 percent, clearly ranks below West Germany and France at 7.7 and 7.3, respectively. West Germany, on the other hand, has not achieved the average R&D intensity in any of the high technology industries; Japan has reached the average in pharmaceuticals, and France in electronics.

It should be noted that the hierarchy of R&D intensities among economies in the high technology sector is proportional to the degree of government funding for industrial R&D. In 1983 the government of the United States financed 32 percent; Great Britain, 30 percent; France, 22 percent; West Germany, 16 percent; and Japan, 2 percent.[18] In other words, *government-financed* R&D expenditures in the United States alone were equal to the *total* R&D expenditures of Japan and exceeded the *total* R&D expenditures of West Germany by 50 percent.

The primary domain of both German and Japanese research efforts is in areas classified as medium technology by the OECD, an area in which the strength of the United States and Great Britain declines considerably. West Germany ranks at the top in such areas as chemicals, mechanical engineering, and plastics and rubber, while the United States leads in automobiles and Japan in nonferrous metals. Japan and West Germany, however, lead medium technology in terms of the worldwide division of labor in R&D. The United States and Great Britain have traditionally devoted themselves to the development of the high technology sector.

A recent study by the Fraunhofer-Institut für Systemtechnik und Innovationsforschung measured the technical performance of the most advanced industrial nations in selected new products and processes (including solar cells and modules, industrial robots, laser beam sources, sensors, immobilized biocatalysts, and genetically produced therapeutic agents for humans). This study concluded that the level of technical performance is a direct function of R&D input:

> American technology and Japanese technology stand out as opposites: U.S. technology dominates in the most research-intensive sectors of leading-edge technology, while the strengths of Japanese technology lie in product areas involving medium expenditure on research. Compared to these two countries, West German technical standards are balanced and at a high level. In terms of results, West German standards on average exceed Japanese standards in leading-edge technologies and American standards in other consumer technologies.[19]

This contrast is reflected in international trade statistics and indicates that specialization in the narrow and expensive area of high technology by the West Germans was not likely. Rather, a strong position in the relatively wide sector of product groups with less, but nonetheless significant, innovative potential was expected. The German economy has shown great strength in this sector for many years, but not in the narrow area of high technology that was in large part promoted by massive subsidies and huge military procurements. It is not always beneficial to specialize in areas in which other economies clearly enjoy a comparative advantage. Every new technology does not have to be developed in every country. Even in trade of technology-intensive products, it is necessary to take advantage of an international division of labor.[20]

West Germany earns its high factor incomes by offering a broad range of high commodity products and is a more "universal supplier" than either Japan or the United States. West Germany should continue this proven strategy in the future instead of pouring large amounts of money into risky high technologies. Actual events, however, have taken another direction. Participation in the Strategic Defense Initiative, Eureka, and European aerospace projects is both expensive and a symptom of megalomania. When the comparative advantages of other economies in these fields of R&D are taken into account, the potential positive effects on the macroeconomic level of employment and income are very uncertain in West Germany. In the face of the accumulated R&D potential of other, more established competitors, West Germany's prospects for success in the high technology race may be dim.[21]

TABLE 7.7
Intensity of R&D Expenditure in OECD Countries, 1980 (R&D Expenditure as a Percentage of Output)

Industry	United States	Japan	West Germany	France	Great Britain	Eleven main countries
High Technology						
Aerospace	36.1	1.0	21.6	14.1	>20	22.7
Office machines, computers	19.3	5.9	6.5	10.1	10.5	17.5
Electronics and components	14.4	6.2	8.1[a]	11.4	18.2	10.4
Drugs	9.5	8.8	8.3	5.1	12.5	8.7
Scientific instruments	10.5	2.8	2.1	2.5	2.1	4.8
Electrical machinery	7.3	3.5	8.1[a]	1.6	1.8	4.4
Average	15.8	5.0	7.7	7.3	11	11.4
Medium Technology						
Automobiles	3.0	2.8	2.7	2.1	1.8	2.7
Chemicals	1.7	3.0	3.4	1.9	2.1	2.3
Other manufacturing industries	n.a.	n.a.	5.4	n.a.	n.a.	1.8
Nonelectrical machinery	1.8	1.7	2.3	0.6	1.4	1.6
Rubber, plastics	1.2	1.2	1.6	1.6	0.6	1.2
Nonferrous metals	0.7	2.3	0.6	0.6	0.6	1.0
Average	2.0	2.2–2.3	2.7	1.4–1.5	1.5	1.7

			Low Technology			
Stone, clay, glass	1.0	0.9	0.7	0.5	0.5	0.9
Food, beverages, tobacco	0.2	0.4	0.2	0.1	0.3	0.8
Shipbuilding	n.a.	3.6	0.6	0.2	0.6	0.6
Petrol refineries	0.7	0.3	0.5	0.5	0.2	0.6
Ferrous metals	0.6	1.1	0.6	0.3	0.3	0.6
Fabricated metal products	0.6	0.5	0.7	0.5	0.5	0.4
Paper, printing	0.4	0.1	0.2	n.a.	0.1	0.3
Wood, cork, furniture	0.3	n.a.	0.2	n.a.	0.1	0.3
Textiles, footwear, leather	0.3	0.2	0.2	0.1	0.1	0.2
Average	0.4	0.4–0.5	0.4	0.2	0.2	0.5
Manufacturing	2.6	1.6	2.1	1.4	2.0	2.0

SOURCE: Hariolf Grupp and Harald Legler, *Spitzentechnik, Gebrauchstechnik, Innovationspotential und Preise* (Cologne: Verlag TÜV Rheinland, 1987).

[a]Intensity of both industries combined.

NOTES

1. These studies included "Wettbewerbsfähigkeit im Exportgeschäft trotz einiger Schwachstellen gut behauptet," in Deutsche Bundesbank, ed., *Geschäftsbericht für das Jahr 1983* (Frankfurt: Deutsche Bundesbank, 1984), pp. 54–62; Sachverständigenrat zur Begutachtung der gesamtwirtschaftlichen Entwicklung, *Jahresgutachten 1984/85*, Bundestagsdrucksache 10/2541 (Bonn: Verlag Dr. Hans Heger, 1984); Organisation for Economic Cooperation and Development, *Trade in High Technology Products: An Initial Contribution to the Statistical Analysis of Trade Patterns in High Technology Products*, DST/SPR/84.66, DSTI/IND/84.60 (Paris: OECD, 1985); Kommission der europäischen Gemeinschaft, *Die Wettbewerbsfähigkeit der Industrien der europäischen Gemeinschaft* (Luxembourg: Kommission der europäischen Gemeinschaft, 1982); Konrad Faust and Hans Schedl, *Internationale Wettbewerbsfähigkeit und strukturelle Anpassungserfordernisse der deutschen Industrie* (Munich: ifo-Institut für Wirtschaftsforschung, 1983); Hans-Hagen Härtel and Christian Langer, *Internationale Wettbewerbsfähigkeit und strukturelle Anpassungserfordernisse* (Hamburg: HWWA-Institut für Wirtschaftsforschung, 1984); and Ernst-Jürgen Horn, *Weltwirtschaftliche Herausforderung—Die deutschen Unternehmen im Anpassungsprozeß* (Kiel: Institut für Weltwirtschaft, 1983).

2. Organisation for Economic Cooperation and Development, *Gaps in Technology: Comparisons between Member Countries in Education, Research and Development, Technological Innovation, and International Economic Exchanges* (Paris: OECD, 1970).

3. Dieter Orlowski, *Die internationale Wettbewerbsfähigkeit einer Volkswirtschaft* (Göttingen: Vandenhoeck & Ruprecht, 1982).

4. Sachverständigenrat zur Begutachtung der gesamtwirtschaftlichen Entwicklung, *Jahresgutachten 1981/82*, Bundestagsdrucksache 9/1061 (Bonn: Verlag Dr. Hans Heger, 1981).

5. Dietmar Keller and Christian Langer, "Internationale Wettbewerbsfähigkeit bei technologieintensiven Gütern," *Wirtschaftsdienst*, no. 10 (1984): 483–88.

6. Harald Legler, *Trends und Positionen der Bundesrepublik im internationalen Wettbewerb* (Hannover: Niedersächsisches Institut für Wirtschaftsforschung, 1987).

7. Harald Legler, "Ökonomische Aspekte der Auswahl von Hochtechnologiesektoren," in Hariolf Grupp, ed., *Workshop Technometrie* (Karlsruhe: Fraunhofer-Institut für Systemtechnik und Innovationsforschung, 1986), pp. 95–110.

8. Hariolf Grupp and Harald Legler, *Spitzentechnik, Gebrauchstechnik, Innovationspotential, und Preise* (Cologne: Verlag TÜV Rheinland, 1987).

9. Harald Legler, "Zur Position der Bundesrepublik Deutschland im internationalen Wettbewerb," *Forschungsberichte des Niedersächsischen Institut für Wirtschaftsforschung*, no. 3 (1982).

10. This distinction is made in Hans-Hagen Härtel and Eberhard Thiel, *Analyse der strukturellen Entwicklung der deutschen Wirtschaft* (Hamburg: Verlag Weltarchiv, 1981).

11. In West Germany, for example, 50 percent of the total industrial R&D expenditure in these sectors is financed by the government.

12. See Legler, *Trends und Positionen*, pp. 42–43, for further details.

13. Keller and Langer, "Wettbewerbsfähigkeit."

14. $$\mathrm{RWS}_{ij} = \left[\ln \left(\frac{a_{ij}}{\Sigma_j a_{ij}} : \frac{\Sigma_i a_{ij}}{\Sigma_i \Sigma_j a_{ij}} \right) \right] 100, \qquad -\infty \leq \mathrm{RWS}_{ij} \leq \infty;$$

where a = exports, i = country index, and j = product group index. The relative world trade share is also used in Gerhard Fels, Ernst-Jürgen Horn, Klaus-Werner Schatz, and Frank Wolter, *Analyse der Erfordernisse und Konsequenzen einer Aussparungsstrategie im Vergleich zu einer Universalstrategie* (Kiel: Institut für Weltwirtschaft, 1976); a different formula, however, is used here.

15. $$\mathrm{RCA}_{ij} = \left[\ln \left(\frac{a_{ij}}{e_{ij}} : \frac{\Sigma_j a_{ij}}{\Sigma_j e_{ij}} \right) \right] 100, \qquad -\infty \leq \mathrm{RCA}_{ij} \leq \infty;$$

where a = exports, e = imports, i = country index, and j = product group index. The concept of RCA originates from Bela Balassa, "Trade Liberalization and Trade in Manufacturers among the Industrial Countries," *American Economic Review* 56 (1965): 466–73. The formula used here is derived from Frank Wolter, "Factor Proportions, Technology, and West-German Industry's International Trade," *Weltwirtschaftliches Archiv* 113 (1977): 250–67.

16. Grupp and Legler, *Spitzentechnik*, pp. 33–45.

17. Legler, *Trends und Positionen*, pp. 23–27.

18. Organisation for Economic Cooperation and Development, *Science and Technology Indicators, No. 2: R&D, Invention, and Competitiveness* (Paris: OECD, 1986).

19. Hariolf Grupp, Olav Hohmeyer, Roland Kollert, and Harald Legler, *Technometrie—Die Bemessung des technisch-wirtschaftlichen Leistungsstandes* (Cologne: Verlag TÜV Rheinland, 1987), pp. 10–11.

20. Keller and Langer, "Wettbewerbsfähigkeit."

21. Konrad Faust, "Früherkennung technischer Entwicklung aus der statistischen Analyse von Patentdaten," *ifo-Schnelldienst*, no. 30 (1987): 7–12.

8

The Challenge to U.S. Leadership
in High Technology Industries: Can the
United States Maintain Its Lead? Should It Try?

RACHEL MCCULLOCH

At the close of World War II, the United States emerged as the acknowledged global leader in both science and its industrial application.
While U.S. science has been able to maintain that preeminence in most
areas, the nation's technological lead has met increasingly formidable
challenges from abroad. Today, a number of U.S. high technology industries have already lost their accustomed positions in world markets;
a growing share of the commercial benefits from major U.S. scientific
advances is now captured by foreign, rather than American, producers.

In the postwar period, U.S. excellence in science and technology has
been vital not only to the dramatic rise in living standard enjoyed by
most Americans but also to national security and the central role of the
United States in the Western alliance. The erosion of the nation's technological superiority therefore calls into question the ability of the United
States to sustain its leadership role in global institutions. Competitors
abroad, understandably proud of their recent gains at the expense of a
once-invincible economic and military rival, are at the same time uneasy
about the wider implications for international stability of waning U.S.
hegemony.

The future of U.S. high technology industries has thus emerged as a
major focus of public policy. This paper examines the recent performance
of U.S. high technology industries and policy options for maintaining or
improving that performance. In the first section I review postwar trends
in U.S. performance relative to major competitors abroad and the implications of these trends for U.S. trade. In the second section I analyze
the distinctive economic features of high technology industries and evaluate the potential costs and benefits from policies to promote high technology production. In the third section I present an approach for evaluating policy alternatives. In the last section I sum up the implications

Thanks are due to the National Science Foundation, the German Marshall Fund of the
United States, and the Ford Foundation for research support.

of a diminished U.S. lead in science and technology for U.S. international competitiveness and national well-being.

Three decades have passed since the Soviet Union shocked complacent Americans with the successful launch of *Sputnik*. The Soviet triumph touched off a prolonged wave of national soul-searching but also stimulated coherent national action. Moving quickly from collective humiliation to new levels of resource commitment, Americans became the first people to walk on the face of the moon.

Until the 1980s, the commercial challenges to U.S. technological supremacy were less dramatic. Although other U.S. manufacturing industries gradually lost their shares of foreign and even domestic markets to competitors abroad, high technology production appeared to be largely immune.[1] The U.S. trade balance on other manufactured goods had already moved into deficit by 1970, but the overall balance on trade in high technology products continued to grow.

The Balance of Trade in High Technology Products

Despite some significant losses on particular goods, the U.S. trade surplus in high technology manufactured products rose from \$6.1 billion in 1970 to \$26.6 billion in 1980. Net trade in other manufacturing followed an opposite trend, with the deficit on U.S. trade in non–high technology products growing from \$3.8 billion in 1970 to \$9.2 billion by 1980 (table 8.1).

But 1980 proved to be a turning point for U.S. performance in high technology trade. The surplus generated by high technology products narrowed in each subsequent year, falling to \$3.6 billion by 1985. The deterioration was less marked than in other manufacturing industries, where by 1985 the deficit had reached an astonishing level of \$111 billion. However, the pattern was similar, with deterioration of U.S. performance in almost every product category and in almost every major trading relationship.

For both high technology and non–high technology trade, the declining balances have reflected primarily surging U.S. imports rather than falling U.S. exports. In high technology trade, the value of U.S. exports nearly doubled between 1978 and 1985—but imports more than tripled over the same period. For non–high technology manufactures, the contrast between export and import growth was almost as dramatic, with the value of exports rising from \$66.6 billion in 1978 to \$93.5 billion in 1985, while imports soared from \$90.6 billion to \$204.6 billion.

TABLE 8.1

U.S. Trade Balance in High Technology and Non–High Technology
Manufactured Product Groups (in Billions of U.S. Dollars)

Year	High technology products			Non–high technology products		
	Exports	Imports	Balance	Exports	Imports	Balance
1970	10.3	4.2	6.1	19.0	22.8	−3.8
1971	11.4	4.9	6.5	19.0	27.4	−8.4
1972	11.9	6.3	5.6	21.8	33.7	11.9
1973	15.9	7.9	8.0	28.8	39.8	11.0
1974	21.5	9.8	11.7	42.0	49.7	−7.7
1975	22.9	9.5	13.4	48.1	45.5	2.6
1976	25.6	13.2	12.4	51.6	56.4	−4.8
1977	27.3	15.3	12.0	52.9	66.6	−13.7
1978	34.5	20.1	14.4	59.5	86.7	−27.2
1979	43.1	22.5	20.6	77.9	96.3	−18.4
1980	54.2	27.7	26.6	95.0	104.2	−9.2
1981	59.9	33.5	26.6	100.7	115.7	−15.0
1982	57.6	34.1	23.4	89.8	116.5	−26.7
1983	59.7	40.9	18.8	79.9	129.9	−59.0
1984	65.0	58.7	16.2	86.2	173.2	−87.0
1985	68.4	64.8	3.6	93.5	204.6	−111.0

SOURCES: National Science Foundation, "International Science and Technology Data Update, 1986" (Directorate for Scientific, Technological, and International Affairs, Division of Science Resource Studies, 1986), p. 54; and U.S. Department of Commerce, *United States Trade: Performance in 1985 and Outlook* (Washington, D.C.: U.S. Department of Commerce, International Trade Administration, October 1986), p. 131.

NOTE: Based on U.S. Department of Commerce DOC-3 definition of high technology products. Data for 1970–77 are estimates.

The relatively minor reduction in the U.S. high technology trade surplus, in comparison to the marked decline in performance of mature industries, is a reflection of continuing U.S. leadership in many high technology sectors. Producers in the United States operate at a substantial labor-cost disadvantage relative to most trading partners, and the impact of this cost disadvantage on U.S. sales is greatest where comparable goods are available from a number of sources worldwide. The U.S. cost disadvantage was exacerbated in the first half of the 1980s by the rising international value of the dollar.

But in the high technology field, the United States remains the sole source of many leading-edge goods (and services). For these products, labor costs and exchange rates play a smaller role in determining U.S. trade performance. Even so, high costs of U.S. production can influence the decision of U.S. firms to establish subsidiaries abroad. The main "foreign" competition for U.S. high technology products often comes from foreign affiliates of U.S. companies.

The U.S. Share in World Exports

U.S. shares in world production or world exports likewise confirm a decline in the U.S. relative position. This is true both in overall manufacturing and in high technology manufacturing. Part of this decline can be attributed to the influence of "temporary" macroeconomic factors, especially the huge U.S. budget deficit. However, it also reflects a process that can be expected to continue and even to accelerate: an increase in the number of nations with the knowledge base and the industrial capacity to quickly absorb and apply new technologies.

In 1950 the United States accounted for more than 40 percent of total world output and about 17 percent of world exports. By 1980 the U.S. share in global output had dwindled to 22 percent and its exports to 11 percent. These data are used by Bhagwati and Irwin to establish a striking parallel between the postwar decline in U.S. global dominance and the relative decline of Britain in the nineteenth century.[2]

However, the use of 1950 as a base year for the comparison may exaggerate the decline in relative economic strength of the United States. As Baldwin points out, the period immediately after World War II was itself atypical.[3] The United States had emerged from the war with greatly expanded productive capacity, while its erstwhile adversaries and allies alike had sustained extensive losses of capital and human resources. Every U.S. manufacturing industry was able to show a trade surplus, a situation that masked the relative weakness of some. U.S. shares of world activity just after the war were significantly above the corresponding measures for the period just before the war. The U.S. share of total exports of the ten most important industrial countries was 35 percent as late as 1952, while it had been only 26 percent in 1938 and 28 percent in 1928.

Looking specifically at national shares in total world exports of high technology products, the U.S. share has actually risen in recent years and by 1984 was less than two percentage points below its 1965 level (25.2 percent versus 27.5 percent; see table 8.2). The dramatic change in the global market has been the increase in the Japanese share, which rose from 7.3 percent in 1965 to 20.2 percent in 1984. However, the Japanese gains have come primarily at the expense of other nations, notably the United Kingdom, rather than the United States. Table 8.3 shows that in 1984 the United States retained relative strength in most technology-intensive product groups but had declined to a minor presence in radio and television receiving equipment, a category dominated by the Japanese with almost 80 percent of total world exports. These trends indicate that the major change in patterns of global competition in high

TABLE 8.2

World Export Shares of Technology-Intensive Products (Percentages)

Country	1965	1970	1975	1980	1981	1982	1983	1984
United States	27.5	27.0	24.5	22.9	23.0	24.7	25.1	25.2
Japan	7.3	10.9	11.6	14.3	17.4	16.2	17.8	20.2
France	7.3	7.1	8.4	8.5	7.9	8.3	7.7	7.7
West Germany	16.9	16.8	16.8	16.3	14.8	15.5	15.0	14.5
United Kingdom	12.0	9.8	9.6	10.8	9.0	9.4	8.7	8.5

SOURCE: National Science Foundation, "International Science and Technology Data Update, 1986" (Directorate for Scientific, Technological, and International Affairs, Division of Science Resource Studies, 1986), p. 58.

NOTE: Technology-intensive products are defined as those for which R&D expenditures exceed 2.36 percent of value-added (DOC-2/OECD definition).

TABLE 8.3

World Export Shares of Technology-Intensive Products, 1984 (Percentages)

Product field	United States	Japan	West Germany	France	United Kingdom
Aircraft and parts	45.1	0.5	15.2	11.8	14.5
Industrial inorganic chemicals	23.9	4.3	15.0	11.5	12.2
Radio and TV receiving equipment	0.5	79.5	8.2	1.0	2.2
Office and computing machines	35.5	19.1	9.2	5.6	9.5
Electrical machinery and equipment	23.9	19.3	17.3	8.2	9.2
Communications equipment	26.5	35.5	10.4	6.1	6.4
Professional and scientific instruments	13.7	31.2	15.3	5.7	7.4
Drugs	19.6	2.6	15.8	10.7	11.9
Plastic materials, synthetics	14.4	10.1	21.4	9.5	6.9
Engines and turbines	29.0	17.4	16.4	1.9	8.7
Agricultural chemicals	33.7	4.1	13.0	7.2	7.2

SOURCE: National Science Foundation, "International Science and Technology Data Update, 1986" (Directorate for Scientific, Technological, and International Affairs, Division of Science Resource Studies, 1986), p. 60.

NOTE: Technology-intensive products are defined as those for which R&D expenditures exceed 2.36 percent of value-added (DOC-2/OECD definition).

technology products has been less the decline of the United States than the rise of Japan.

Declining U.S. Competitiveness?

Moreover, because the usual indicators of U.S. market losses take no account of the concomitant rise in U.S.-controlled production abroad, these indicators may overstate the decline of the United States as an economic power.[4] The U.S. share of world manufactured exports fell from over 17 percent in 1966 to less than 14 percent by 1983. However, the global share of U.S. multinational *firms* remained unchanged over almost two decades, with gains in exports of majority-owned foreign affiliates compensating for declines in exports from parents.[5] Thus, while U.S. manufactured exports are indeed losing their share of world markets, to a great degree they are losing it not to foreign competitors but to themselves, that is, to foreign subsidiaries of U.S. companies.[6]

This evidence suggests that much of the current discussion of declining U.S. competitiveness does not fit the facts. In particular, analyses that focus on failings of U.S. management and innovation are inconsistent with the sustained market shares of U.S. firms. Rather, the data show that the United States has lost ground primarily as a locus of production. Differences in costs are presumably the main factor underlying the shift abroad by multinational corporations of production activities. Effective policies to improve U.S. competitiveness must address the determinants of these costs in order to upgrade the United States as a site for production.

Implications of the Closing Gap

While the postwar scientific and technological advances of Europe and Asia are undeniably impressive, these gains were made possible in large part by the existence of a technology gap between the United States and other industrial nations. Even in those cases where considerations of national security prompted the United States to limit foreign access to its advanced technology, scientists abroad were often able to duplicate U.S. results at a small fraction of the original cost. Thus, as other nations achieve parity with the United States in scientific and technological endeavors, global patterns of innovation and dissemination will undergo corresponding changes.

Like other nations, the United States has always derived substantial benefits from imported scientific and technological knowledge. In the postwar period, however, the significant U.S. lead in most areas meant that this source of advance was of only secondary importance. Although catch-up abroad entails painful adjustments for the U.S. economy, it also means a potential increase in U.S. gains from technological imports. Although the specter of other nations closing the technology gap is evidently distasteful to some nationalistic Americans, over the long term it offers the opportunity for mutual gains through expanded two-way trade in new knowledge. Other consequences include greater U.S. participation in international cooperative research projects and commercial joint ventures, a trend already well under way.

The Role of Domestic Research and Development

Critics of U.S. policy argue that the United States has fallen behind in research and development (R&D) relative both to other major nations today and to its own past efforts. This assessment is based largely on comparisons of R&D spending as a share of gross national product (GNP), a measure that shows other nations catching up to or even surpassing the United States. Yet the United States still spends far more in total than any other Organisation for Economic Cooperation and Development (OECD) nation, a reflection of the nation's much larger size. (The Soviet Union, not an OECD member, is estimated to allocate an amount comparable to that of the United States.)[7]

Recommendations intended to restore the U.S. competitive edge in high technology production almost always include measures to spur domestic R&D. This prescription reflects two implicit assumptions: first, that more R&D means more innovation and productivity growth; and second, that these assumed results of U.S. R&D activity influence mainly *domestic* productivity growth and thereby boost U.S. international competitiveness. However, there is scant empirical evidence to justify this critical assumed link between a nation's aggregate R&D and productivity gains relative to competitors abroad.

In the past, lack of ability to absorb and apply new knowledge was the major factor preventing foreign firms from sharing equally in the commercial benefits from U.S. R&D. Today, however, new technical knowledge is quickly transmitted abroad and applied by foreign as well as domestic firms. In particular, subsidiaries abroad of U.S. multinationals can be expected to enjoy a level of technological advancement similar to that of the U.S. parent.

Absorptive capacity, rather than national boundaries, is the key to determining the implications of U.S. R&D for the international competitiveness of American producers. On the other hand, U.S. firms can now benefit from new knowledge resulting from foreign R&D activity. Narrowing of the technology gap between the United States and other industrial nations thus means expanded opportunities for two-way trade in knowledge as well as products. And the recent growth in offshore research activities undertaken by U.S. multinationals and in U.S. research activities of foreign multinationals further blunts the significance of comparisons between U.S. and "foreign" R&D spending.

MOTIVES FOR PROMOTING HIGH TECHNOLOGY PRODUCTION

The United States is one among many nations currently seeking to promote domestic high technology industries. This goal of government trade and industrial policies has become commonplace not only for most of the industrialized nations but also for many less-developed countries. In some cases, the cost as conventionally measured of maintaining the sectors in question appears to be staggering (although perhaps less than for the ubiquitously sheltered agricultural sectors of industrial nations). And notwithstanding large expenditures, many such attempts are ultimately unsuccessful in creating an economically viable domestic industry. Thus, it is important to identify the broader objectives the United States and other nations seek to foster through support of high technology production.

Policies to Raise National Income

Economists' theoretical analyses of trade policy usually assume as a starting point the goal of maximizing national income or, more precisely, its present discounted value. On this basis, there are two fundamental justifications for departures from laissez-faire, both resting on an assumed divergence of social and private benefits. The first justification, which entails gains for one country at the expense of its trading partners, is the optimum tariff argument. A country that is large relative to the world market can improve its terms of trade (the price of its exports relative to that of its imports) by restricting the volume of trade; the optimum tariff sets the level of trade restriction to balance these terms-of-trade gains against the accompanying reduction in trade volume.

However, the same logic suggests that large suppliers should shun export subsidies (which would increase industry profits but lower national income). Since subsidies to production and export are endemic in high technology industries, it is safe to conclude that maximization of national income through terms-of-trade manipulation is not the relevant consideration underlying support of these industries.

A recent variant of this reasoning views trade and industrial policies as means by which a nation can increase its share of worldwide economic profits ("rents") in oligopolistic industries.[8] As in the case of terms-of-trade manipulation, one country's gain from such a strategy is likely to mean corresponding losses abroad. However, the implications for global efficiency are ambiguous, since the starting point is not (as in the standard optimal tariff analysis) a Pareto optimum. I return to this point in the third section.

The second theoretical justification of government intervention to increase national income requires that a productive activity generate benefits not fully captured by the producing firm. Under these conditions, the market-determined level of the activity may be too low relative to its value to society, and there is a case on narrow efficiency grounds for a subsidy to production. However, direct production subsidies are rarely employed, or even proposed. Rather, the alleged spillover becomes the basis of an argument for import restrictions or export incentives. These policies do provide an implicit subsidy to domestic production, but they also provide an implicit tax on domestic consumption. Their use can therefore be justified on second-best grounds if the social benefit from the production subsidy outweighs the social loss from the consumption tax.

Assumed spillovers or externalities from high technology production are frequently cited as the main rationale for policies to promote these industries (and recently, more broadly, to promote any "complex production"). Appeals based on learning curves, forward linkages, strategic activities, and maintenance of an industrial base are all updated versions of the traditional infant-industry argument for protection and subject to the same qualifications.[9]

Two important qualifications must be met for protection to be justified along these lines. First, there must actually *be* an externality. In particular, this means that the mere existence of learning-by-doing is not enough; it must be impossible for firms to fully capture these benefits. This could be true because of problems of technological appropriability or because private capital markets are imperfect in their ability to finance large, risky, long-range projects.

In addition, the size of the expected benefit must be sufficiently great to offset, in present-value terms, the cost of the policy needed to produce the benefit. This condition is more likely to be met if the productive activity can be encouraged directly rather than through trade intervention, since the latter entails additional cost. The additional cost is still greater, and the case for intervention correspondingly weaker, if the facilitating policy is maintained after the infant has matured.

The externalities argument does seem at least potentially relevant to the case for government suppport of high technology industries. In particular, the fruits of R&D may not be captured fully by the innovating firm, especially in industries such as electronics, where the market is served by a large number of small firms. On the other hand, there is no clear evidence that as a consequence of appropriability problems, firms do in fact engage in a suboptimal aggregate level of R&D; rivalry among firms may induce duplication of R&D efforts.

Furthermore, as in any efficiency argument for government intervention, the potential for a welfare gain from an optimal policy does not ensure that the actual policies adopted with this motive will be socially beneficial. And because the affected domestic industry almost always benefits from preferential policies regardless of whether the broader national interest is served, an activist trade or industrial policy is likely to divert substantial industry resources into lobbying. A final consideration is that policies that promote the growth of particular high technology sectors (targeting) or of high technology industries as a group will, except in the very long run, drive up the costs to all users of specialized inputs, for example, the salaries of scientists and engineers.[10]

Other Policy Goals

A more basic question concerns the appropriateness of the assumed ultimate goal used in most economic analyses: maximization of national income. It is clear that national policies are also shaped by other criteria, including the distribution of earned income and the composition of domestic production. With respect to the former, U.S. policy to a large extent aims to maintain the status quo, that is, to slow the process by which changes in competitive conditions worldwide (whatever their cause) are translated into corresponding changes in U.S. earnings or employment patterns.

The second criterion, composition of domestic production, also figures prominently in national policy-making, although it is rarely stated in this way. Arguments about American deindustrialization and about the strategic role of particular industries usually reflect implicit assumptions about the desirable composition of the nation's output. The national debate about causes and consequences of "loss of international competitiveness" has as its heart the question of how the composition of employment or production ought to be determined. Also important is that issues of distribution and of industrial composition are intimately related; an accelerated shift away from the manufacturing industries (or from mature industries to newer ones) entails important redistributive consequences by region, sex, race, education, and union status.

Issues Involved in the Promotion of High Technology Industries

The high technology manufacturing sector consists of individual industries, each with its own distinctive economic features and policy concerns. The common defining feature is the high share of R&D activities relative to sales, or of "professional, technical, and kindred" employment relative to total employment. However, efforts to promote specifically these industries raise several issues that are much more important than for other types of industrial policy.

First, these are the industries in which the United States has had its clear competitive advantage in recent decades and which together account for the lion's share of U.S. manufactured exports. Access to superior technology has allowed American producers to remain internationally competitive despite labor compensation far higher than in other nations. Thus, there is a strong belief, both in the United States and elsewhere, that high technology production has been the main *cause* of the nation's economic and military strength and that loss of U.S. competitiveness in these industries must mean a corresponding reduction in both the U.S. standard of living and the nation's military might.

Second, for many high technology products, R&D expenditures constitute a substantial fraction of the total cost of production. These large costs of R&D in turn create significant economies of scale. Aircraft is an extreme case of this, in which it is estimated that the total market worldwide can sustain only two, or perhaps three, profitable firms. Furthermore, once the R&D costs associated with a given product or process have been incurred, a private or government-controlled firm may find it optimal to sell at a price that is well below full average cost per unit. If firms or nations price in this way, resulting financial losses to rivals tend to drive some from the industry and thus curtail future competition and innovation.

Third, both technological barriers to entry (proprietary technology in the form of patents, copyrights, and trade secrets, but also absorptive capacity) and pervasive scale economies tend to restrict the number of competitors worldwide at any given time. This means economic profits need not be forced to zero through competition among firms. An additional implication of limited entry is that from a social point of view, production may be too low, that is, the cost of additional output from the industry would be more than justified by its value to potential consumers.

Finally, these industries are perceived as having important links to the nation's defense capabilities. In aircraft as well as semiconductors and computers, past U.S. defense and space expenditures are credited with an important role in facilitating the subsequent commercial dominance of the domestic industry in world markets. But for aircraft, that dominance is threatened today by the success of the European Airbus consortium, while in semiconductors and computers, the Japanese have become an increasingly formidable presence.

Moreover, the implications for the United States of increased R&D activity abroad are more complicated in industries with clear links to defense. The *economic* benefits from one nation's superior products or processes are typically shared worldwide through trade, so that the United States is likely to benefit not only from its own R&D efforts but also from those of other nations. In contrast, the *military* value of new products and processes depends critically on their superiority to what is available elsewhere. From the point of view of defense, a rival nation's gains must always come at the expense of the United States.

Although each of these considerations appears to play some role in shaping national policies toward high technology industries, it seems that the last one, broadly conceived, offers the best explanation for the evident willingness of many nations to promote these industries even at considerable expense in terms of forgone national income. In these industries, world ranking makes an important difference. For the United States, moving from first to second means a fundamental adverse shift in the world strategic balance. For the major economic rivals of the United States, the challenge to U.S. worldwide preeminence in high technology production implies a challenge to U.S. political and military hegemony as well as to established commercial interests.

For minor industrial nations (e.g., Sweden, which has its own national aircraft producer) or for less-developed countries (e.g., Brazil, which has supported a domestic industry in both aircraft and computers), it is evident that the motivation must be somewhat different. Again, however, part of the explanation may hinge on the implications for the nation's political and strategic relationship with the United States and other superpowers. Having a viable domestic industry in, say, aircraft or computers elevates a nation from the dependent status of technological followership, even though the twin goal of leadership may be, at least for the present, unattainable except in relation to other minor nations.

In those industries such as aircraft where sellers are few worldwide, buyers' fears of economic or political exploitation may be justified. However, in light of the strong incentives for sellers to supply their products at a price below full average costs, political costs of dependency seem far more likely than economic ones. This is particularly true when the United States is the relevant external supplier, given the nation's extensive use of temporary trade embargos and the very broad definition of "strategic" importance used in licensing exports with potential military applications.[11]

The Economics of High Technology Production

Arguments for special treatment of high technology industries are usually based in part on the distinctive economic features of these industries' production processes and cost structure. The key role of R&D in these industries has at least three important implications for the role of policy.

First, extensive R&D often means a relatively long period of time between the decision to market a new product and the first sales of that product, and an even longer time until the new product "breaks even." In the case of aircraft, it is estimated that the first positive net cash flow associated with a new model occurs five to ten years after the start of development. In pharmaceuticals, legally mandated product testing almost always means significant delays in bringing a new product to market.

A related characteristic of high technology production is the potentially higher risk than in mature industries. This great risk entails both technological uncertainty with respect to the feasibility of producing the planned product and uncertainty concerning market conditions at the relatively remote date when the product is ready for sale. In the case of aircraft, sales have been affected by unforeseen changes in fuel costs and real interest rates, noise-abatement policies, and deregulation of the U.S. industry. For nuclear power, falling energy prices and conservation have reduced demand, while regulatory difficulties have led to costs several times greater than originally projected.

Both the long period until profits are realized and the greater financial risk suggest that even where the dynamic benefits could potentially be captured entirely by the innovating firm, private capital markets may be unwilling to provide the required financing for major development projects.

Finally, because R&D expenses represent fixed costs that do not depend on the total volume of output produced and because of learning-curve effects, there are typically strong economies of scale in production—the cost of each *additional* unit produced of a given model will be much lower than the average cost per unit (which will itself be a decreasing function of the length of the production run). The firm's profits will thus depend on its ability to spread fixed costs over a sufficiently large volume of output. Another consequence of this cost structure is the incentive to sell products below full average cost, especially in the early stages of a production run. This practice may cause special problems when a profit-motivated firm must compete with government-supported enterprises abroad.

The Problem of Interface

Competition between profit-motivated U.S. firms and enterprises owned or heavily subsidized by foreign governments is not a problem unique to high technology industries. Steel and shipbuilding are examples of mature industries in which governments worldwide have chosen to participate actively, attempting to mitigate the domestic consequences of secularly declining demand and global excess capacity. However, the particular characteristics of high technology industries make the problem of interface between a basically market-oriented domestic industry and competitors underwritten by foreign governments even more complicated than for other manufacturing activities.

As already noted, foreign governments may see special reasons for market-share protection of their high technology industries. Furthermore, the cost structure of these industries presents particular problems in maintaining a competitive market. In light of pervasive scale economies, there are strong economic incentives for import restrictions, dumping, and export or production subsidies. As U.S. firms view the situation, the key economic question is not how many suppliers are needed to meet world demand for a particular product, but, rather, how many different manufacturing entities, each competing for a favorable share of a finite market, can the world industry support?

U.S. reliance on the market as the major mechanism for allocating productive resources entails a belief that investors should be rewarded for risk taking through higher-than-average anticipated profits. In particular, this means the possibility of losses as well as profits from any given undertaking. However, high technology industries pose special problems because profits earned by U.S. firms are likely to depend more on actions of governments (both foreign and U.S.) than on the conventional ingredients of industrial competitiveness. While as a society we may be comfortable with lower profits for an entrepreneur who guesses wrong about tastes, technology, or costs, it is quite different to say the same about losses caused primarily by actions of foreign governments. The long-term survival of the U.S. market-based system may be threatened if domestic firms must compete on equal terms with enterprises bankrolled by foreign treasuries.

From the foreign perspective, however, that support may be deemed necessary in order to avoid economic and political domination by the United States. In aircraft, computers, and semiconductors, foreign governments point to the influence of U.S. military procurement in maintaining the profitability of U.S. firms.[12] Thus, there are really two aspects of interface: between profit-oriented and government-underwritten suppliers, and between defense-related and civilian sales.

ALTERNATIVE POLICY REGIMES

A wide variety of policy measures may be used to enhance the competitive performance of high technology industries. Because these industries are often characterized by oligopolistic rather than highly competitive markets, because of the important role of governments both as consumers and as producers, and because multiple criteria (economic, political, and strategic) are used in evaluating outcomes, economic theory can offer few firm guidelines concerning the potential costs and benefits of policies to promote high technology production or to protect national shares in global markets for specific products.[13]

Rather than attempting here to catalog every possible outcome—in any case, an impossible task—it may be helpful to enumerate the most important dimensions along which the outcomes of alternative policy regimes may be measured.

Specifically, policy outcomes may be judged on the basis of their effects on market competition (number of firms worldwide and in a specific market), cost of production, product variety available to consumers, and national share of global economic profits for the industry.

The last of these is easiest to evaluate. The industries in question are

ones in which positive economic profits (supernormal profits) may be sustained indefinitely. Therefore, other things equal, a country will benefit
from increasing its share of the market and, thereby, its share of the
(relatively fixed) pool of global profits. Although these gains will arise in
the form of higher profits of the relevant national firms, they will normally be shared more broadly through factor payments and taxes. However, one nation's gain in this dimension is necessarily another nation's
loss.

Competition among nations for the fixed total can only reduce world
welfare and may well reduce welfare for each competing nation (the latter is not assured, even when all nations retaliate optimally to their competitors' profit-grabbing tactics). Because of the certainty of global losses
and the likelihood of national losses from competition of this type, there
is a clear case for international agreements to limit at least the most
obvious forms of it.

Again holding other considerations constant, more firms serving a given
market means more competition and greater economic efficiency. In this
case, however, the gains come in the form of benefits to consumers from
a larger volume of production and lower price. Economic profits are expected to decline as the number of competing firms increases, although
the possibility of exit ensures an adequate expected return.

For industries in which the number of firms has no important relationship to cost per unit or to product variety, more competing firms
will always be economically beneficial. This suggests that market share
protection has greater expected benefits (or lower social costs) when it
increases national firms' share in an integrated global market than when
it reserves a particular segment of the market for its own firms. By this
logic, the Airbus market competition strategy is preferable from an efficiency point of view to a restricted-market approach (along the lines of
the U.S.-Japan semiconductor agreement) that achieved the same sales
volumes for Airbus and Boeing.

This analysis of competing suppliers would be sufficient in an industry
in which costs were unrelated to the level of output (constant returns to
scale) or tended to increase with the level of output, and each firm sup-
plies an identical product. For the high technology industries, however,
neither situation is typical. Policies that increase the number of competing firms serving a given market have the advantage of allowing choice
among a greater range of related products. Unfortunately, the issue of
cost per unit tends to cut in the opposite direction. When strong static
and dynamic economies of scale exist, the larger the number of firms,
the higher the cost per unit. Ignoring for a moment the issue of variety,
the social optimum would be achieved with a single producer selling its
product at marginal cost. However, this arrangement requires a subsidy
to that firm in excess of the full cost of R&D. The distributional and
political issues raised by this solution of the natural-monopoly problem

are well known. One possible compromise is average-cost pricing, typical in public utilities.

In mature industries, a major problem associated with regulation of natural monopoly is lack of incentive for cost minimization and an associated incentive for overcapitalization. Implementation of a regulatory approach in high technology sectors is even more problematic. Complete underwriting by government of fixed costs, uncertain in both size and technological outcome, dilutes the incentives to produce marketable results at minimum cost. This is true whether the actual R&D is undertaken by a profit-oriented firm or by a government agency. Furthermore, government bureaucrats are thereby placed in the position of making technological and business judgments about which projects ought to be undertaken. The history of the U.S. government's role in innovation suggests that this arrangement virtually guarantees failure.[14]

On the other hand, complete reliance on the market is also likely to be unsatisfactory, for several reasons. As already noted, both appropriability and capital market problems may prevent the private sector from undertaking some worthwhile projects. One workable compromise for the United States is to encourage cooperative ventures in which government support plays a role (particularly in the "generic" research where appropriability problems are likely to be greatest) but profit-oriented enterprises are encouraged to participate actively. A related approach already used in the United States is to encourage industry R&D indirectly via support for university research activities.[15]

Even these mixed strategies have disadvantages, at least from a static perspective. One is the high probability of duplicative R&D effort unless the government limits its support to just one firm or group per project. But since such limits would eliminate some of the benefits from fostering private-government cooperation, this would presumably be the appropriate choice only where capital costs are very large. Furthermore, to the extent that the reward to successful innovators comes through control over eventual output and price, there will still be the usual incentive to supply a volume of output below the social optimum. If the quid pro quo for government participation were some form of mandatory licensing, this problem could be reduced but not eliminated.

At the international level, exactly the same economic problem of natural monopoly arises, except that it is further complicated by implications for the national distribution of supernormal profits already mentioned. In terms of trade regimes, global productive efficiency is best served (ignoring the issue of variety) by concentrating production in a single firm. Efficiencies of scale make market share protection an economically rational strategy for any individual country that has a potentially competitive supplier. But, again, competing efforts to achieve these economies of scale will actually result in the opposite: high-cost production from an excessively large number of competing suppliers worldwide.

Here the case is even stronger for international rules limiting policies to capture scale economies for national producers.

Furthermore, there are potential efficiency gains from measures that encourage international cooperative ventures among firms serving a given national market. As long as national policies toward trade allow the world to remain in effect a single integrated market, possible losses from a reduced number of competitors are likely to be more than offset by supply-side savings. This suggests that market segmentation strategies implemented by tariffs, quotas, voluntary export restraints, or other bilateral agreements are inferior on efficiency grounds to production or export subsidies that have the same effect on the number of surviving competitors.

U.S. PROSPECTS AND OPTIONS

The evidence on recent U.S. performance in high technology industries is mixed. Some alleged U.S. problems simply reflect the postwar recovery and technological catch-up of other nations, that is, a return to normal conditions from highly atypical ones. But if the nation's competitiveness problems have been exaggerated, it is nonetheless clear that the era of unquestioned U.S. economic hegemony is over. Today, Japan and the European Community rival the United States in important dimensions of economic achievement. Yet the United States remains the acknowledged leader of the Western alliance in both economic and security matters. One possible reason is the apparent reluctance of other economically powerful nations, specifically Japan and West Germany, to assume the burdens and costs of an active leadership role. That reluctance may be another legacy of the unique circumstances that propelled the United States into its postwar hegemonic role.

The decline of the U.S. technological lead entails important changes in the economic relationship between the United States and its major trading partners. As these nations become more similar in terms of technology base, abundance of capital and skilled labor, and per capita income, intraindustry trade is likely to grow. In particular, two-way trade in technology and in technology-based services should become increasingly important as other nations move from adaptation into innovation. And in the mature industries and even some that are now considered high technology sectors, all the industrial market economies are likely to be squeezed by a new tier of competitors in Asia and elsewhere.

Likewise, for all the industrial economies, problems of sectoral adjustment will continue to generate strong pressures for import protection and other forms of assistance to industries losing ground to newcomers. Contrasting national approaches to the nurturing of high technology production will remain a major source of sectoral trade conflict between the United States and its trading partners.

Simple policy prescriptions are unlikely to emerge from any analysis that captures the important features of high technology production and international competition. Nonetheless, some broad guidelines for policy do emerge. The key distinguishing features of alternative policy regimes are the number of competing firms in a given market or worldwide, cost efficiency, product variety, and national distribution of economic profits.

These considerations suggest the utility of international agreements that limit counterproductive efforts to increase any one nation's share of world production in a specific industry, whether to get a larger share of economic profits or to capture greater economies of scale. They also imply that market share protection is more likely to be deleterious to world and national welfare when it segments the international market. Import barriers or explicit turf agreements are thus less desirable than production or export subsidies. This is a particularly interesting conclusion in light of current General Agreement on Tariffs and Trade rules, which allow import barriers and at least tacitly accept turf agreements but actively discourage the use of subsidies. Similarly, U.S. trade law contains explicit provision for countervailing any foreign subsidy but has been less successful in combating the greater damage resulting from foreign barriers to imports.[16]

Finally, it is evident that potential world and national gains are greatest from policies that encourage international cooperation in high technology ventures while limiting the potential harm from reduced competition among suppliers by maintenance of an integrated world market.

Can the United States Maintain Its Lead? Should It Try?

Many Americans are reluctant to accept a future in which the United States is but one among several leaders in the high technology industries. By redoubling its efforts, could the United States return to its one-time position of unquestioned technological preeminence? Even with vastly increased resources allocated to R&D, this kind of advantage probably can no longer be sustained—by the United States or any other country—in a world that has become highly interdependent and in which many nations command the physical and human resources necessary to participate in research and production at the technological frontiers. The advantage gained by being first in any innovation, whether for a firm or for a nation, is likely to be short-lived, thanks to the greatly increased speed with which new technical knowledge now becomes available to potential competitors all over the globe.

But even if it cannot succeed, the U.S. effort to maintain technological leadership is likely to have important positive consequences, not only for the United States but for its trading partners as well. R&D and the resulting scientific and technological advances will continue to provide the primary basis for economic growth and a rising standard of living. Vigorous competition, whether among firms or among nations, can quicken the pace of technological advance worldwide and thus enhance economic prospects both at home and abroad.

NOTES

1. High technology industries are usually defined either in terms of the proportion of "professional, technical, and kindred" workers in total employment or the ratio of research and development expenditures to total sales.

2. See Jagdish N. Bhagwati and Douglas A. Irwin, "The Return of the Reciprocitarians: US Trade Policy Today," *World Economy* 10, no. 2 (June 1987): 109–30.

3. See Robert E. Baldwin, "U.S. Trade Policy since World War II," in Robert E. Baldwin and Anne O. Krueger, eds., *The Structure and Evolution of Recent U.S. Trade Policy* (Chicago: University of Chicago Press, 1984), pp. 3–27.

4. Similar arguments apply in the case of the United Kingdom and other European nations with extensive direct investments abroad.

5. Robert E. Lipsey and Irving B. Kravis, "The Competitiveness and Comparative Advantage of U.S. Multinationals, 1957–1983" (National Bureau of Economic Research Working Paper no. 2051, October 1986).

6. Of course, some U.S. sectors did better than the average while others lost ground to foreign competitors. The largest loss of export market share both for U.S. production and for U.S. multinationals came in motor vehicles, not a high technology industry by the usual definitions. The largest gain over the period was in chemicals and allied products, a high technology sector.

7. See chap. 1 for a review and analysis of trends in R&D spending.

8. For a helpful review of the issues and literature, see Gene M. Grossman and J. David Richardson, "Strategic Trade Policy: A Survey of Issues and Early Analysis" (Princeton Studies in International Finance, Special Papers in International Economy, no. 15, Department of Economics, Princeton University, April 1985).

9. For numerous examples, see the papers in Paul Krugman, ed., *Strategic Trade Policy and the New International Economics* (Cambridge: MIT Press, 1986).

10. For a theoretical analysis of this point, see Avinash K. Dixit, "The Cutting Edge of International Technological Competition" (unpublished paper, Princeton University, October 1985).

11. See Hanns-D. Jacobsen, "Political Implications of High Technology Cooperation between Industrialized Countries" (unpublished paper, J. F. Kennedy Institute, Free University of Berlin, July 1987).

12. On the significance of U.S. defense-related R&D and production, see chap. 1.

13. For an excellent account of the ambiguous *economic* considerations and references to the relevant technical literature, see Grossman and Richardson, "Strategic Trade Policy." For an analysis of the many possible outcomes in a very simple case of two countries and two firms, see Avinash K. Dixit and Albert

S. Kyle, "The Use of Protection and Subsidies for Entry Promotion and Deterrence," *American Economic Review* 75, no. 1 (March 1985): 139–52.

14. See Richard R. Nelson, "Government Stimulus of Technological Progress: Lessons from American History," in Richard R. Nelson, ed., *Government and Technical Progress: A Cross-Industry Analysis* (New York: Pergamon Press, 1983), pp. 451–82.

15. See Richard R. Nelson, "Institutions Supporting Technical Advance in Industry," *American Economic Review Papers and Proceedings* 76, no. 2 (May 1986): 186–89.

16. "Reciprocity" trade legislation now under consideration in the United States has never, to my knowledge, been justified in terms of its potential contribution to maintaining integrated world markets. Of course, bilateral, product-by-product reciprocity would probably lead to market share agreements rather than open markets.

9

Geography Is Not Destiny:

The Changing Character of Competitive

Advantage in Automobiles

GEORGE C. EADS

Over the past two decades, coinciding roughly with the emergence of the Japanese as major producers of automobiles and the breaking down of intra-European barriers through the formation of the European Community, motor vehicles have become a truly worldwide industry. The number of significant players has increased dramatically, trade in completed vehicles has become very important, and the significance of the once-dominant North American producers has declined. As one industry analyst put it, "Rather than being the center of the universe, the only thing that America is today is a very, very large car market with a lot of players."[1]

Some analysts see this as merely a transitional phase. Recent predictions have been made that motor vehicle production will become increasingly concentrated in both low-wage, Third World countries and Japan. According to this scenario, developed countries will come to rely more and more on imported vehicles to meet their needs. Several newly industrialized countries (NIC)—in particular, Brazil, Mexico, Korea, and Taiwan—are betting heavily on this outcome. That is, in the terminology of this conference, the "followers" will take over leadership in motor vehicle production from the "leaders."

In one brief paper, I cannot hope to provide a complete treatment of how competition in this important industry is likely to develop in the future. The most I can do is to suggest that the pattern of competition is unlikely to be as simple as the "conventional wisdom" summarized above might indicate. To state my thesis simply: geography is not destiny.

This paper is divided into two sections. In the first, I examine how recent exchange rate changes and the growing realization that cost advantage is more company-specific than country-specific are affecting competitive relations within the industry and how these changes will influ-

I would like to thank Jim Trask and Mustafa Mohatarem of the General Motors Economics staff for their comments on drafts of this chapter.

ence where adjustment from current industry overcapacity will occur over the next several years. I conclude that contrary to the conventional wisdom, the burden of capacity reduction will not necessarily fall almost exclusively on the traditional North American producers. Some Third World and Japanese producers will also have to bear a share of the adjustment burden.

In the second section of the paper, I examine the role that automation has played so far and might play in the future in determining successful competitive strategies for motor vehicle producers. Although it is not generally recognized, the impressive Japanese reductions in labor-hours per vehicle have not stemmed extensively from their heavy use of automation. While some Japanese plants are heavily automated, many are less automated than some of those of the traditional North American producers. There is as much variation in automation within countries as between countries. Instead, the Japanese manufacturers' lower costs are due principally to their improvements in the organization and management of the production process.

This does not mean that higher levels of factory automation—in particular, the ability to efficiently manufacture a large variety of models in a single plant and to change models inexpensively through the use of flexible manufacturing techniques—is unimportant. Indeed, it is likely that the next redefinition of "best manufacturing practice" in motor vehicles will come from the successful marrying of improved management techniques with increased automation, primarily automation that increases flexibility in manufacturing. Several companies in the United States, Japan, and Europe are working to develop such combinations. However, it is still too early to conclude which of the various approaches will turn out to be superior and how different the outcomes may be. One impact of the recent strengthening of the yen (which has put Japanese wages much more on par with wages in other developed countries) and the growth of North American "transplants" may be to increase the pressure on Japanese automakers to perfect such a marriage.

WHO WILL BEAR THE CAPACITY ADJUSTMENT BURDEN? THE CONVENTIONAL WISDOM

The argument I refer to as the "conventional wisdom" regarding who will bear the burden of capacity adjustment in motor vehicles has three major elements. First, anticipated increases in worldwide capacity in motor vehicles are said to be in excess of reasonable estimates of demand growth. Second, due to the low costs of Japanese and Third World producers, the additional output will most likely be marketed in North America and, to a lesser extent, Europe. Third, traditional North American and European producers will therefore bear the brunt of any adjustment that is required to bring capacity and demand into approximate balance. Let me examine each of these elements in turn.

Worldwide Capacity-Demand Balance

Table 9.1 presents one estimate of the 1990 capacity-demand balance for passenger cars on a worldwide basis. This comparison is restricted to passenger cars, as information on truck capacity is not sufficiently consistent to permit a comparison for these vehicles. The demand figures reflect the current long-term outlook of the General Motors (GM) Economics staff. The capacity figures have been compiled by the GM Economics and Marketing and Product Planning staffs from a variety of sources. They reflect GM plant closings announced to date and are intended to reflect potential supply based upon two-shift, straight-time operation with normal provision for vacations and model changeovers. Quite obviously, however, a given plant or firm can "stretch," especially in the short run, achieving output levels considerably in excess of rated capacity. Indeed, some GM plants are designed to permit operation on a two-shift, three-crew basis, allowing them to run 120 hours per week instead of the usual 80. Moreover, through "continuous improvements," firms can increase the effective capacity of their facilities. Of course, the ability to stretch assembly capacity may be limited by component capacity. Thus, the capacity figures shown in table 9.1 should be considered only a rough approximation of true effective capacity.

The difference between estimated capacity and forecast demand provides a rough estimate of potential worldwide excess capacity in 1990. I feel it necessary to qualify this estimate heavily not only because the capacity figures on which it is based are themselves imprecise but because even with quite precise capacity estimates, it would be erroneous to infer excess capacity merely by subtracting demand from estimated capacity. Prudent capacity planning demands that firms have the ability not only to meet general surges in demand but also to deal with strong

TABLE 9.1
Projected Worldwide Passenger Car Capacity and Demand for 1990
(Millions of Units)

	North America	Europe	Japan	NICs[a]	Other	Total
Capacity	10.6	13.6	8.7	3.4	1.0	37.3
Demand	12.1	12.2	3.4	1.6	2.3	31.6
Difference						5.7

SOURCES: GM Economics staff and GM Marketing and Product Planning staff.
[a]Newly industrialized countries: Mexico, Brazil, Korea, and Taiwan.

demand for specific models, although different firms choose various means to meet this requirement. Some firms deliberately build costly flexibility into plants, while some deliberately plan for overcapacity in certain strategically important segments. No set of gross measures, such as those shown in table 9.1, can fully capture these business decisions. Therefore, the "bottom line" estimate of worldwide excess passenger car capacity for 1990 of 5.7 million units should be taken as only a rough approximation at best.[2]

Meaningful country-by-country comparisons are even more difficult to make. But the figures in table 9.1 clearly show the rationale of the conventional wisdom argument. Despite recent net increases in North American capacity, projected 1990 North American demand still exceeds estimated North American capacity. In contrast, capacity significantly exceeds demand in both Japan and the NICs while Europe shows only a minor amount of excess capacity.

Excess Capacity Targeted at North America and Europe?

As already noted, the standard assumption is that any excess of supply over local demand is targeted at North America or Europe.[3] Europe is seen to be less in danger than North America only because of its stronger tradition of effectively controlling motor vehicle imports. The implication is that only by adopting similar limitations can the North American industry hope to survive at anything like its current size.

It is true that most of the projected net capacity growth is in North America (largely from transplants) and in Third World countries planning to export to North America. However, the ability to achieve these plans rests on the corollary assumption that low wage rates or other country-specific advantages in countries like Japan and, especially, Third World producers such as Korea, Taiwan, Brazil, Mexico, and Yugoslavia translate more or less automatically into an ability on the part of firms located there to produce low-cost motor vehicles of quality that will sell in the North American and European markets. As I will show, it is this latter assumption that is open to serious question.

Current Competitiveness of Japanese Producers Operating in Japan

There can be no doubt that in past years Japanese motor vehicle manufacturers have enjoyed a major labor cost advantage over North American and some European producers. Most Japanese producers have enjoyed a significant advantage in labor productivity as well. Their capital costs and certain other input costs (steel, for example) have also been lower. And this lower cost has not led to any sacrifice in product quality; Japanese cars today enjoy a worldwide reputation for quality.

Not surprisingly, therefore, researchers have concluded that Japanese producers have enjoyed a considerable cost advantage over traditional North American and European producers. Table 9.2 shows one such calculation made by the GM Economics staff. At the yen value prevailing in late 1984, ¥240 per dollar, Honda is calculated to have enjoyed a landed cost advantage over GM on a compact car of approximately $2,300.

Of course, not all Japanese producers are as efficient as Honda or Toyota, the two firms by which the efficiency of Japanese motor vehicle manufacturers has typically been measured. But given the magnitude of the cost advantage at ¥240 to the dollar, interfirm cost differences probably made relatively little difference in the competitiveness of Japanese motor vehicle manufacturers as a group vis-à-vis their North American counterparts.

But, as we all know, the dollar is no longer valued at ¥240. Recently it has traded at ¥140 or lower, and some have predicted that it will decline still further. Table 9.2 shows that this change had a major impact on the cost advantage of even the most efficient Japanese producers such as Honda. Of course, over longer periods, significant additional efficiencies are probably attainable by the Japanese. In the next section I discuss the role that improved manufacturing technology may play. But at yen/dollar exchange rates near current levels, even Honda's landed cost advantage over GM on a compact car has almost disappeared. And it has more than disappeared in the case of a compact pickup when the 25 percent U.S. tariff on this product is factored in.[4]

A major cause of the disappearance of the Japanese cost advantage is the impact of exchange rates on the wages paid by Japanese motor vehicle producers. Table 9.3 reproduces data from the U.S. Bureau of Labor Statistics showing average hourly compensation costs in the auto industry (wage rates plus fringe benefits) for the United States and Japan. Although trends in hourly compensation in national currency units are not identical, most of the narrowing in these rates over the past few years is due to changes in exchange rates. It can be seen that at the exchange rates prevailing in early summer 1987, average hourly com-

TABLE 9.2

Japanese Landed Cost Advantage on a Compact Car Relative to GM
(U.S. Dollars per Vehicle)

Cost advantage over GM	¥240/$	¥190/$	¥160/$	¥140/$
Import	2,300	1,800	1,000	400
Transplant	1,700	1,300	800	500
Difference	600	500	200	−100

SOURCE: GM Economics staff estimates.

TABLE 9.3
Automobile Industry Average Hourly Compensation Costs
in Selected Countries

Country	1985 hourly compensation cost in dollars[a]	1987 hourly compensation cost in dollars[b]
United States	19.63	19.88[c]
Canada	13.10	13.95
Brazil	1.73	[d]
Japan	8.14	14.46
Korea	1.87	2.01
Taiwan	1.86	2.62
West Germany	12.08	20.61
United Kingdom	7.04	10.00

SOURCE: U.S. Bureau of Labor Statistics.
NOTE: Hourly compensation cost is the total cost of an hour worked, including base pay, overtime, fringe benefits, and profit sharing or bonus. It applies only to production workers (hourly employees).
[a]Calculated at 1985 average annual exchange rates.
[b]Calculated at exchange rates prevailing in early summer.
[c]The number shown is for the motor vehicle and parts industry, standard industrial classification 371, which includes both unionized and non-unionized firms. Hourly compensation costs for the unionized firms are higher. Specifically, GM reports in its 1986 annual report that its 1986 hourly labor costs for U.S. hourly employees were $24.00.
[d]Not available.

pensation in the Japanese motor vehicle industry was 72 percent of the average compensation in the U.S. motor vehicle industry, was nearly identical to that of Canada, and substantially exceeded hourly compensation rates in most major European countries except West Germany.

More importantly, the labor cost changes shown in table 9.3 and other increases in Japanese factor costs have substantially magnified the significance of differences in productivity among Japanese auto firms. Nissan is reputed to be in financial trouble, having reported last year the first annual operating loss for a major Japanese auto producer. And Nissan is by no means alone. The highly efficient Japanese producers such as Honda and Toyota, however, are by all accounts in much better financial shape. Nevertheless, in any "crisis" there are clearly weaker Japanese producers who would bear the brunt of any adjustment that was required in Japan.

Competitiveness of Third World Production

As table 9.3 shows, changes in hourly compensation most likely have not affected operating costs in the Third World nearly as much as in

Japan. Does this mean that Third World producers (often Japanese or Japanese affiliated, but also North American and European affiliated) are now in a position to take up any slack created by the Japanese?

Some have assumed this to be true, but I do not believe that the picture is so clear. For one thing, it was the Japanese voluntary export restraint (VER) on auto exports to North America that encouraged the building of some of this Third World capacity. With the increased Japanese capacity in North America and the strengthening of the yen, the VER is no longer providing such an "umbrella" protecting U.S. automakers. Second, in a significant number of cases, the vehicles being produced have major Japanese content, so the strengthening of the yen has an indirect but significant adverse impact on the competitiveness of these products.[5] Third, low hourly compensation costs do not automatically translate into low production costs. Wages aside, there are many costs of doing business in Third World countries. The low compensation costs are themselves sometimes more than offset by low productivity, especially where the production technology being employed is not properly matched to local skills.

In addition, there is the important task of ensuring high quality of output. The Japanese were aided in this task by having to compete in a large, competitive, and quality-conscious domestic market. Few, if any, Third World producers have similar opportunities to hone their competitive instincts. Instead, from the very first, the overwhelming bulk of their output is intended for export directly to North America.

Finally, economic instability, sometimes indigenous and sometimes linked to high levels of indebtedness, can play havoc with the business plans of firms operating in the Third World. These risks are of different types and vary by country. One faced by all developing countries today is the risk of trade sanctions. Another is the risk of currency fluctuations not directly related to market conditions. In most developing countries, currencies are overvalued.

Rapid depreciation or price controls aimed at preventing currency depreciation can complicate operations. Where currencies are deliberately kept *under*valued, the very insulation from the direct, market-based exchange rate fluctuations that prevents wages from keeping pace with wages elsewhere may open exports to the charge of subsidization, with the potential for countervailing duties. This is a particularly acute threat for Korea and Taiwan at present. Developed countries are much less willing to look the other way these days in cases of exchange rate manipulation in the name of export promotion as well as other Third World country activities that also arguably constitute subsidization.

For all these reasons, I believe it is a mistake to assume that production in Third World countries is invariably less costly than production in North America or Europe. This is not to say that properly situated and well-managed Third World facilities cannot be highly profitable sources of products for export to developed countries. However, competitiveness is determined by more than merely low hourly compensation costs or the availability of attractive subsidies. In any adjustment crisis, it should not be assumed that Third World producers would be immune from pressures to reduce capacity.

Competitiveness of North American Transplants

A new extremely important competitive phenomenon is the set of facilities known as the North American "transplants." There is little doubt that the original impetus for the development of these facilities was a desire to defuse protectionist pressure within the United States. In 1980, as Japanese auto imports achieved an unprecedented 20 percent share of the U.S. market, there was significant sentiment in Congress for the passage of some form of "local content" legislation. The purpose of this legislation, as stated by its strongest proponent, the United Auto Workers (UAW), was to eliminate the "unfair advantage" of the Japanese producers by forcing them to build motor vehicles in the United States rather than to export them from Japan. It was believed that the Japanese cost advantage was the result of some combination of lower Japanese wage rates and a labor market environment in Japan that permitted Japanese motor vehicle manufacturers to squeeze very high rates of productivity out of Japanese workers. In this line of argument, any Japanese cost advantage would disappear once the Japanese manufacturers were forced to pay American wages and use American (and presumably unionized) workers.

The supporters of forcing the Japanese to construct assembly plants in the United States evidently hoped that the Japanese would repeat the experience of Volkswagen when it built a U.S. assembly plant in 1978. Volkswagen's facility was a conventionally managed, UAW-organized facility in Westmoreland, Pennsylvania. It evidenced no particular competitive advantage over the plants of traditional U.S. manufacturers.[6] Indeed, Volkswagen announced in late 1987 that it was closing this plant and ending its North American assembly operations.

Domestic content legislation did not pass Congress. Around 1980, however, both Nissan and Honda announced plans to build assembly plants in the United States. In 1983, GM and Toyota announced plans for a joint venture. Subsequently, several additional assembly facilities, as well as numerous component operations, have been announced. By 1992, these facilities plan to turn out nearly 2.5 million vehicles annually—a figure approximately equal to Ford's North American passenger car assembly capacity (fig. 9.1).

The expectation that the Japanese cost advantage would disappear once

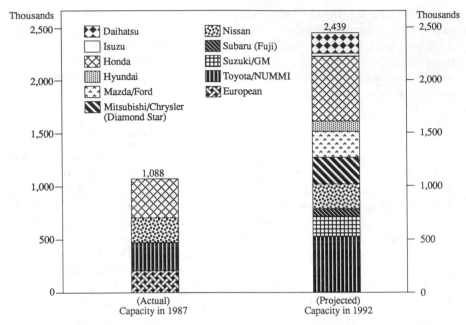

FIGURE 9.1. North American production by foreign manufacturers (straight-time, light vehicle assembly capacity; includes foreign joint venture production and foreign-owned production for sale by domestic firms.

Japanese manufacturers moved production to America was not realized. Indeed, the pressure on Japanese producers to locate in the United States turned out to be fortuitous from their point of view, for it positioned them advantageously when the yen began to strengthen against the dollar.[7] As table 9.2 shows, at the yen/dollar exchange rates prevailing in mid-1987, the Honda Marysville facility could actually produce a compact car for less than it cost to produce the same car of equal quality in Japan and deliver it to the United States. This was also true of the cars produced at GM's California-based joint venture with Toyota, known as New United Motor Manufacturing, Inc. (NUMMI).

As is the case in Japan, not all Japanese transplant facilities in North America are equally efficient. Specifically, Nissan's Smyrna, Tennessee, plant is reported to be somewhat less efficient than either NUMMI or Honda's Marysville facility. And the most efficient plants in Japan are probably still somewhat more efficient than the most efficient Japanese-owned plants in North America. But the gap has greatly narrowed. And as these Japanese-owned North American plants increase their North American content, replacing now-expensive Japanese components with now-inexpensive North American components, their costs will be further reduced.

Productivity Improvements by Traditional Domestic Manufacturers

The traditional domestic North American producers are certainly not standing still. Much attention has focused on some of Ford's new automobile products such as the Taurus and Sable in North America and the Scorpio in Europe. The importance of these products to Ford's greatly improved profitability should not be underestimated. Ford's cost-cutting moves, however, are of even greater significance to its competitive viability.

Between 1978 and 1985, Ford reduced its worldwide employment by nearly 30 percent and raised its total car and truck output per employee by more than 20 percent. Salaried employment at Ford was cut for twenty-eight consecutive quarters, and capital expenditures were held to a minimum.

In part, Ford's achievement reflects its circumstances in the early 1980s. At this time, Ford faced the choice of improving its efficiency or going bankrupt. But its improvements in efficiency could not be based on investments in new plants and equipment since the company did not have the resources to undertake a major program of plant modernization. Instead, Ford was forced to focus on productivity improvements that could be obtained through labor force rationalization and internal restructuring.

Now that its profitability and cash availability have significantly improved, Ford is increasing its investment outlays. Recently Ford's chief financial officer was quoted as saying that modernization and expansion, including increased use of automation, would have "first use" of Ford's new cash reserves.[8]

These are investments that GM has already made. Our program of modernizing nearly all of our assembly plants and press facilities is now virtually complete. We have announced the closing of many of those plants that we have not modernized. We are reducing the number of our car platforms while making the individual cars built on these platforms more distinctive. We have a program well under way that will achieve a 25 percent reduction in our North American salaried staff. And we are working closely in both the United States and Canada with the unions to develop new contracts embodying productivity-enhancing features.

In Europe, signs of our turnaround are already clearly evident. We have been gaining ground on Ford in terms of market share, and our profitability has increased sharply. In the United States, our new products, such as the Chevrolet Corsica and Beretta and the GM-10 (each of which is being produced either in new or in totally remodeled factories), are expected to do for us in the United States what the redesigned Kadett, Omega, and Senator are doing for us in Europe.

Thus, GM and Ford have adopted sharply different strategies to enable them to compete in the decade of the 1990s, with each company's

strategy being determined in large part by its initial challenges and resources. Ford's approach has shown the quickest payoff and has demonstrated that a traditional North American producer can achieve significant improvements in efficiency, thereby improving its competitiveness.
It may still be the case that the typical Ford facility in North America
today is not as efficient as Honda's or NUMMI. But Ford clearly can no
longer be automatically ranked as a high-cost North American producer.[9]

The Conventional Wisdom Revised

The picture of the worldwide competitive situation in motor vehicles
that emerges from even this cursory look is thus quite a bit more complex than the conventional wisdom would suggest. Yes, there does appear to be excess motor vehicle assembly capacity worldwide given likely
future demand patterns. And yes, there has been rapid growth in capacity in the Third World countries. But there has been a surprising
amount of net capacity growth in North America, where foreign-owned
firms have been building capacity significantly faster than traditional North
American producers have been shutting it down. And as labor and other
factor costs in Japan have risen with the strengthening of the yen, efficiency differences among producers have been magnified to the point
where it is not now possible to claim that *all* Japanese producers are
more efficient than *all* traditional North American producers. In particular, the most efficient of the foreign-owned North American facilities
and even certain of the facilities of traditional North American producers
appear to be competitive on a worldwide basis. Certainly, it is now in-
appropriate to lump the traditional producers together when ranking their
cost competitiveness.[10]

The implications of this revised picture for the distribution of adjustment pressures to the worldwide overcapacity situation in motor vehicles
are profound. These pressures are not likely to be focused exclusively
on any one geographic area, such as North America or Europe. Instead,
high-cost producers *wherever they are located* will feel the most severe
competitive pressure. And the experiences of Toyota, Honda, and Ford
show that production in North America can be highly profitable. In particular, Ford's experience illustrates that high-cost producers have alternatives other than merely folding up their tents and retreating. Cost reduction may involve capacity rationalization. It certainly means reducing
overhead costs by simplifying management, but it need not mean permanently reducing market share.

In such a competitive environment, the role of trade policy is also
different. Where low-cost producers are spread around the world, or where
they can enter either de novo or through merger or joint venture, the
ability of trade policy to fundamentally alter competition in an industry

such as motor vehicles is significantly reduced. If draconian enough, trade restrictions can keep an industry alive in the sense of protecting its aggregate output. But if that industry is composed of firms of widely differing efficiencies, low-cost producers will displace high-cost producers, regardless of the degree of trade protection and provided internal competition is not restricted. If high cost is a reflection of inefficiently high labor input, industry employment will also decline. In short, adjustment will take place in spite of any trade restrictions.

What trade restrictions *can* do is shift relative adjustment pressures among high-cost producers in various countries and alter trade flows in ways that create important profit opportunities for low-cost producers. The movement of the transplants into North America as a response to the Japanese VERs is a reflection of this.

The trade environment can have another important impact. If adjustment pressures begin to be spread around the world rather than being concentrated primarily in North America and Europe, some Third World countries might be tempted to adopt a strategy to subsidize production either directly or indirectly. This would be especially true if these same governments had intervened to build up an export-oriented motor vehicle industry through a variety of national development policies and were reluctant to see this capacity sit idle. Today, such behavior is not likely to be tolerated to the extent it might have been in the past. Countries attempting to implement such policies can be certain of being subjected to countervailing duty complaints and, possibly, to being charged with targeting in the sense implied by Section 301 of the U.S. Trade Act of 1974. Countries such as Korea, Brazil, Mexico, and Yugoslavia would appear to be especially vulnerable to such trade actions.

Implications for Traditional North American Manufacturers

The recent shift in exchange rates means that a restoration to international competitiveness of traditional North American producers is possible—and perhaps possible over a much shorter period of time than some might have thought. More importantly, in order to restore this competitiveness it will not be necessary for such producers to abandon their North American production base. Both Japanese motor vehicle manufacturers and Ford have managed to produce results in North America using North American workers and paying North American wages that rival cost levels anywhere in the world. This is not to say that restoring competitiveness will be easy or that the changes required of both management and labor will be minor. But as I have already indicated, the need to make such changes is currently recognized by both the companies and the unions, and important results have already been achieved.

AUTOMATION AS A SOURCE OF COMPETITIVE ADVANTAGE

In this section, I explore whether automation has been or might become a critical source of competitive advantage in the motor vehicle industry. As I noted at the beginning, automation has been proposed as an antidote for high developed-country wage costs. It is argued that (1) only by significantly reducing the labor content of motor vehicles can companies manage to retain production in the developed countries and (2) the only way that labor content can be reduced is through automation.

How Critical Is Automation to Low Costs?

Thus far at least, the second part of this argument has not turned out to be correct, at least not in the United States. In Europe, some significant automation-related productivity advances have been achieved. Fiat's Termouli engine plant and Volkswagen's Wolfsburg passenger car assembly plant are reported to be the most automated auto plants in the world. In addition, some of the specialist European producers are in the forefront of efforts to develop flexible manufacturing systems to overcome the scale economy advantages of the mass market producers.

However, automation is not the only source of significant productivity improvements. The cost reductions achieved by the North American transplants and Ford have *not* been obtained through increased automation but instead through improved organization and management of the production process. To see how this has been accomplished, let us briefly examine GM and Toyota's joint venture, NUMMI.

How Does NUMMI Achieve High Productivity?

NUMMI has demonstrated that the "secret" of Japanese efficiency rests primarily on management and organization, not on advanced technology.[11] Consider NUMMI's relationship with its work force. In contrast to Nissan's and Honda's U.S. facilities, which are not unionized, from the beginning of the NUMMI joint venture there has been close collaboration with the UAW. However, the three-year NUMMI labor agreement, which was signed in July 1985, differs in important respects from traditional GM UAW contracts. There is only one unskilled labor classification, compared with the average of 80–100 in U.S. auto plants. The general classification promotes a flexible work force capable of performing many different tasks. Absenteeism is strictly controlled; the employee is responsible for being present at work. All this reduces costs and helps enhance quality.

Consider also how NUMMI gradually built up to full production. NUMMI did not add a second shift until one full year after the first Nova was built. NUMMI's acceleration period lasted for approximately eighteen months, considerably longer than start-up time for most GM plants. This time was used to ensure that quality was not compromised and that operators were fully trained and prepared for their responsibilities. The slow acceleration allowed for a gradual hiring of employees, for a high level of confidence to develop in the supplier community, and for problems to surface and be resolved during lower-volume periods.

At NUMMI, workers are organized into small teams. The teams are responsible for production, quality, training, and achieving continuous improvement in the production process. The concept of continuous improvement of the production operation to eliminate waste is viewed as each person's responsibility. This is supported by a "Just-in-Time" production strategy, which produces only the necessary items in the necessary quantities and at the necessary time. Just-in-Time production, which is extended to NUMMI's suppliers, is explicitly designed to eliminate the waste of overproduction and inventory accumulation that occurs when upstream processes produce ahead of their downstream customers. Through the elimination of stocks of inventory that hide problems, product quality is improved by highlighting problems and forcing corrections quickly and permanently. The central focus of the NUMMI quality control system is to satisfy the requirements of the "customer." The customer may be the purchaser of the vehicle, an assembly line station, or the next process in building the car.

At NUMMI, decisions are made at the lowest level possible. Consensus decision making is institutionalized through the system of expenditure and policy approval. Affected departments are required to demonstrate their approval of a proposal before it goes to upper management. This strategy recognizes that no element of the production and management system operates independently and that the manufacturing process will shut down unless the elements of the system function in harmony.

NUMMI's strategy of human resource development complements its organizational and decision-making strategies. During three days of preemployment testing, workers are screened for skill aptitudes and work attitudes. NUMMI devotes a significant amount of time to educating and training team members and supervisors on a continuing basis. Education at NUMMI is defined as teaching someone how to solve problems. Everyone is encouraged to discover problems, and a common and constructive approach to problem solving is provided. The common understanding of the production and management system and the role of each employee in it helps employees to know what to expect from their coworkers. This commonality of purpose and approach enables managers to delegate decision making to those closest to the problem.

NUMMI employs only 2,200 hourly and 300 salaried employees to build sixty cars per hour, a much smaller work force than is characteristic of most U.S.-owned auto plants. A comparable plant in Japan, however, can build cars at the same rate with about 10 percent fewer employees.

The tenets of Toyota's management theory seem to have been applied successfully at NUMMI, but it is important to remember that NUMMI is experimental and young.[12] Both factors suggest caution in interpreting results. Also, the system requires close cooperation with suppliers and, particularly, with labor. As yet, we cannot be sure of the durability of this cooperation.

Manufacturing Technology as a Future Source of Competitive Advantage

NUMMI demonstrates that it is possible to achieve significant reductions in cost through improved organizational and management techniques.[13] Ford's attainment of productivity levels similar to those of NUMMI in some of its plants without adopting the specific NUMMI management techniques demonstrates that there are alternative paths that produce similar results. But in both cases, high levels of automation do *not* seem to be a key part of the story. Neither NUMMI nor the Ford plants that were studied represent the state of the art in manufacturing technology. At both, one sees fewer robots and less extensive automation than in some of GM's newest plants.

Some of this conservatism with respect to automation is deliberate. Automation is expensive and does not automatically reduce costs. In a recent *Automotive News* interview, Robert Eaton, vice president and group executive, GM Technical Staffs, acknowledged a "plant automation backlash" that stems from the U.S. auto companies trying "too much, too fast."[14] Despite this increased caution, no major automaker today can afford to ignore the cost-reducing and quality-enhancing possibilities that automation affords; in the same interview, Eaton indicated that increased automation is clearly coming in the motor vehicle industry. I have already referred to Ford's commitment to increased automation.

There are different types of automation and different ways of utilizing it. In the assembly of complete vehicles and also in the manufacture of many components, what appears to be exciting most interest within the industry today is not automated factories that reduce labor content to zero but flexible manufacturing techniques that reduce the cost of being able to handle a variety of products on the same assembly line.[15]

Flexible manufacturing has become a necessity for medium-size and specialist manufacturers. By definition, these firms do not produce sufficient volumes to benefit from economies of large-scale production. However, the declining minimum efficient scale in manufacturing permitted by flexible manufacturing could give them a much more "level" playing field on which to compete. Indeed, flexible manufacturing, combined with the demand for greater product variety, could provide specialist producers with a significant competitive advantage in high-income markets.

It is not difficult to see why this is so. Near the beginning of this paper, I referred to one problem in estimating excess capacity as being the need to be able to respond to model-specific fluctuations in demand. If consumers all of a sudden want Chevrolet Corsicas and you only have the capacity to produce Cadillac Sevilles (two cars built off totally different platforms), you lose sales. Some firms currently design their factories to be able to switch between models. Firms with few plants, such as Chrysler, have no choice but to do this if they are to be able to offer a range of products.

As economists have long known, flexibility to switch between models is not without costs. Flexible manufacturing techniques offer the potential of enhanced flexibility at substantially lower costs. If this potential can be realized, firms can match capacity to expected demand much more closely, saving on both capital and labor costs.[16]

Even variations in the frequency with which various options are ordered by the customer raise costs because they require overstaffing the assembly line. Option packaging (which reduces option variability) and improved scheduling practices can reduce this overstaffing and thus reduce cost. But they also reduce the ability of manufacturers to tailor a vehicle to the customer's individual specifications—an important marketing advantage. Flexible manufacturing techniques applied to assembly have the potential to reduce the cost of offering a wide range of customer-ordered options.

At a few GM assembly plants, traditional conveyors have been replaced with automatic guided vehicles (AGV), which radically alter the traditional concept of the assembly "line." Each AGV carries a vehicle being assembled. Workstations do not occur in sequence but in parallel. Thus, different vehicles can be scheduled through different assembly areas at different rates while still maintaining a smooth overall production rate. Problems can be bypassed; the "line" need not be shut down when problems develop.

AGVs also offer other potential improvements in manufacturing flexibility. For example, annual model changes should be significantly less expensive because it should not be necessary to rip apart factories and replace conveyor systems if AGVs are being used. But AGVs are expensive. As with any other system of automation, their use does not automatically bring about reduction in cost. It is a major challenge to employ the proper combination of advanced automation and traditional scheduling techniques to balance the cost reduction available from smooth line flow with the increased operating and marketing flexibility that comes from being able to offer a broader range of options and to manufacture more types of vehicles in a single plant.

In particular, the various stages of automation in an assembly plant must be controlled and coordinated if they are to work together efficiently. To do this, it may be necessary to use computers to integrate the various manufacturing steps. But even though many manufacturing processes are now computer controlled, the computers involved typically cannot speak to each other. To overcome this difficulty, GM is sponsoring the development of Manufacturing Automation Protocol (MAP). MAP will provide translation elements between computing devices that use different programming languages. We believe that MAP is the key to making computer-integrated manufacturing a reality and thus is a key to obtaining the full benefits of flexible manufacturing.

Next State of the Art: Advanced Automation and Improved Management Systems

People who study the motor vehicle industry are generally convinced that the next state of the art in motor vehicle manufacturing will consist of combining advanced automation with improved management practices, possibly of the sort described in connection with NUMMI. But there are different strategies by which this combination could be effected. Toyota and Honda are known to be actively exploring the use of much higher levels of automation in their operations, building incrementally on their current manufacturing systems. Ford has a less well-defined management system but also generally introduces automation incrementally. In contrast, GM is taking a more comprehensive approach that combines improved management techniques (building on the lessons it has learned from NUMMI but not parroting it) with much higher levels of automation.

It is still too early to determine which of the various approaches will turn out to work best—or even if a single "best" will exist. Recent exchange rate changes and developing trade pressures may even affect the outcome of this race.

Japanese auto manufacturers have been exploring the possibility of the greater use of automation for quite a while. Some are making use of quite high degrees of automation in selected applications. The impact on Japanese wages of the strengthening of the yen will obviously increase the appeal of automation in Japan. Automation represents one of the major opportunities for Japanese motor vehicle manufacturers to reduce their costs in Japan and avoid pressures to move their own assembly operations to other countries. Increased use of automation will also help them to avoid surrendering the low-cost end of the product spectrum to Third World producers. Finally, the fact that they are increasingly involved in production in high-wage North America provides a third reason for exploring higher levels of automation.

The traditional North American firms recognize that overseas manufacture is no panacea, and this, together with their renewed determination to become world-class manufacturers again, puts pressure on them to move quickly to achieve an effective integration of advanced technology and improved management techniques.

CONCLUSION

Other papers presented at this conference have been written from the perspective of an individual *country*, exploring such topics as the ability of leader countries to maintain their traditional technological advantages and what might be required to enable follower countries to catch up with them. In this paper, I have deliberately shifted the focus to *companies*. This is because in a number of industries, especially those that are more technology- or skill-based than natural-resource-based, competition is becoming much more company-specific than country-specific. The ability to organize and manage production and to appropriately incorporate new technology into the production process as well as the product is becoming more important than location in determining competitive success.

This is not to say that individual countries and their policies for promoting economic growth and technological development are irrelevant—far from it. But as financial markets are liberalized, as technology is more easily transferable across national boundaries, and as more companies adopt a worldwide strategic perspective, there is a growing tendency for companies to identify less with countries and for individual company success to become less and less dependent upon country success. In such an environment, the type of influence that a country can have on a company's behavior changes significantly.

The importance of distinguishing between country and company success is emphasized in a paper by Lipsey and Kravis in which they studied the competitiveness of U.S. multinational corporations from 1957 to 1983.[17] The authors focused on the share of world exports of manufactured goods accounted for by U.S. multinationals during this period. They noted that a decline in the U.S. share of worldwide manufactured exports has been cited as one indication of the decline in U.S. competitiveness, and the shortsightedness of U.S. managers has been one explanation for this decline.[18] Lipsey and Kravis reasoned that if U.S. management practices have somehow been flawed, the decline in the share of worldwide manufacturing output accounted for by U.S. multinationals should roughly parallel the decline in the share of manufacturing exports accounted for by the United States as a country. In fact, this expected result was not found. U.S. multinationals continued to hold a steady share of world manufacturing exports throughout the period studied. This led Lipsey and Kravis to speculate that it was the decline in the relative attractiveness of the United States as a place to manufacture rather than any fundamental flaw in management practices that likely was the cause of the declining U.S. share of manufactured exports.[19]

Researchers seeking to understand what permits leading countries to remain leaders and following countries to catch up in terms of living standards need to keep in mind the limitations of what countries can actually do. Countries establish the environment within which companies compete. Companies, by and large, do the actual competing. In the course of doing this, they develop much of the technology that, when embodied into their products, their manufacturing processes, or both, helps to generate the increased productivity upon which improved living standards so critically depend. The policies that countries adopt with respect to investment or the taxation of research and development can influence how aggressively the companies located within their borders seek out and apply these new technologies. Thus, a country's policies might be said to "determine" the rate of technological advance within its borders, but only indirectly.

A nation's political and social environment also sets important limits on management's ability to organize production efficiently and, perhaps of even greater importance, to adjust the organization of production to reflect changing market conditions over time. Policies that facilitate or retard structural adjustment therefore also affect productivity, but, again, only indirectly.

Finally, a nation's attitude toward risk taking as reflected in its various policies can change the attention that management pays to keeping abreast of and rapidly incorporating changes in organization or technology. For example, if a country's political system emphasizes equity over efficiency and rewards the preservation of existing stakes over efforts to change them, it is hard to see how managers in such a country can be faulted for failing to stay abreast of changing organizational or technological innovations. And if a country makes it easier for a firm to obtain trade protection than to undertake the difficult and often painful adjustments necessary to restore its competitiveness, is it fair to fault management for choosing the former route? Country-specific policies are therefore important to the ability of firms to perform well in international competition. But nations seeking to alter their competitive performance must be aware of the constraints they face, especially in a world of multinational corporations, mobile technology, and increasingly unfettered capital markets.

No, geography is not destiny—especially in today's highly competitive and technologically dynamic motor vehicle industry.

NOTES

1. Maryann Keller, as reported by the *Detroit News*, 10 June 1987, p. 2C.

2. According to an *Automotive News* article (18 May 1987), Ford's estimate of world automotive industry excess capacity in 1990 is 6 million units. I understand that Chrysler's estimate is 7 million units.

3. In this paper, I use the term *targeted* in a somewhat different sense from its common use, at least currently in the United States. I do not necessarily mean to imply that imports are being purposefully directed by governments with

the intent to injure North American (or European) auto producers in the sense meant by Section 301 of the U.S. Trade Act of 1974, though neither do I necessarily rule out this sort of behavior. My use of the term is intended merely to suggest that at present it is relatively more profitable for imports to go to North America or Europe than elsewhere and that production capacity has been constructed, at least in part, with this in mind.

4. The duty actually applies to light commercial vehicles. As the yen has risen and the current voluntary export restraint has ceased to bind, Japanese manufacturers have been reclassifying certain dual-use vehicles as "cars" rather than "trucks" in order to escape the tariff. The U.S. duty on automobiles is 2.5 percent.

5. For example, Ford's Mexican- and Taiwan-assembled Tracers sold in North America use engines and most components built in Japan by Mazda.

6. Whether because of shrewd timing or just plain luck, Volkswagen *did* enjoy a major, if temporary, advantage over its European rivals due to the Westmoreland plant. The plant went on line just as the deutsche mark and other European currencies strengthened. Volkswagen was thus able to avoid many of the increased costs that injured its European competitors.

7. In this respect, their situation is like Volkswagen's in 1979. However, unlike Volkswagen, the Japanese have introduced new and more efficient production systems.

8. *Detroit Free Press*, 5 May 1985.

9. Ford is by no means the only traditional automaker showing dramatic improvements. Peugeot and Fiat have shown equally impressive improvements while operating in political and social environments different from Ford and from each other. However, in each case, the firm's current prosperity is underpinned by significant improvements in productivity combined with very successful new products (the Peugeot 205 and the Fiat Uno).

10. Of course, if the U.S. dollar were to strengthen significantly, the overall position of U.S. auto manufacturers would again decline. However, this would not eliminate what appear to be emerging differences between companies. Thus, even if the dollar were to strengthen again, U.S. companies would not be affected equally.

11. This is an extremely brief summary of an extensive body of information gathered by various GM staffs concerning the lessons of NUMMI. Most of this information is considered proprietary.

12. Several GM plants are currently introducing elements of NUMMI's management and production practices. Cost savings and quality improvements are being realized through the introduction of Just-in-Time production, self-inspection by employees, and the organization of workers into teams. In addition, innovative labor agreements have been negotiated in some areas that reduce the number of job classifications and allow for greater worker flexibility.

13. On the issues discussed in this section, the reader might wish to consult a survey, "Factory of the Future," published in *The Economist*, 30 May 1987.

14. *Automotive News*, 8 June 1987, p. E-16.

15. *Flexible manufacturing* need not mean a high degree of automation. Toyota has more variation and flexibility in its comparatively low technology Takaoka plant than is possible in many much more highly automated plants of other manufacturers. (Flexibility in this case means an ability to handle a variety of

platform, body, and engine combinations.) However, as the term is generally used today, *flexible manufacturing* implies high levels of automation.

16. The North American auto manufacturers all have contracts with the UAW guaranteeing workers a substantial portion of their salaries and benefits while on temporary layoff. The Japanese automakers practice lifetime employment. Both, therefore, treat labor as a quasi-fixed cost.

17. Robert E. Lipsey and Irving Kravis, "The Competitiveness and Comparative Advantage of U.S. Multinationals, 1957–1983" (National Bureau of Economic Research Working Paper no. 2051, October 1986).

18. On the decline in share of U.S. manufactured exports as an indicator of loss of competitiveness, see, for example, Bruce R. Scott and George C. Lodge, *U.S. Competitiveness in the World Economy* (Cambridge: Harvard Business School Press, 1985), pp. 18–27. On the shortsightedness of American managers as a cause for poor U.S. performance, see, for example, Pat Choate and J. K. Linger, *The High-Flex Society: Shaping America's Economic Future* (New York: Alfred A. Knopf, 1986), pp. 97–106.

19. Lipsey and Kravis, "Competitiveness and Comparative Advantage of U.S. Multinationals," pp. 23–26.

Part Four

SUMMARY

10

The Benefits and Burdens
of the Technological Leaders

MERTON J. PECK

Although this volume deals primarily with the three technological leaders—the United States, Japan, and the Federal Republic of Germany—it is well to remember that most Organization for Economic Cooperation and Development (OECD) countries are active players in the technology leadership game. The common perception supported by survey evidence, however, is that the United States and Japan are the winners in the high technology sweepstakes while West Germany maintains a strong third (table 10.1).

Yet several chapters in this volume and discussions among its authors raise the following questions: Is technological leadership all that important? With the internationalization of knowledge, production, and markets, does it matter who is number one, two, or even three? These are critical question for if not, all the furor in the press and political circles over technological competition is simply much ado about nothing. I argue that technological leadership matters, though perhaps not enough to justify the protectionist proposals and promotional policies that have been advanced in the last few years. It is a complicated question to which the first section of this chapter, utilizing the points raised in chapters 1, 4, and 8, by Nelson, McCulloch, and Itoh.

In the second section, I examine the apparent erosion of the U.S. position as technological leader, a central concern in the chapters by Nelson and McCulloch (chaps. 1 and 8) and less directly in the chapter by Eads (chap. 9). The perspective in the third section is that of the challenger, Japan, which is the focus of chapters 2 and 6, by Taylor and Yamamura and Nakatani. In the fourth section, I turn to West Germany, which represents an interesting in-between case: Germany is neither a leader nor a challenger but is still a major player in technological competition, as demonstrated in the chapter by Legler (chap. 7).

THE UNCERTAIN REWARDS OF LEADERSHIP

Economists are uncharacteristically uncomfortable in discussing technological leadership. Even though they hesitate to say so, they are not

TABLE 10.1
Ranking in High Technology: An Assessment
by Chief Executives of More than 200 European Firms

	United States	Japan	West Germany	Scandinavia	United Kingdom	France
Computing	1	2	3	4–5	6	4–5
Electronics	1–2	1–2	3	4	6–7	6–7
Telecommunications	1	2	3	4	5–6	5–6
Biotechnology	1	2	3	4	5	a
Chemicals	1	2	3	4	5	6–7
Metals and alloys	2	1	3	4	5–6	5–6
Engineering	1	2	3	4	5	6
Manufacturing	1–2	1–2	3	4	5	6
Robotics	2	1	3	4	6	5
Mean rank	1.3	1.7	3.0	4.2	5.4	5.8

SOURCE: John Marcum, "High Technology and the Economy," *OECD Observer*, no. 131 (November 1984): 5; as reproduced in R. D. Norton, "Industrial Policy and American Renewal," *Journal of Economic Literature* 24, no. 1 (March 1986): 32.
[a]Not available.

sure it matters. And, indeed, if one believes in the instant transmission of knowledge and the purely competitive model, technological leadership is not important. Technology, of course, is knowledge. And if knowledge is available to all, it hardly matters whether the discovery occurs in Cambridge, England, or Cambridge, Massachusetts. It is equally available in Tokyo, the Silicon Valley, or Cologne.

This model fits relatively well in the case of basic research, but basic research is not a major factor in the competition between nations or firms. What counts is the development of marketable products and usable processes, the knowledge required for which is hoarded by firms and nations. The economic value of knowledge depends largely on exclusivity; if every competitor and every nation obtains the knowledge immediately, its private economic value would soon be competed away. Indeed, the entire concept of leaders and followers (as found in table 10.1, for example) rests on the differential availability of knowledge and on how quickly and how well it is applied to products or processes. Note that even if knowledge is equally available to all, some firms might apply that knowledge sooner or at a lower cost. This is most obvious in the case of new knowledge embodied in new equipment in which the rate of application depends on the rate of investment.

While capital-embodied knowledge is the example most familiar to economists, sociologists have found many barriers to innovation within organizations and societies. Indeed, entire societies can be labeled traditional or innovative depending on their receptivity to change. Some forms of social organization favor and others discourage technical change, though inertia is so pervasive as to make the differences primarily of degree. There is good reason, of course, for the inertia; most change involves uncertainty, and history is replete with cases of failed innovation.

The differences in the availability of knowledge and its rate of application undermine the economists' model of pure competition, which assumes all firms have equal access to the factors of production, including knowledge. But, when conditions of imperfect competition prevail, rents can be collected from the successful use of new knowledge. In this case, it can pay to be a technological leader. This is true even without considering the static and dynamic economies of scale examined in chapters 4 and 8. The existence of scale economies, however, enhances the potential benefits of technological leadership. The simplest case is that of static economies of scale, in which technological knowledge can be considered a fixed factor of production and a higher rate of output allows research and development (R&D) costs to be allocated over many units without additional expense.

Dynamic economies of scale are associated with the learning curve. The more of an item a firm produces, the more it learns how to reduce unit cost or improve the product. Note that this kind of cost reduction depends on cumulative volume rather than the rate of output, and the learning is assumed to be firm specific. Latecomers do not tap into the learning curve established by the leader but must accumulate their own experience. And while the traditional learning curve develops for a single product, there is considerable evidence that it can apply across products as well. In developing the 747 commercial aircraft, Boeing's major asset was its experience in developing the earlier 707 model. A further advantage for the leader is that with product differentiation, a firm can establish a market position from which it cannot be easily dislodged. All these considerations are incentives for firms to become innovators. It pays—the profits of successful innovations are well documented in the economic literature. And a nation that is consistently a technological leader will earn the profits of innovation as one of the rewards of international trade, a point explained in both chapters 4 and 8.

It also pays to be a fast follower, that is, to successfully imitate an innovation as quickly as possible. Generally, the successful fast follower does not rely on a straight me-too product; they do better if they can improve on the initial innovation. Being a very latecomer with a more or less generic product is not very profitable, unless the firm or nation has access to a low-cost factor—typically labor. Indeed, very latecomers will be producing what Itoh calls borderline and basic technology goods, in which a major factor is low labor costs and in which high-wage countries lack comparative advantage.

The potential benefits of innovation explain why firms and nations seek to become technological leaders. But leadership is not costless and involves major uncertainties. Many aspire to technological leadership and even fast followership, but few succeed. It is easily forgotten that in the late 1960s the British prime minister, Harold Wilson, called for a "white-hot technology revolution" and established the Ministry of Technology to set Britain on the path toward technological leadership. The effort failed.[1]

The uncertainties, of course, lie in the unpleasant fact that innovation is not a process in which inputs and outputs are well correlated. One can spend vast sums on R&D and achieve nothing; only educating one's children is as hazardous. One reason for this is the interactability of nature; another is that successful innovation rests on a complex social network. Still another factor is the existence of rivals constantly introducing new and competing knowledge. Harold Wilson might have succeeded if other nations had stood still.

Still, high-income countries may have no choice but to participate in technological competition, particularly in the long run. Consider other trade-creating factors that require differences in the factors of production among nations. If capital markets continue the trend toward internationalization, differences in capital costs among nations will eventually disappear. If old knowledge is widely diffused, differences in the application of standard industrial techniques will also disappear. And, as the education levels of the labor force of various countries converge, human capital differences will become less important. Natural resource differences are important in such sectors as agriculture but are hardly a basis for large-scale international trade. What remains is technology. That is why technological competition in the twenty-first century will be so important.

THE DECLINE OF THE UNITED STATES

Both the Nelson and the McCulloch chapters (chaps. 1 and 8) conclude that the United States lost its dominant position as technological leader during the 1960s. World War II made the United States a technological leader, and the United States was able to strengthen that position as other nations struggled to reconstruct their war-battered economies. As these immediate postwar conditions receded, the United States was certain to face more competition. Both McCulloch and Nelson make much of the inevitability of the relative decline of the United States and in that they are right. Yet one can push the argument only so far, particularly because the U.S. decline has continued into the 1980s, thirty-five years after World War II.

Nelson lists four factors leading to the U.S. decline: (1) increasing internationalization of technology, allowing many other nations to benefit from U.S. research; (2) greater world trade, which gave other nations access to a mass market, previously possible only for the United States; (3) a rising level of education abroad, making education of the labor force comparable to that of the United States; and (4) declining commercial spillover from defense R&D, thus reducing the advantage of large U.S. defense expenditures. I have no quarrel with the last three points; I do with the first. This point is fundamental in understanding technological rivalry at both the national and the firm level. McCulloch also notes that new technical knowledge is quickly transmitted abroad, where it is applied by foreign as well as domestic firms. Yet the rapid diffusion of new knowledge would argue that firms could become free riders on the R&D efforts of others. A firm could simply wait as others bear the R&D costs and rely on McCulloch's quick transmission to keep them abreast of rivals. Yet the data in her chapter show nondefense (and therefore largely company financed) R&D expenditures rising in all five major industrial countries. Why?

The answer lies, I think, in an earlier point. The knowledge for industrial application still retains strong elements of exclusivity—the essence of economic value. Technological knowledge has sufficient characteristics of a private good, the benefits from which can be appropriated by an innovating firm, to lead to substantial and rising R&D expenditures as reported by McCulloch.

This proposition is given solid empirical support in the studies of my colleagues. They set out to determine the mechanisms that create appropriability for new products and processes, relying on a survey of 650 R&D executives from a wide range of industries. These R&D executives were asked about the effectiveness of alternative means of protecting competitive advantages of new or improved processes and products. The striking feature of the findings is that the most effective methods of realizing profits from innovation were given as lead time, moving quickly down the learning curve, and superior sales or service efforts rather than the much more familiar method of patent protection.[2] Today, therefore, it would seem that exclusivity primarily takes the form of a head start for the innovator and not permanent possession of special knowledge. In one sense these results support McCulloch's argument. The survey revealed that the imitation lag required to duplicate an innovation was typically one to three years. At the same time, Nelson's internationalization of markets makes even such a short lag important. At one time, if a firm could imitate an innovation abroad in its home market in three years, there was a good chance it could dominate that market. Now such a firm is likely to find the foreign innovator already selling in its home market. Furthermore, having a three-year-old product in many high technology industries, such as semiconductors, is almost like having no product at all. Each successive generation of products is so superior to its predecessor that there is little demand for the older products. This situation leads firms and nations to take technological competition seriously. Indeed, internationalization may intensify technological rivalry rather than mute it.

McCulloch also raises the issue of the multinational firm. What does it mean to think of IBM as a U.S. firm when over half of its sales occur abroad? Particularly striking is the trend to separate development from production or even to locate the various stages of the production process for one product in different countries. It is conceivable that a nation could be a leader in a high technology product and still have few exports and little domestic employment and income to show for it. In most high technology products, however, there is still an advantage in locating development and production together. As products and processes are modified as experience accumulates, extensive interaction between the R&D and production organizations may be required. It is primarily the U.S. production of such relatively old products as television sets that has moved offshore and not the rapidly changing products.

As one looks to the future, the fundamental question is whether large firms will lose their national identity to such an extent that national economic policies will no longer affect them. If this should occur, then some of Nelson's concerns would take a different form. Should Nelson's concerns about the quality of American primary and secondary education be justified, firms will simply relocate to countries with better educational systems. Similarly, if the American university system is an asset for high technology firms, firms of every country will locate in the neighborhood of American universities. In such a world, nations can pursue policies to attract high technology firms from throughout the world, and firms would locate various parts of their operation in countries with the most advantageous policies for particular operations.

Internationalization, however, seems unlikely to go as far as to eliminate the national identities of the majority of firms even in the twenty-first century. Fujitsu will still be located primarily in Japan and be a different kind of firm than Texas Instruments. Firms have grown up in particular societies, and they retain strong links to those societies, which fundamentally shaped their characteristics. This is apparent in management practices and personnel policies, as well as in ties to other firms, financial institutions, and government agencies. Nakatani's paper on Japanese business groups and Nelson's concerns about the impact of takeovers of U.S. firms underline the distinctive national characteristics of business firms.

Given that nations can and do pursue implicit and explicit technological policies with substantial impact on national firms, what can be said about U.S. technological leadership and U.S. public policy to make the United States more technologically competitive? McCulloch concludes that technological leadership is an obsolete notion, that "this kind of advantage [technological leadership] probably can no longer be sustained—by the United States or any other country—in a world that has become highly interdependent." Nelson appears to agree with McCulloch when he concludes that we are now in a world of near-equals.

I agree, if by leadership one means the U.S. position in the 1950s, which is better characterized as dominance than leadership. If leadership is defined as being first in a race with other competitors, however, it retains its significance. And such leadership can be the basis for a large worldwide market share and higher exports, as the United States demonstrates in large commercial aircraft and Japan in certain semiconductors. As already discussed, I believe that there are still substantial private benefits to innovation, and some of these surely accrue to the nations in which innovating firms are located. Otherwise, it is difficult to understand the rivalry for technological leadership that has occurred in the last decade at both the firm and the national level.

McCulloch is dubious about whether public policy can affect technological competition and counsels seeking "agreements that limit counterproductive efforts to increase any one nation's share of world production in a specific industry, whether to get a larger share of economic profits or to capture greater economies of scale." That is difficult to do, though the postwar reduction in tariffs gives some hope. One limitation on such agreements is that technological leadership is influenced by a wide range of domestic policies, including patent policy, competitive policy, educational measures, and government support of R&D. As Itoh points out, international agreements concerning traditional domestic policies raise difficult questions of national sovereignty.

I suspect that the future will be similar to the past. Nations will seek technological leadership and adopt policies—some wise and some not—to achieve that goal. We can hope that protection will be a minor theme in that policy and that measures, such as R&D subsidies, promoting technical change will play a major role. Technological competition is not a zero-sum game. It can be, as it has been in the past, a major factor in raising the well-being of all.

The chapter by George Eads (chap. 9) addresses a single industry—motor vehicles—rather than a nation. As such, it is a valuable supplement to the Nelson and McCulloch chapters, particularly since it raises important considerations not discussed in the other two chapters.

The first of these is the importance of exchange rates. Eads shows that at ¥240 to the dollar (about the rate in 1984), the Japanese cost advantage for compact cars landed in the United States was $2,300; at ¥130 to the dollar (the 1987 rate), the cost advantage disappears. A nation's cost advantage is critically dependent on exchange rates and can disappear in just a few years. Thus the discussion of comparative advantage in various types of goods that underlies, say, Itoh's chapter, should rec-

ognize how transitory comparative advantage can be in a world of fluc-
tuating exchange rates.

Second, Eads shows, using Ford as an example, how quickly an individual firm can change its cost position through various measures. Ford
raised its output per worker by 20 percent between 1978 and 1985 with
minimum capital investment. The measures largely involved capacity rationalization and overhead reduction. Simple measures apparently still
matter even in a world of high technology.

Third, Eads finds both high- and low-cost firms in each nation. There
is no meaningful national average, and implicitly, firms matter more than
nations. This is perhaps his most important point. In adjusting to predicted excess capacity, he concludes that "high-cost producers *wherever
they are located* will feel the most severe competitive pressures." He
also indicates that low-cost producers can be located in North America
and high-cost producers can be located in Japan or Third World countries.

The last point Eads makes in his chapter undercuts the preceding
proposition that nations matter. He holds that firms or even plants are
the units that count in competition. I think there is some merit in this
view, but only some. What a firm must do to offset, say, American
unionized wages is considerably more than what is required for a Korean
firm. Still the successes he reports demonstrate that high management
may matter as much as high technology.

The generally optimistic tone of the Eads paper for U.S. prospects
contrasts with the more somber tone of McCulloch and Nelson. I would
side with Eads but for rather different reasons. In technology there tends
to be stability in relative position. In many industries the leader of today
was the leader one, two, even five decades ago. Eastman Kodak is one
example; IBM another. And the nation that is the leader in the past is
the leader today; for with all the rise of other nations, table 10.1 shows
that the United States is still the leader.

The reason is, I believe, a generalized learning curve for both firms
and nations. Reaching a number one position in a high technology industry requires that a firm create a successful R&D organization and
production, sales, and service capabilities that can capitalize on innovation. These become major assets in the next round of competition. Similarly with nations, technological leadership requires an education, basic
research, and financial infrastructure attuned to the demands of high
technology industries. Hence, I would conclude that the United States
will enter the 1990s with a head start from a number one position. Yet
there is still a race, and national position can change dramatically. If
table 10.1 were constructed for 1960, Britain would likely be number
two and Japan close to the bottom. Now Japan has a clear second. As
McCulloch points out, the relative decline of the United States is largely
the other side of the relative rise of Japan.

JAPAN: THE CHALLENGER

Japan's rise to become a major technological power in only two decades is remarkable and, to most, surprising. Perhaps it should not be so. In the Meiji period the country transformed itself into an industrial power, and World War II showed that Japan was capable of producing complex weapons such as the Zero fighter aircraft. In the 1960s Japan moved so effectively into high technology products that it reached number two in the technology race by the 1980s.

The Taylor and Yamamura chapter (chap. 2) does not relate this history but rather focuses on the current situation. They provide an assessment of Japan's technological position in three broad areas: (1) communications, broadly defined as electronics, computers, and telecommunications; (2) biotechnology; and (3) new materials. The first two can be associated with sectors in table 10.1 in which Japan is ranked number two after the United States, whereas Taylor and Yamamura often place them first. There is no contradiction here—being number two in a broad sector such as electronics necessarily means a number one position in particular products.

Taylor and Yamamura go on to examine four factors that might constrain or promote Japan's future technological progress. They give rather short shrift to government policies to promote innovation, concluding that the strength or weakness of Japan as a competitor in the twenty-first century will depend more and more on aspects of Japanese society and its economy and not on public policy. In general, this judgment is likely correct, as the difficult fiscal situation, increased internationalization, and doubts about the wisdom of "administrative guidance" have reduced the ability of the Japanese government to direct industries and firms.

Still even the modest role of the Ministry of International Trade and Industry (MITI) can be significant, particularly in organizing cooperative R&D projects. Some, like the VLSI project, have been a major contribution to international competitiveness. The projects are organized as research associations and often include most of the large firms in the industry. The research itself is assigned partly to the individual laboratories of the participating companies and partly to a central laboratory largely staffed by member companies. The projects last several years and have very specific objectives and usually involve applied research, with subsequent commercial applications left to the individual companies. Such cooperative research can reduce duplicative efforts and lead to a sharing of information. Companies supply most of the project funding, and as Taylor and Yamamura point out, government subsidies are small.

While these R&D projects have attracted much attention outside Japan, most Japanese R&D occurs outside these projects in individual company laboratories without government subsidy. Indeed, among OECD countries Japan is distinctive in the modest role of government financing of R&D. Japan has relied primarily on the private sector to both finance and carry out R&D. Even the limited role of the government, however, may be an asset in future technological competition.

As for broader aspects of Japanese society, these seem to have served the high technology industries well. Taylor and Yamamura are, however, less optimistic about the future, as they see the "catch-up" phase of Japan's development coming to an end. They conclude that Japan must now create its own capacity to produce basic scientific innovations that lead to technological breakthroughs. However, they have doubts about Japan's ability to do this. They argue that the organizational structure best suited for catch-up innovations is quite different from that which facilitates radical innovations. Incremental innovations are said to benefit from R&D professionals with a specific knowledge of the firm and its products, a hierarchical and formal structure, and intense loyalty to the firm—all features of a Japanese corporation, with its emphasis on permanent employment, seniority-based wages, and rotation of engineers from R&D to production. In contrast, radical innovations are said to require organizations that are informal and collegial and researchers that are cosmopolitan, that is, with numerous contacts outside the firm. What is needed, say Taylor and Yamamura, is the very difficult transition from a bureaucratic to an entrepreneurial climate within Japanese corporations.

I would tend to be more optimistic regarding the ability of Japanese corporations to make the transition. Japanese corporations have already demonstrated an ability to create subsidiaries and affiliates to carry out specific functions. Many of these take advantage of specialized labor— part-time workers, women, the retired, and other groups outside the standardized employment and wage patterns of the large parent corporation. They could do the same for the specialized R&D personnel that require special organization. The "stigma" of subsidiary employment could be offset if these R&D corporations offered high pay. (Most employees in Japanese subsidiaries now receive lower wages and benefits than employees in the parent firm.)

Nakatani's chapter (chap. 6) examines a unique feature of Japanese industrial organization—corporate groups. As he points out, groups involve ties between corporations, including mutual shareholding and long-term buyer-seller relationships; they offer certain advantages for technological innovations, risk sharing, freedom for long-term profit maximization, and a network for R&D activities. Corporate groups afford some of the advantages of an American-style conglomerate without the necessity of common ownership and centralized control. Group ties in Japanese business date back to the prewar period and remain important today. Nakatani, however, does not address the issue of whether group ties will weaken with the increasing internationalization of the Japanese economy. Another omitted question is whether the potential advantages of the group for R&D exchange remain largely hypothetical. Notably, well-known joint research projects, such as the VLSI project, involved firms from diverse groups but within the same industry.

Despite potential group advantages, I still share the Taylor and Yamamura concern that the future may not be as favorable to Japan as the past. Japanese corporations achieved high returns on R&D because they focused on incremental innovations, in which the risks are less. This strategy required the importation of technology, and even as Japan achieved a remarkably strong position in such fields as electronics, its payments for licensing technology in the form of know-how and patents to the United States were four times its receipts from technology sales to the United States.[3] The cost of relying on technology purchased from abroad may increase significantly as foreign companies anticipate that the sale of technology will strengthen competition from Japanese firms. A decline in availability of imported technology, as noted by Taylor and Yamamura, would force Japanese firms to spend more on high-risk, radical innovations, which, in turn, would reduce the profits from R&D.

Another problem relates to basic research. Japan is viewed as a free rider on U.S. basic research, particularly that occurring in U.S. universities. Indeed, in terms of publicly funded university research, Japan's government expenditures are one-fifth those of the United States, adjusting for the size of the two economies.[4] Since university research is freely available, it is hard to see how Japan can be precluded from access to its results, though various measures, largely relating to U.S. government laboratories, have been proposed. The more serious problem for Japan may be that radical innovations require close university-industry cooperation, a practice better established in the United States than in Japan.

The most serious problem for Japan, however, may be the rise of old-fashioned protectionism, particularly that directed at Japanese high technology products. High technology products often require worldwide markets to be economically viable. Taylor and Yamamura are correct when they state that the international climate could be the most significant barrier to Japanese success in the twenty-first century. I am less sure of their concluding observation, however, that "the future of the Japanese economy rests in its own hands."

WEST GERMANY: DOING WELL IN MEDIUM TECHNOLOGY PRODUCTS

Legler's chapter (chap. 7) reminds us that high technology products are not a homogeneous group. Indeed, there is a good case for dividing them into high technology products per se and what he calls high commodity products. The distinction is made primarily by R&D intensity (industry R&D expenditures as a percentage of industry sales). High technology products have R&D intensities of more than 8 percent; high commodity products, from 3 to 8 percent. Products of the electronics and aerospace industries are leading examples of high technology products; automobiles and chemicals are leading examples of high commodity products.

Legler uses the concept of revealed comparative advantage (RCA)—the difference between a nation's net export surplus (or deficit) for a product group and its new export position or export position in manufactured products as a whole—to show competitive position. Legler finds that West Germany's RCA in high technology products has declined somewhat from 1976 to 1986; the U.S. RCA declined between 1976 and 1980 and then stabilized, whereas Japan's RCA has steadily improved. The levels are of as much interest, however, as the changes. In high technology products, Japan and West Germany still had negative RCAs in 1986, while the United States had a positive RCA. The record is different in high commodity products, where West Germany is second and the United States is third. The U.S. RCA for this group showed a continual decline from 1976 to 1985.

There is, however, a problem with RCA as a measure of competitive position. The measure is a relative one, and it is possible that a nation may actually be gaining competitive advantage in high technology products while its RCA is declining if the nation is gaining markets even faster in other manufactured products. The problem is particularly marked for both Japan and West Germany since automobile exports have such a dominant position in the total of manufactured exports. Thus, the surge in automotive exports in Japan and West Germany would reduce the RCA for high technology products. Stated alternatively, a nation will show a negative RCA for a product even though it is gaining export share in that product if its RCA is rising even more rapidly in other products. A negative RCA for Japanese high technology products then is not inconsistent with Taylor and Yamamura's report on the international success in these products.

Still the distinction Legler makes between high technology and high commodity products is a useful one. Differences in R&D intensity, however, are only part of the story. In high technology products, product cycles are short and depend on large R&D expenditures. Competition depends critically on offering the latest products—a 16 K random access memory is inferior to a 64 K product no matter how well made, serviced, or priced. In high commodity products, competition is more multidimensional. Eads demonstrates that exchange rates and manufacturing efficiency are crucial for competition in the automotive industry. Japanese success in that industry did not rest on its R&D efforts but in the more prosaic aspects of efficiency.

Legler shows that West Germany has been more successful in high commodity than in high technology products. In high commodity products, West Germany's tradition of workmanship and manufacturing efficiency and its established position have been major assets. And, of course, from the viewpoint of its balance of trade and economic prosperity, such success is as good as that in the high technology products. Yet these are what Itoh calls borderline technology goods, which are more vulnerable to competition from low-wage countries than high technology products.

A CONCLUDING COMMENT

What generalizations can be drawn from these seven chapters about the leaders in technological competition? We can say that the era in which one nation can be the dominant technological power is over. The United States held that position for the two decades after World War II only because of special circumstances, which are unlikely to be repeated. Yet in the era of many players, some nations and firms will be more successful than others, even though there will be several competitors.

In this competition, success today is a major asset for success tomorrow. The static and dynamic scale economies support this tendency; but it is only a tendency. Technological opportunities have been overlooked by established firms, allowing new firms to enter successfully. Japan's rise shows that a nation can dramatically change its technological standing.

Nations will undoubtedly carry out public policies with the objective of increasing their technological competitiveness. But this volume suggests that these policies, even though they might pass a cost-benefit test, can only have a marginal impact. Success depends on the policies of individual firms and on many other factors: the primary and secondary educational system, basic research and training at universities, characteristics of industrial organization, monetary and fiscal policy, to name only a few. These features of society change in response to many factors, of which technological competition is but one.

Given the diversity of sources for technological change and the likelihood of domestic oligopoly in many high technology industries, international competition serves economic welfare, as painful as it may be for the industries facing such competition. Thus, preserving the openness of the international economy may turn out to matter most for technological competition, from which we can all benefit.

NOTES

1. Merton J. Peck, "Science and Technology," in Richard Caves, ed., *Britain's Economic Prospects* (Washington, D.C.: Brookings Institution, 1968), p. 448.

2. For more detailed discussion of the survey and its results, see Richard C. Levin, Alvin Klevorick, Richard R. Nelson, and Sidney G. Winter, "Appropri-

ating the Returns from Industrial R&D" (paper presented at the Brookings Panel on Economic Activity, Washington, D.C., December 3–4, 1987).

3. Data are for 1985 for North America, but my interviews indicate that almost all payments and receipts relate to the United States. Statistics Bureau Management and Coordination Agency, Japan, *Report on the Survey of Research and Development* (Tokyo: Statistics Bureau, 1985), pp. 144–46.

4. Calculations are based on data from Organisation for Economic Cooperation and Development, *OECD Science and Technology Indicators* (Paris: OECD, 1982), and supplemented by data in National Science Foundation, *Science Indicators* (Washington, D.C.: U.S. Government Printing Office, 1985), and Statistics Bureau, *Report on the Survey of Research and Development*. Data are for R&D expenditures in natural science, engineering, medicine, and agriculture, fields in which most university basic research is government supported in both countries. This comparison takes into account the relative gross national product of each country using purchasing-power parity exchange rates.

Contributors

PETER F. COWHEY, Professor of Political Science, Department of Political Science and Graduate School of International Relations and Pacific Studies, University of California, San Diego

GEORGE C. EADS, Vice President and Chief Economist, General Motors Corporation

GÜNTER HEIDUK, Professor of Economics, Faculty of Economics, Duisburg University

ERNST-JÜRGEN HORN, The Kiel Institute of World Economics

MOTOSHIGE ITOH, Professor of Economics, Faculty of Economics, University of Tokyo

HARALD LEGLER, Lower Saxonian Institute of Economic Research, Hannover

RACHEL MCCULLOCH, Professor of International Finance, Department of Economics, Brandeis University

IWAO NAKATANI, Professor of Economics, Faculty of Economics, Osaka University

RICHARD R. NELSON, Professor of Economics, School of International and Public Affairs, Columbia University

MERTON J. PECK, Professor of Economics, Yale School of Organization and Management, Yale University

SULLY TAYLOR, Assistant Professor of International Business, Portland State University

KOZO YAMAMURA, Job and Gertrud Tamaki Professor of Japanese Studies, Henry M. Jackson School of International Studies, University of Washington

Index